DEVELOPMENT OF WRITING

Counting with pebbles. Drawings and painting[...]gs	
Counting with tokens made of baked clay, shaped to indicate commodity.	Unmarked clay tokens
Tokens incised to indicate commodity. Thumb-size clay tablets with number and some-times outline of animal incised.	Incised tokens Incised clay tablets
Pictorial script. Sumerian was largely monosyllabic, so a sign was potentially both word and syllable. Signs gradually represent sounds (or ideas), instead of illustrating things.	Early pictorial tablets
Cuneiform could have recorded language but did not yet do so.	Clay tablets still a kind of shorthand for clerical memoranda
Cuneiform records language.	Royal inscriptions, treaties, religious texts, literature, history
Cuneiform had become the script of Akkadian and some other languages in Mesopotamia	Full range of developed cuneiform tablets, inscriptions, etc.

THE PERIOD OF THE FIRST WRITTEN LAWS:

The laws of Ur-Nammu, king of Ur.

Laws of the city of Eshnunna.

Tablets containing written laws

Laws of Lipit-Ishtar, king of Isin.

A school exercise showing ten laws.

Laws of Hammurabi, king of Babylon.

The original pillar is now in the Louvre

JOHN SASSOON

ANCIENT
LAWS
AND
MODERN
PROBLEMS

In vain thy reason finer webs shall draw,
Entangle Justice in her net of Law,
And right, too rigid, harden into wrong ...

ALEXANDER POPE, *An Essay on Man*, 1733–4

JOHN SASSOON

ANCIENT LAWS AND MODERN PROBLEMS

*The balance between justice
and a legal system*

LONDON

THIRD MILLENNIUM PUBLISHING

THIRD MILLENNIUM PUBLISHING
Shawlands Court, Newchapel Road
Lingfield, Surrey RH7 6BL

Published in the year 2001 by Third Millennium Publishing
Copyright © John Sassoon 2001

A catalogue record for this book is available
from the British Library

ISBN 0-9536969-9-5

Set in Century Schoolbook
Designed and produced by
Pardoe Blacker Limited
Lingfield · Surrey

Printed in Hong Kong
by Midas Printing Limited

CONTENTS

DEDICATION

To
ELWYN BLACKER
Without whose encouragement
and active support
this book would never
have happened

INTRODUCTION

THE LEGAL SYSTEMS of modern democracies appear to be in something very like disarray. Few would think of looking at the ancient laws of around four thousand years ago for ideas about what has gone wrong and what might be done. That, basically, is what this book is about.

I am the textbook outsider: outside the community that studies ancient Mesopotamia; outside any community that studies law. But maybe that is the only way a book of this kind could be written; maybe that explains why such a book does not seem to have been written before.

This book is not a history of law. It extracts from the surviving laws of the city states of Sumer, Akkad and Babylon an idea of what their underlying concepts of justice might have been. It reflects on the nature of their societies including their notions of justice, and compares them with some aspects of modern societies. Ancient legal systems are necessarily interpreted with the aid of imagination but not, hopefully, of fantasy. If this exercise aims a spotlight at some modern orthodoxies, that may be no bad thing.

Such a ground plan needs for its basic material surviving original laws from a single culture and a definable period. Although reference is made to development since the stone age, the core material is the surviving laws from the peak of the Sumerian cities to Hammurabi of Babylon from, say, 2100BC until, say, 1800BC.

History is normally told from the point of view of a modern scholar looking backwards, so the past reaches us as an entertaining video with minimum impact on our thoughts or our lives. The relevance of the past is a matter of choice for each generation, so if we find the past to be irrelevant that reflects our own choice that for us it shall be so. It is a common belief that the past has gone away; but even a cursory glance reveals that elements of past societies, conflicts, decisions, are still there, still active components of today's problems and attitudes. The lessons of past experience are waiting to be consulted but indifferent if they are not. Too deep a searching of the past can suffocate the present and make it impossible for modern people to live their own lives and grow according to their nature, because that requires the freedom to make their own mistakes. But one persistent illusion needs to be confronted: that the past is another country whose inhabitants were somehow primitive, a belief that bolsters a second illusion that where our ancestors were primitive we are civilised and superior.

It is becoming apparent that during the brief five thousand years of written records there have been no such beings as primitive people anywhere on the planet. Modern man with his full range of intellect has been all over the earth, and his primitive ancestors have been extinct, for far longer than even the remote precursors of writing. Though ancient history may deal with a distant past, it is the study of written records and therefore of modern man. For instance, the intelligence available and brought to bear on the problems of governing a city has not changed noticeably during the passage of a few thousand years; people were people then and a city was a city, and reason and intelligence are clearly visible in the ancient solutions to the problems of government. What has changed are the numbers of those to be ruled and the practical means of administration available to rulers; and it is these that have altered the kinds of solution arrived at. Ancient laws tell of a search for truth and justice by simple and direct means which did not always succeed; modern laws will tell our descendants about a more complex society whose laws were usually effective but in which truth and justice were not always the first objectives.

Discussion today of the problems our city dwelling ancestors faced tends to be conducted in a special tone of voice which implies that the ancient issues are not to be taken seriously, not because they no longer arise but because the principles our ancestors brought to bear on those issues are not part of any of today's orthodoxies; and that special tone conveys, tactfully, the further message that the more sacred of today's orthodoxies are not to be questioned under the pretext of studying the past.

There are plenty of excellent histories which depict the ancient world as it appears to modern eyes; but apparently none that attempt to understand the ancient world by trying to visualise the modern world as ancient eyes might have seen it; nor is there any recognition that an exercise of that kind might contribute to our understanding of ourselves. In spite of the conjectural element, that is what this book is going to do. But there is a word of caution. To imagine the ancient world as that world may have seen itself has to involve the temporary suspension of adherence to many of today's values. Some of those most deeply and sincerely committed to today's values may find that difficult.

Generally, the most ancient world in history will be presented through the medium of their surviving laws in the conventional order, from today's standpoint looking backwards; but the attempt to understand those laws will then involve considering what the ancient world might have thought about some of our solutions to the problems they faced and which were evidently common to us both. Just as we record our contemporary history in the hope that it may serve as an example or a warning to our descendants so we need to, and can, learn from our ancestors once we have accepted both that they were modern men and women and that they faced many of the same problems as we do.

The easiest point from which to start a discussion of the ancient world is their laws, because their laws have sometimes survived in original when

THE EPIC OF GILGAMESH: these fragments of a tablet illustrate some of the
problems faced by those who set out to translate that epic, or indeed any tablets.

other indications of their ways of life have vanished or reach us only at second hand. A comparison of some of the principles which underlie the most
ancient legal systems with those which underlie the most modern raises two
questions which neither our historians nor our lawyers appear to have
addressed: the first, how did our ancestors manage to solve, or avoid having
to face, so many of the social and legal problems which baffle us? The second,
how has it come about that thousands of sincere, intelligent, devoted, trained,
honest men and women who are our barristers and judges find themselves
running, and consciously running, a system which in the course of its normal, correct operation can produce injustice on a magnificent scale?

Let it be said that our barristers and our judges are among the most
intelligent and sensitively ethical of all our people and that our system

produces excellent justice for most of the time. So what has gone wrong for part of the time, and how on earth has the growing catastrophe apparently escaped their notice for so many decades, even centuries?

A study of the ancient world will not solve modern problems but it may throw some light on them. Many considerations tending in different directions will go into the stand taken on the various issues. Among those considerations are, first, that we are dealing with sincerity not malice; another, that some of the problems that arose millennia ago are not dead and irrelevant but are still facing us and are still unsolved; a third, that some of the worst problems facing legal systems are not legal problems at all but the result of principles adopted by the societies they serve; fourth, that though our ways of dealing with those problems are different from those of our ancestors, our objectives are often, though not always, the same while modern methods are sometimes more and sometimes less successful than the ancient methods; fifth, that in the ancient world justice was individual while today it is social ... The list goes on and it contains more than laws; but when trying to strike a balance and seek an answer to the main questions it will be found, surprisingly often, that the problem comes down to this: that several of the basic principles of civilised society, which we have traditionally defended with our lives, are now turning out to be incompatible with each other. Freedom and equality, for instance, are twin ideals that can now be seen to be contradictory if they are pursued far enough; the rule of law and individual justice can, similarly, be irreconcilable.

Discussion is going to be enlivened by introducng a fictitious, but not necessarily unrealistic, scribe from the ancient world with whom communication can occasionally be established and who joins in from time to time with his own opinions both on his world and on ours.

The facts about the ancient world will not, of course be universally agreed, but what has been taken for this purpose as fact is derived from the body of archaeological and philological knowledge and opinion, and that in turn is derived largely from the surviving original tablets. The facts about the modern world will similarly not be universally agreed which confirms, if that be needed, that all knowledge is subject to interpretation.

ACKNOWLEDGEMENTS

I ACKNOWLEDGE my debt to the authors of the works listed in the Bibliography on page 211. I also owe far more than is readily apparent to Mrs Anna Partington, philologist, specialist in ancient near-eastern languages and their modern relatives, for our ongoing and wide-ranging debate by correspondence, full of penetrating comment on many topics. I acknowledge in the text her hitherto unpublished philological explanation quoted in Chapter 11.

Quotations from the English translations of ancient laws and other works in J.B. Pritchard (Ed), *Ancient Near-Eastern Texts*, are reprinted by kind permission of Princeton University Press and detailed in the list of references.

For all that goes into putting an untidy text together I owe a special debt to Cindy Edler of Pardoe Blacker Limited, as well as to other members of Elwyn Blacker's outstanding team.

I owe a particular debt to my daughter Joanna Sassoon who made some suggestions for Chapter 1 which have been gratefully adopted; and to my wife, Rosemary, whose unfailing encouragement has been essential to the making of this book.

PHOTOGRAPHIC CREDITS

The publishers would like to thank the following for their assistance in providing images and for giving permission to reproduce copyright material. Every effort has been made to locate copyright holders but in a few instances this has not been successful.

page 9 Epic of Gilgamesh: fragments of tablet. British Museum, London.
page 16/17 The ziggurat of Ur: modern restoration. Comstock Photo Library.
page 23 Mesopotamian world map depicting the campaigns of King Sargon of Akkad (*c.*2371–2315BC), 24th century BC (stone). British Museum, London/Bridgeman Art Library.
page 31 Writing on a nail; terracotta cone on which Lipit-Ishtar, king of Isin, records duties of an Old Babylonian ruler. British Museum, London.
page 32 Ur-Nammu, king of Ur around 2100BC; cylinder seal found at Babylon *c.*2050BC, Post Akkadian. Werner Forman Archive.
page 35 00327 Code of Hammurabi: the god Shamash dictating his laws to Hammurabi, king of Babylon, Mesopotamia, found at Susa, Iran, *c.*1750BC. Louvre, Paris/Bridgeman Art Library.
page 39 A legal tablet in its envelope, from the Middle Babylonian period. British Museum, London.
page 40 The Lion Gate at Boğazköy, entrance to Hattusas, the ancient capital of the Hittites, Turkey.
page 43 Royal Standard of Ur, 'Peace' side from the Sumerian Royal Graves of Ur, Early Dynastic Period, 2750BC (mosaic). British Museum, London/Bridgeman Art Library.
page 46 God of Justice and the Sun; cylinder seal, showing the sun-god Shamash holding a toothed saw. British Museum, London.
page 54 Captives in manacles; diorite fragment of an Akkadian victory stele from Susa. Louvre, Paris.
page 64 Akkadian serpentine cylinder seal depicting the goddess Ishtar in a presentation scene, *c.*2200BC; Babylonian amethyst cylinder seal showing three lines of inscription 'Ishtar Lamassi, daughter of Lushtammar, slave girl of Ninisina', 18th century BC; Babylonian lapis lazuli cylinder seal showing a suppliant goddess in a presentation scene *c.*1900–1700BC. Bonhams, London, UK/Bridgeman Art Library.
page 71 An ordinary couple; terracotta plaque from Ur, about 1800BC. British Museum, London.
page 82 The role played by Ur-Nanshe, king of Lagash, in the construction of a temple; limestone wall plaque. Louvre, Paris/Bridgeman Art Library.
page 91 A school exercise book from *c.*2000–1500BC. British Museum, London.
page 111 Enheduanna, daughter of Sargon of Agade who became high priestess of Nanna, the patron god of Ur, *c.*2300BC. The University Museum, University of Pennsylvania.
page 115 Painted terracotta statue of a woman, *c.*1800BC. British Museum, London.
page 120 Small votive statue of a Sumerian woman, *c.*2500BC. British Museum, London.
page 122 Head of a king, possibly Hammurabi, king of Babylon, *c.*1750BC. Louvre, Paris/Bridgeman Art Library.
page 135 A representation of Hammurabi carved around 1760BC; the fragment was probably found at Sippar. British Museum, London.
page 138 The laws of Hammurabi; detail of the column inscription. Louvre, Paris/Bridgeman Art Library.
page 153 The remains of Uruk, the home of Gilgamesh and the largest city of the third millennium BC.

CHAPTER 1

EMERGENCE FROM PREHISTORY

T HE WORD 'HISTORY' when applied to mankind, has at least two
meanings: it can mean the actual succession of events; or it can
mean those events or aspects of mankind's story that historians
select as relevant to a theme and choose to present. The former is what happened; the latter is what is taught. But it is the latter that paints the picture for the reader's mind and enlightens or deceives him – unless he be
alert – according to the imagination, the judgement and the intention of the
historian. The judgement and detachment of a master was surely displayed
by Edward Gibbon when he published, as early as 1788, these thoughts
about the nature of human progress in *The History of the Decline and Fall
of the Roman Empire:*

> His progress in the improvement in the exercise of his mental and cor-
> poreal faculties has been irregular and various; infinitely slow in the
> beginning, and increasing by degrees with redoubled velocity: ages of
> laborious ascent have been followed by a moment of rapid downfall; and
> the several climates of the globe have felt the vicissitudes of light and
> darkness. Yet the experience of four thousand years should enlarge our
> hopes and diminish our apprehensions; we cannot determine to what
> height the human species may aspire in their advances towards perfec-
> tion; but it may safely be presumed that no people, unless the face of
> nature is changed, will relapse into their original barbarism.[1]

Beyond the starts and stops of the grand scene, the temporary empires, the
destruction of cities, lay the continuum of ordinary lives, a less eventful subject that is easily overlooked by historians intent only on recording change.
The few moments when recorded history happened hide the long intervals
when it did not, and thus the tale is stunted. The decision to omit material
which the historian sees as irrelevant to his purpose makes it possible to
present a coherent picture, but it can distort more than one perspective.

To try and see Sumer, Akkad and Babylon and their laws as part of
the real continuum it is necessary to envisage the slow emergence of civilisation from the old stone age to the early cities and to identify some of the
prehistoric elements on which modern civilisation is built.

The story of Sumer has been written many times, based on objects actually
found, such as astonishing buildings, sculpture, wealth, records of empire,
but with scarcely a word about the problems of ordinary men and women – as
though these were neither history nor interesting. The surviving laws, which
are widely available, tell us that neither people nor relationships have

changed much in four thousand years. But if laws are mentioned at all in the histories it is probably for their legal procedures rather than the picture they paint of ancient lives. These laws reveal how our predecessors coped with many situations that still baffle us: for instance, what did they do with a rebellious teenage son, or a daughter who went on the street and came back pregnant? Their laws also throw a dim but fascinating light on prehistoric societies where most of their problems and some of their laws originated; they can still provoke discussion of many an unsolved problem today.

Too often studies of ancient laws reflect a legal outlook that combines a dismissive tone with the faintest of praise. Some fasten, rightly, on the

FIVE PRE-FLOOD CITIES

After kingship had descended from heaven, Eridu became the seat of kingship. In Eridu Alulim reigned 28,800 years as king; Alalgar reigned 36,000 years — two kings reigned 64,800 years. Eridu was abandoned, and its kingship was carried off to Badtibira.

In Badtibira, Enmenluanna reigned … Badtibira was abandoned and its kingship was carried to Larak.

In Larak … its kingship was carried off to Sippar.

In Sippar … its kingship was carried off to Shuruppak.

In Shuruppak, Ubartutu reigned 18,600 years as king — one king reigned 18,600 years.

Total five cities, eight kings reigned 241,200 years.

The Flood then swept over the land. After the Flood … Kish became the seat of kingship …

From the Sumerian King List, translated by S. N. Kramer. The huge numbers are not understood; they cannot be regnal years. Similar numbers, though not quite so large, appear in lists of early ancestors in the Bible. In the Sumerian King List for the city of Uruk, for instance, Gilgamesh (usually taken as *c*.2800BC) is listed as reigning for 126 years, but his son and successor Urnungal reigned only 15 years, and thereafter the reigns are 9, 8, 36, 6, and 36 years. The use of apparently unrealistic numbers appears to have declined and ceased during the first quarter of the third millennium BC. If the large numbers are a code, it awaits decipherment. The history, as opposed to prehistory, of Sumer and Akkad is often held to begin with the post-Flood kingdom of Kish, for which twenty-three kings are listed in the King List.

role of superstition which called on the gods to resolve problems to which there was no answer – as though we never have recourse to Deity. They forget that ancient legal systems did not depend on chance for most of the time and that they did recognise all of the time that an honest search for the truth is a precondition of justice. A study of ancient laws tells us that prehistory was not primitive, and it casts light on how even the basic concept of justice is far from simple.

Discoveries fundamental to the development of the modern world had mostly been made far back in prehistory by men and women of clearly modern intelligence: the use of fire, pottery, the domestication of animals, the wheel, farming, metallurgy, are obvious examples. Less generally recognised as prehistoric discoveries, because the evidence they leave is indirect, are the concepts of number, of writing and of law. Of these, the rule of law and, probably, number date from the old stone age, while if writing in the full sense came only later, at least the urge to write can be detected as probably the earliest of all.

So when does history start? The answer that history starts when prehistory ends is uninformative and, when you look at it closely, untrue. The past is known most fully by the written word, but the remains of its artefacts can suggest the outline of a longer tale. Much of our knowledge of the earliest writing comes from the rubbish dumps of the prehistoric Sumerian city of Uruk where the inhabitants threw away the written tablets they no longer needed.[2] Prehistory and history may merge into each other, but writing has to be described as a prehistoric invention if prehistory is defined, as it often is, as the age before writing. Merging apart, the end of prehistory is nowhere a straight line separating myth from fact. The invention of writing was a period lasting many centuries during which a script gradually emerged which could record language and be applied to an ever-widening range of new activities. Prehistory did not end all at once in all fields but was

> *To Nanna-Mansim speak! This is what Sumrustum says:*
> *As soon as this tablet of mine has been read to you,*
> *Buqumtum will drive one slave and four sheep to the*
> *Akkadians. Let him pass on! He must not be held up!*

From a collection of letters between *c.*2000 and 1500BC, translated by Albrecht Goetze. Clearly Nanna-Mansim was not literate, so he would have to find someone to read the tablet to him. This would probably not be too difficult since the cuneiform script and scribal training had been around for at least five hundred years, and scribes spent much of their time, and presumably earned much of their income, reading and writing letters for those who could not do it for themselves. It is not certain that Sumrustum, the sender, was himself literate.

THE ZIGGURAT OF UR: the ziggurat (or stepped tower) was built by Ur-Nammu, king of Ur around 2100 BC. This is a modern restoration of part of the building. The ziggurat was previously restored in the 6th century BC by the Chaldean kings of Babylon, of whom Nebuchadnezzar was one. The technology available to the original builders included the slight outward curvature of its principal lines, vertical and horizontal, so that from a distance they looked straight. Until recently, this technique was thought to have been invented by the Greek builders of the Parthenon more than fifteen hundred years later.

hesitatingly overtaken by written records in different fields at different times in different places. Accounting systems, for instance, ceased to be prehistoric in Uruk some seven centuries before written history appears.

The early city of Uruk consisted of a main urban centre surrounded by satellite villages or small towns.[3] A little after 3500BC there was a dramatic growth in population which cannot be explained by natural increase, though no one can say who the immigrants were or where they came from. The main city centre expanded, public and ceremonial buildings grew; some of the satellite towns themselves acquired satellites as, in turn, did some of their satellites until the whole became a web of interdependent population centres – in administrative terms a conurbation. By about 3000BC the Uruk conurbation has been estimated at twenty-five to fifty thousand population and by 2800BC perhaps one hundred thousand – larger than Athens or Rome in their heyday.[4] To hold all this together, to feed and defend the people, to plan and finance what on any scale was a major urban undertaking, a far more complex administration had to be created; and the technology on which it must rest could no longer be a system of information storage based largely on memory.

The new arrivals may well have been Sumerians and they may indeed have possessed a superior culture or ability, however politically incorrect that elitist idea may now seem. But their mere presence and the administrative crisis caused by a suddenly increased population would have been quite enough by themselves to set the storekeepers of Uruk searching for a solution to a predicament which threatened their craft, their livelihood and their status – and they were not long in finding one. They developed first a pictographic script and, soon after, added a phonetic element which was the real beginning of writing as the recording of language.[5] These inventions produced immediately a script that could convey a full meaning to those who knew the circumstances, but it was many centuries before a script was to emerge which could be read accurately by strangers. Population pressure provided the impetus for the invention of writing, but intellect and creativity were needed to exploit it. Whether writing was invented by the original inhabitants or by the new arrivals, or whether indeed the new arrivals were a wave of the original population is unknown: but it is now established that a long-held belief is correct and that the language of the earliest tablets is Sumerian.[6]

Writing can of course be said to have begun with the origin of the first process that was to lead to it: a sign which had a meaning and conveyed a message and which, more significantly, also reflected the beginning of a need to write. That could be the cave paintings of 35,000 years ago or, even earlier, signs to mark a route. The outline of a fish can decorate a jar, or it can indicate the jar's contents or ownership, though it is now impossible to say what significance was in fact attached to it. Pebbles may have been used for counting in the old stone age and clay tokens in the neolithic. All these can be seen as precursors of writing but they were not writing itself. Writing is more than isolated images, stone pebbles or clay tokens with meaning, because writing in the full sense can record a language.

Scripts that could record language, such as syllabaries or the alphabet, were the middle stages of a far longer evolution of recording systems which began with small stones and is far from ending with the computer. Numerical information necessary for community life may have been recorded and processed in the old stone age by arranging and counting pebbles, as implied by Nissen *et al.*[7]; but from the beginning of the neolithic, about 8000BC[8], stones were gradually replaced by little moulded clay tokens. The progressive adoption of farming was producing agricultural supplies whose distribution needed to be controlled, as well as settlements whose future operations needed to be planned: small, deliberately shaped, tokens made these possible. As farming centres increased in size, manufactured goods including metals entered the economy, and tokens patterned with a pointed stylus were made and used; while from the shapes of tokens as well as from the patterns on them some of the earliest pictorial signs were derived.[9]

Later precursors of writing abstracted from tokens the numerical and descriptive information they contained and wrote it on clay tablets, thus intellectualising it. That opened the way for the further development whereby pictures meaning things became ideographs meaning ideas. The last of the building blocks of a full script was in place about a century later when the phonetic principle was introduced so that cuneiform, partly ideographic and partly syllabic, could record language. Gradually, over centuries, writing released the past from the constraint of human memory and thereby enlarged the storehouse of knowledge, a prerequisite for the expansion of knowledge itself. The potential scale of human enterprise was multiplied; but in doing so, writing opened the way to deterioration by neglect of the faculty of human memory.

To the ancient mind in its own setting, time stretched infinitely backwards into the past as it did forwards into the future. The ancient records of past time were held in the living memory, taught by the old, learnt by the young, recited regularly and updated at intervals. The ancient world knew their own history with an objective accuracy more precise and more comprehensive than modern historians will generally allow, because their childhood training had developed the faculty of memory and taught them as second nature how to interpret and operate their memory systems. Most of the ancient memory systems died with those who knew them, but a few were partly written before their guardians had vanished. Of those, just one or two have survived by chance to tantalise the modern world with an expectation of mystery where the ancient world had recorded fact. Modern knowledge of those systems is necessarily derived from secondary and written sources that were, and are, open to contamination as memories held in living minds were not. Remnants of the ancient memory systems survive in the lists of ancestors in the Bible and in fragments of documents such as the Sumerian King List, whose numbers presented as lives or reigns are sometimes so impossibly large that modern scholarship cannot understand them and dismisses them as myth. Remnants of the techniques by which memories were stocked and information preserved survive in the doctrine of sacred writings and in the consequent insistence on precise, literal accuracy regardless of understanding or subsequent scholarship when a document is being copied or a record transmitted.

Memory is hard work. Like any other faculty it is strengthened by exercise and withers with disuse. What we underestimate is the crucial part played by memory in the thinking process. Memory is not just the storage and recall of fact, but the faculty which enables us to relate facts to each other and feed a coherent picture into our minds. Without memory there would be no thinking. Our ancestors over five thousand years ago began to transfer the contents of memory from the mind to tablets which, collectively, were a machine with greater capacity and more accurate recall. By relieving the pressure this threatened the faculty of memory by which alone mankind could use the information which writing gave him. In this sense, writing threatened to start a process of deterioration which in evolutionary terms could result, in time, in the destruction of our unique human intellectual capacity. That threat is more menacing today than it was in the ancient world because we are abandoning the practices designed to exercise memory which our ancestors maintained. There are some signs that the danger is now being felt, but no sign that what is felt intuitively is truly understood. In the ancient world, when memory was all they had, the danger of neglecting it was clear. Writing could not be halted nor would they have wished, or needed, to do so; but they did recognise that memory training was concerned with the preservation of intellect and they conducted their education systems accordingly. Memorising and precise copying were the basis of the scribal school (Eduba meaning tablet house) curriculum in Sumer and in its successors, Babylon and Assyria, as A.W. Sjoberg reveals when he quotes from an ancient tablet about the school curriculum:

> The whole vocabulary of the scribes in the Eduba
> I will recite for you, I know it much better than you.[10]

Exercising the memory not only preserved their knowledge but kept their memories virile; and it was a practice whose roots lay far back in prehistory.

The origin of the city was once thought to lie in defence. More recent information suggests a different process. The old stone age – the golden age of hunting and gathering, the Garden of Eden – had its disciplined society, its laws, hierarchies, planning, trade and the arithmetic to support them; but its population was controlled by nature at a level which nature unaided was able to support. The old stone age did not have the means to sustain uncontrolled population increase. That changed around 8000BC with the discovery of farming and the arrival of the new stone age, or neolithic. From then on increases in population could be sustained by increasing agricultural production, apparently without limit. In a sense, the whole of subsequent history is the tale of how mankind has tried to adjust to the possibilities and the pressures thus released.

In the growing towns storage must have been a problem, so it is not surprising to find the temple precinct used for that purpose and the temple priests, as a result, playing a controlling part in the recording, storage and distribution of produce. Engraved stamp and cylinder seals impressed their designs on to clay to establish ownership. Temple buildings expanded, and to maintain the physical and administrative substructure of the growing towns an ominous measure of far-reaching significance appeared: taxation.[11] The origins of a coercive but effective system of government for a city state may be traced to the way early municipal administrations reacted to population pressures in the late fourth millennium BC.

Religious experience and organised religion had long been central to personal and public life as the existence of temples in the earliest settlements and the number of surviving figurines make clear. Each later city,

He who saw everything to the ends of the land,
Who all things experienced, considered all!
The hidden he saw, laid bare the undisclosed.
He brought report of before the Flood,
Achieved a long journey, weary and worn,
All his toil he engraved on a stone stela.
Of ramparted Uruk the wall he built,
Of hallowed Eanna, the pure sanctuary.
Behold its outer wall, whose cornice is like copper,
Peer at the inner wall, which none can equal.

Opening lines of the Epic of Gilgamesh (translated by E.A. Speiser), probably written down about 2000BC. According to the Sumerian King List, Gilgamesh was fifth king of the city of Uruk. Inanna was goddess of love and battle; she was the city god of Uruk, where her temple was called 'Eanna'.

and probably each prehistoric settlement, had its patron or city god. The city god of Uruk was Inanna, Queen of Heaven and Goddess of Love, and her temple in Uruk was known as Eanna. The concept of a city god suggests the possibility that in the early cities economic as well as religious power may have been vested in the priesthood, a question which the incomplete records leave open. But the scale on which government had to be conducted in the growing cities and a possibly circumstantial origin of temple power must soon have caused a civil power to arise or, if already there, to separate. Surviving records indicate partnership rather than conflict between crown and temple. Political power rested, or came to rest, with the crown, but the temple owned and operated many, but not all, of the storehouses. It was in the storehouses that records and accounts were kept, and from the storehouses that their civil service keepers exercised power over the daily lives of citizens.

The story of the city states of Sumer is one of conflict between cities, combined with strict internal control within them. The stability inside the cities lasted virtually unchanged for three thousand years. The area south of modern Baghdad down to the shore of the Gulf was home to two peoples: the Sumerians whose language was not semitic and the Akkadians whose language was. The word semitic was coined in the eighteenth century AD to describe, broadly, the family of languages of which Arabic and also Hebrew are members. It acquired political and social connotations when it was used to denigrate some, but only some, of the speakers of those languages. A 'semitic language' is an acceptable technical description of Hebrew as well as of Arabic; but the term 'anti-semitic' means hostile to Jewish people only, while saying nothing about any attitude towards the Arabs. For this reason, the word 'semitic' is being used less and less, but it is still widely accepted in a linguistic context.

The Sumerians lived mainly in the southern half of that part of the Tigris/Euphrates valley that lies between modern Baghdad and the Gulf, and the Akkadians lived mainly in the northern part. Though they clearly came from different origins, Akkadians and Sumerians intermingled culturally, and if the Akkadian kings with Sumerian names and Sumerian kings with Akkadian names say anything it is that over the centuries they intermarried until their cultural differences became blurred and, in the end, vanished. But that did not stop cities from fighting each other: give football fans clubs and they will mimic war; give people independent cities and they will indulge the real thing. The need to control inter-city violence often coincided with the pursuit of empire and the thousand years from, say, 3000 to 2000BC. was punctuated by attempts by individual cities to establish dominance over the whole area as well as to extend their influence outside it. From c.2300BC to c.2150 Akkad, under Sargon the Great and his dynasty,

A MAP OF THE WORLD as seen from Babylon, c.600BC, illustrating the conquests of Sargon King of Akkad, c.2300BC. It is a flat earth; the outer circle represents the Salt Sea, the river flowing from north to south is the Euphrates and the rectangle is the city of Babylon.

> Gilgamesh opened his mouth,
> Saying to Enkidu:
> 'Who, my friend can scale heaven?
> Only the gods live forever under the sun.
> As for mankind, numbered are their days;
> Whatever they achieve is but the wind!
> Even here thou art afraid of death. . .'
>
> Enkidu was created by a goddess, Aruru, and is described as 'Shaggy with hair is his whole body ... He knows neither people nor land ... With the gazelles he feeds on grass, with wild beasts he jostles at the watering-place.' He may symbolise a pre-Sumerian population of Sumer. He has great strength, is lured into the city of Uruk and becomes the bosom friend and travelling companion of Gilgamesh. Here Gilgamesh is addressing Enkidu before they set off to slay the monster Huwawa.

dominated Sumer and spread their influence over the region, followed from c.2100 to c.2000BC by a Sumerian revival known as the Third Dynasty of Ur, when Ur was the capital city and civilisation reached an astounding peak. But three of the five kings of that Sumerian dynasty had Akkadian names. After c.2000BC when the cities had been destroyed by invaders until, say, Alexander the Great and his Macedonians and Greeks occupied Babylon in 323BC, dominance was, with some intervals, exercised by Babylon, Assyria and then Persia but, the character of life inside the cities did not change.

The question how did the ancient cities manage to preserve their internal structure intact for thousands of years has frequently been asked. There is no obvious answer but there are two certainties: the rule of law was older than any city; and the thread of law was never broken.

The rule of law is a characteristic of all societies, however ancient, however offensive or even however criminal. The kind of law will vary, but if a society exists there must be law within it. We have no direct evidence for laws in the old stone age, but laws there must have been because stone age society endured. That is an inference; perhaps there are others. We might hazard that stone age laws must have been strict because life was precarious and dissent, beyond a certain stage, could not have been permitted. We might add that laws must generally have been fair because they were accepted over long periods of time.

We can be fairly sure there were no legislative assemblies in the modern sense to make laws, but there is evidence from the early third millennium BC for the already established existence of other assemblies whose decisions were formal and powerful. The most celebrated example is to be found in the text 'Gilgamesh and Agga', translated by S. N. Kramer,[12] who explains that Agga, king of the city of Kish, had sent Uruk (Erech) an ulti-matum, and the question was whether Uruk should fight or surrender. Gilgamesh, the historical king of Uruk, wanted to fight, saying:

> The lord Gilgamesh before the elders of his city
> Put the matter, seeks out their word . . .
> '. . . Let us not submit to the house of Kish, let us smite it with weapons.'

The elders, disconcertingly, voted for appeasement:

> The convened assembly of the elders of his city
> Answer Gilgamesh . . .
> '. . . Let us submit to the house of Kish, let us not smite it with weapons.'

So Gilgamesh tried another route:

> A second time . . .
> Before the men of his city, put the matter, seeks out their word . . .

Kramer suggests that there were two assemblies in Uruk, the elders and the men of the city, and that the 'men of his city' were 'the arms-bearing men'. The armed men voted for war, so war it was; but that seems not to have been successful:

> Erech – its judgement was confounded because Uruk was besieged and the issue was settled by negotiation.

So, in the city of Uruk in the first quarter of the third millennium BC, there were at least two assemblies, the elders, and the arms-bearing men. Each seems to have had power to make this decision freely and irrespec-tive of the king's wishes. The councils may well have been advisory. In this

Utnapishtim said to him, to Gilgamesh:
'I will reveal to thee, Gilgamesh, a hidden matter
And a secret of the gods will I tell thee:
Shuruppak – a city which thou knowest,
And which on Euphrates' banks is situate –
That city was ancient, as were the gods within it,
When their heart led the great gods to produce the flood.'

Gilgamesh has found and met Utnapishtim, and asked him how he obtained eternal life. Utnapishtim's reply starts by impressing on Gilgamesh how very ancient, even then, the Flood was and that Utnapishtim's story begins before the Flood. The Sumerian King List names five cities as existing before the Flood, of which Shuruppak, the home of Utnapishtim/Zuisudra is one.

> To the king, my lord, my pantheon, my Sun-god, say: Thus Milkilu, thy servant, the dirt under thy feet. At the feet of the king, my lord, my Sun-god, seven times, seven times I fall. Let the king, my lord, know the deed which Yanhamu did to me after I left the presence of the king, my lord. Now he seeks two thousand shekels of silver from my hand, saying to me: 'Give me thy wife and thy children, or I will smite!' Let the king know this deed, and let my lord send to me chariots, and let him take me to himself lest I perish!

A letter from a cache of diplomatic correspondence found at Tel el-Amarna in Egypt, dating probably from just before 1500BC. They are written in the cuneiform script and the Akkadian language. Translated by W. F. Albright and George E. Mendenhall. Milkilu was prince of Gezer, and Yanhamu was 'a high Egyptian official of Canaanite (possibly Hebrew) origin, who seems to have been the Egyptian governor of Palestine at the beginning of the reign of Akhenaton'.

The elaborate formal salutation was normal for royal correspondence. The accusation against Yanhamu is not corroborated and cannot be confirmed. The request for Egyptian arms and protection was entirely normal.

case, the arms-bearing men, together with the king, could and did overrule the elders, which may reflect prudence in face of a balance of power on the ground rather than a formal relationship established by constitutional law. We do not know whether the inability of Uruk to withstand the subsequent siege reflected military weakness, or disunity caused by lack of enthusiasm in the council of elders.

There is no suggestion that such city councils were recently established. Their presence in early third millennium BC Uruk may well point to the existence of similar councils in the very earliest cities, and behind them to very ancient pre-city clan and tribal councils going back thousands of years.

Most laws probably started as court decisions and the ones that survived were those that worked. We can surmise that stone age laws and, indeed, government must have been appropriate to the conditions and problems of the societies they served.

Some things we can say for certain: stone age laws must have been transmitted by word of mouth and preserved in memory, and a knowledge of the laws must have been taught to every young person as a matter of course. We can surmise that, even so, legal problems will have arisen, and if surviving pre-literate societies are a guide, there will have been private individuals interested in the law, who were neither chief nor elder, from whom advice will have been available. The function of solicitor is older than that profession, and no doubt the barrack-room lawyer is older than the barrack room.

We can be bold if not rash: stone age society must have had procedures for determining guilt, though probably not for declaring innocence. They were small societies, perhaps fewer than one hundred persons; so they all knew each other and each was needed. A resentful dissident could poison relationships and endanger the whole: so the truth may have mattered more than the procedure for obtaining it. The chief will probably have been judge and he will have needed to hear the case for, as well as against, the accused. The accused will have been given his say because the continued functioning of the group will have depended on both verdict and penalty being accepted. It is doubtful whether any appeal will have been allowed: to whom would an appeal have been addressed? The separation of judge from chief will probably have come later when communities expanded and the need for an appeal process had become obvious. It is likely too that penalties will not have been over harsh. For instance, if each individual was needed the death penalty will have been rare indeed, and fines payable as restitution are likely to have been preferred as the pre-Hammurabi laws indicate.

The form in which the earliest surviving written laws are framed, as though distilling the essence of established judgements, suggests a continuity both in the laws and in the principles on which they are based. If so, ancient laws, including written laws when they appeared, will have added up to a coherent system of social control based on ethical principles and enforced by public opinion. But neither oral nor written laws were comprehensive in the modern sense of providing a law for every foreseeable situation. One coherent principle that pervaded so many of the earliest written laws was the principle of property. The ancient concept of property included people as well as things, and underlay most of criminal, civil and family law. It is fashionable to belittle ancient laws as mere custom – arbitrary conventions that arose from necessity without real forethought. One glance at the careful and precise wording of the surviving ancient laws dispels that illusion.

If the ancient oral laws continued to apply inside the early cities the thread of law from stone age to city may well have been maintained substantially unbroken. The earliest written laws – and by inference their predecessors – tended to deal with the application of a small number of general principles to a wide range of problems which had actually arisen. Such a framework can easily adjust to changing circumstances by adding new laws, and by discontinuing old ones as they became obsolete. That the surviving laws of Sumer, Akkad and Babylon may have been a substantial continuance of oral laws going right back to the old stone age is, of course, surmise; but it is not necessarily wild surmise.

And there is room for one further surmise. As cities grew, elders who knew the laws and taught them to their young could no longer communicate their knowledge to thousands. A small number of local courts whose decisions everybody knew were overtaken by dozens of courts whose decisions no one knew, and in the resulting confusion of laws civil order was threatened. In the growing cities, new social structures arose that needed new kinds of law, as Hammurabi of Babylon in particular recognised when drafting his code. At some point, someone in one city must have decided that the time had come when the principal laws must be written and published. Nobody knows when this might have been, but sometime after c.2500BC is probable when the cuneiform script had developed sufficiently for the writing of laws to be feasible. Nobody knows which city was first, or even whether it was an Akkadian or a Sumerian city. All that is known is that the earliest law tablets we have contain some of the written laws of the Sumerian city of Ur. They were published in the name of Ur-Nammu, first king of the third dynasty of Ur, shortly after 2100BC though they may have been collated in fact by his son and successor Shulgi.[13]

The first act of writing laws had a far reaching effect on the status and the nature of law itself. It meant that henceforth the practical demands of civil order must prevail over the temptations of individual justice so far as to ensure that the same laws be applied in the same way throughout a jurisdiction. It meant that the courts would increasingly become bound by written laws and that judges would lose much of their ancient discretion in the individual case. It meant that the meaning of justice had been changed by a necessary reaction to population pressure and that, in turn, opened the way for further changes in the meaning of justice in response to different pressures in the future. The act of writing laws down planted the seeds of conflict between public policy and the individual which, four thousand years later, has still to be resolved.

It had still to be resolved, of course, in the cities of Sumer and Akkad, including Babylon, whose laws continued to reflect an ancient bias towards individual circumstance and whose court records as a result contain not one single mention of any written law or code.

The fact that the surviving records show that court judgements were generally consistent with the surviving written laws may suggest the continuation of an ancient oral law whose concepts of justice informed the new written law. The most ancient written laws provoke many thoughts about the balance of conflicting principles, and raise the question whether our legal ancestors may have been perfectly aware of the hornets they were releasing by deciding to write their laws in the first place. The order in which writing was applied to the various fields of activity is uncertain, except that administrative records were clearly the first. The probability that laws were among the last to emerge from prehistory may tell us something about the foresight of our ancestors.

CHAPTER 2

THE LAW CODES

THE REMAINS OF THE LAWS of Sumer, Akkad and Babylon in the late third and early second millennium BC open a window on to a different world. Ancient civilisations faced in principle, or at least in embryo, many of the same problems as we do, but they lacked the means of identifying and focusing on them. In their eyes justice consisted of truth and common sense, so they sought the facts and trusted their judges. Ancient laws are often condemned because some of their penalties were horrific, among which mutilation and the branch of talion which punished the innocent were the worst. But that hardly justifies dismissing the laws wholesale as arbitrary and unworthy of the name of law. A law and its penalty are different things, even though the one is part of the other; while to condemn ancient laws because some of their penalties are no longer acceptable reflects not only confusion but a complacent view of modern legal systems.

Few have time or motive to read through laws four thousand years old, so opinions are bound to be formed by the drops of information that happen to come to hand; and cruel penalties are particularly vivid and accessible. In fact, according to the surviving court records, a wide discretion does not seem to have led to eccentric judgement: the ancient courts had to grapple with moral issues when modern courts can take refuge in a written law. Even a casual look at the most ancient of the Mesopotamian legal systems reveals them as surprisingly moderate and humane, while the cruelty by which they are so often characterised appears to have arrived centuries later and from outside the region. If some of their eventual penalties and some of their methods make us shudder, the reasons why they were adopted are not primitive. That is why an attempt to envisage how our remote ancestors might have reacted to some of our ways of tackling the same problems can be interesting and, occasionally, instructive.

Many can recall the name of Hammurabi as the author of the collection of laws which bears his name. Not so many know that the oldest surviving

> Do not return evil to your adversary;
> Requite with kindness the one who does evil to you,
> Maintain justice for your enemy,
> Be friendly to your enemy.

From 'The Instructions of Shuruppak' c.2500BC. This sentiment also appears, much later, in the Bible.

laws are three hundred years earlier than Hammurabi and that many of the laws not only come down from prehistory but still form part of most legal systems today.

Code is an ambitious word to use of these collections of laws, because even when complete they cannot have recorded the whole body of the law in any field. Nor did they presume to lay down the law in detail for individual cases, and thus circumvent the judges and their age-old discretion. These laws do not look as though they have emerged from a legislature, worded in general terms and describing situations that are foreseen rather than actual. On the contrary, each looks like a court judgement in a real case, complete with relevant details, carefully worded so as to illustrate how a principle should apply in the particular circumstances of that case. It is left to another judge's discretion how that principle should be applied in subsequent but similar circumstances.

The collections of laws assembled and published by cities were intended to inform citizens how legal problems, or some of them, were likely to be resolved. But the element of guesswork remained considerable, and Hammurabi was clearly being optimistic when he wrote in the Epilogue to his laws:

> ... Let any oppressed man who has a cause come into the presence of the statue of me, the king of justice, and then read carefully my inscribed stela, and give heed to my precious words, and may my stela make the case clear to him; may he understand his cause; may he set his mind at ease![1]

No ancient court could plead law as an excuse for injustice, or for failing to take its own steps to reach the truth. Those who accuse the first great law-givers in history of inability to see beyond the particular or of ignorance of principle have not understood the meaning of their laws nor the rationale behind having them written down and published. Nor can they have asked themselves which of our modern statutes can claim to be comprehensive in the market-place or the street.

In earliest times, each tribal or clan group had its laws. They formed part of the oral tradition and are referred to by the modern world, rather loftily, as 'customs'; and 'custom' is the word most generally used to describe the laws of our diminishing number of surviving prehistoric societies. As these separate legal systems arose within broadly the same social and economic circumstances, they were similar in content.[2] When, in Mesopotamia for instance, the smaller clan or tribal groups came together into towns and then, in the second half of the fourth millennium BC into great cities, the laws merged together as easily as the people.

The ancient accounting signs used by the masters of trading caravans for communicating with their merchants and their customers were developed into cumbersome but effective writing systems, and became the sinews of the new city administrations. Within the cities, scribal communities controlled the knowledge of writing and therefore the machinery of public affairs. Feeding the people, protecting them and providing them with justice are three pillars on which any ordered society must rest, and among the cramped crowds of the ancient cities it was the knowledge of writing and of the written law held by their scribal communities which made food and justice available to all. The oral tradition did not vanish overnight, but as the city judges took new decisions or confirmed important old ones they tended to be written down. It was these cases which kings such as Ur-Nammu, Lipit Ishtar and Hammurabi gathered together into the embryos of statute law. The difference between the ancient oral laws and the new written ones, between what we nowadays disparage as custom or recognise as law, starts with the use of writing. The influence of writing on the nature of law has already been noted and will be referred to again.

WRITING ON A NAIL. On this clay 'nail' buried in the plaster of a building is a reference to the prologue to the laws of Lipit-Ishtar.

The early collections of laws reflect in large measure the prehistoric legal systems. At the time when laws were first written down legal prehistory was, almost literally, yesterday. The form in which these ancient laws reach us makes it clear that the judges were expected to be guided by the law but were not bound by it; they were free to consult individual circumstance and use their sense. In this, of course, the ancient world contrasts sharply with the modern whose laws lay down the hypothetical circumstances to which they apply, often in minute detail, and intentionally leave as little as they can to the discretion of the judge. If there is conflict today between written law and apparent justice, it is the written law, or the judges interpretation of it, that must prevail. One by-product of the supremacy given to the written law is the modern tradition that anything is permitted that the written law does not specifically forbid. The ancient world had courts of justice, the twentieth century generally has courts of law; and there lies a family of controversies we shall return to.

Here is an early law from the laws of Ur-Nammu during the last years of the third millennium BC:

> If a man, in the course of a scuffle, smashed the limb of another man with a club, he shall pay one mina of silver. (Ur-Nammu, law 16)

The part-time judges who administered laws like these had two jobs: to find the truth, and do justice. Thousands of years were to pass before a third element was added: to serve the law. But when it came, that third element reflected a change in the status of the law by which the law had acquired first an existence then a supremacy of its own, had been deified and, finally, equipped with a then necessary priesthood consisting of full-time judges and a profession of advocacy. That apparatus has proved mighty enough to control millions and subtle enough to leave individuals free; but, almost unnoticed, priesthood status has suppressed the traditional discretion of the judge until justice, even truth itself, can be smothered. A Sumerian lawyer/scribe looking at our world with the penetration of an independent mind would have understood the problem, and grasped that its cause lay not in giving our legal priests too much power, but too little.

Four collections of laws, none of them complete, have been recovered from Sumer and Akkad; while the fifth, the great collection of Hammurabi, was found by French archaeologists in Susa, capital of Elam, where it had lain a war trophy for over three thousand years. The English language translations are taken from ANET 1955 and 1969, and the translators of the individual collections are named below. The five collections of law are:[3]

THE LAWS OF UR-NAMMU

Ur-Nammu was the first king of the third dynasty of Ur (2112–2095BC). It now looks as though these laws may have been written by his son and successor, Shulgi (Kramer 1983), but they continue to be known by his father's name. The written laws date from about 2100BC, though many of them are likely to be far older oral laws; the tablets on which they have survived are school copies made around 1750BC. There are twenty-nine

UR-NAMMU, king of Ur around 2100BC, initiated the earliest surviving collection of written laws. This comes from an impression of a cylinder seal, found at Babylon, showing the king seated and by then deified.

detectable laws of which twenty-three are decipherable. They are written in Sumerian and translated into English by J.J. Finkelstein.

THE LAWS OF ESHNUNNA

The laws of the Akkadian city of Eshnunna. They date from about 1975BC, just after the destruction of Ur. There are sixty-one detectable laws of which fifty-nine are decipherable. They are written in Akkadian and translated by Albrecht Goetze.

THE LAWS OF LIPIT-ISHTAR

Lipit-Ishtar was the fifth king of the dynasty, and city, of Isin. He reigned from c.1934 to 1924BC. It was in Isin that Sumerian civilisation lingered on after the destruction of Ur in about 2000BC. These laws date from about 1930BC and there are thirty-eight detectable laws, of which twenty-two are decipherable. They are written in Sumerian and the English translation is by S.N. Kramer.

A LAW FRAGMENT

A school exercise dating from about 1800BC. The ten laws copied are clearly Sumerian laws. They are written in Sumerian and the English translation is again by J.J. Finkelstein.

THE LAWS OF HAMMURABI

Hammurabi was sixth king of the first dynasty of Babylon. He reigned from c.1792 to c.1750BC. The list of date formulae for the reign of Hammurabi gives for year 22: 'The statue of Hammurabi as king granting justice', which fits the stele bearing his laws with his image in bas relief at its top. In round figures we take the date of publication of his laws to be c.1770BC. The stele on which Hammurabi's laws are engraved is now in the Louvre. He was a semitic speaking Amorite, and he ruled both Sumer and Akkad from Babylon, following the kings of Isin and Larsa. These laws consolidate and reflect the legal framework traditional in both Sumer and Akkad – indeed the whole region – though their penalties are sometimes markedly more severe than those of the older codes, a problem which we will discuss. There are two hundred and eighty-two detectable laws, of which two hundred and fifty-eight are decipherable and one is partly decipherable. They are written in Akkadian and translated by Theophile J. Meek.

Three substantial collections of later laws from the wider region of Mesopotamia or beyond have also survived, at least in part. They are the Edict of Ammisaduqa (who was Hammurabi's great great grandson and king of Babylon c.1646–1626BC), a collection of Hittite laws, and a collection of middle Assyrian laws. A study of these laws is essential to the historian of early law, but they add little more than the main collections above to our knowledge of the status of law or the meaning of justice in the earliest cities of Mesopotamia. A brief look at each of these collections will illustrate the point.

In the introductory note to his translation of the Edict of Ammisaduqa, J.J. Finkelstein[4] tells us that it had been customary for many centuries in Mesopotamia for a king to '... proclaim an act of "justice" or "equity" at the beginning of his reign and at intervals of seven or more years thereafter ...'; that these proclamations concerned mainly the remission of debts of various kinds, and that the Edict of Ammisaduqa is the only substantial surviving text of such a proclamation.

The Edict of Ammisaduqa consists of twenty-two paragraphs of which the first is introductory, giving the purpose of the tablet. Of the remaining paragraphs, eleven grant remission in various degrees to variously specified debts (paras. 2–4 incl., 11–17 incl. and para. 20); one, paragraph 19, is doubtful but probably a remission; seven paragraphs detail circumstances which might be held to qualify for remission but do not do so (5–10 incl. and 21); and two paragraphs (18 and 22) are general laws whose force does not appear to derive from the edict. Paragraph 18 deals with the lady innkeeper who uses dishonest weights and is analogous to Hammurabi's law 108, and 22 concerns the regional governor who abuses his power by conscripting a soldier for harvest or other labour and is analogous to Hammurabi's law 34. The penalty in each of these two cases is death, but the reason for their appearance in this edict is not clear.

The edict was issued once only on a specific occasion for a specific purpose. Finkelstein suggests that the practice of making edicts of this kind may go back to before 2500BC,[5] and that 'some of the provisions' of earlier edicts may have been incorporated into the laws of Hammurabi and the earlier collections. That emphasises that the edicts themselves were considered a genre apart from mainstream legislation. They demand a mention, but their exceptional nature and the probability that they were a source for, rather than a part of, general legislation makes it precarious to use them as bases for conclusions about the general character of legal regimes as evidenced by the law 'codes'.

The main body of Hittite laws[6] were found in Hattusas, capital city of the Hittites, in what is now Turkey. They are written in the cuneiform script and the Hittite language on two tablets, each with one hundred laws, not all decipherable, and a number of related fragments. Tablet I also contains twenty-one later versions of laws 3 to 18 inclusive and 44 to 48 inclusive; and there are twelve laws, some on each tablet, which combine the new with the old version in a single law, for example '... they would formerly give one

KING HAMMURABI OF BABYLON receiving his laws from the sun god Shamash,
carved at the head of a stele engraved with his laws, now in the Louvre, *c.*1770BC.

mina of silver. Now he shall give 5 shekels of silver . . .' (from Hittite law 91).
The later versions soften the severity or improve the humanity of the older
laws they replace, but the older versions are still recorded. Some of these
laws may well be very old, but it is conceivable that the tablets might date
from between *c*.1400 and *c*.1200BC, the period of the Hittite empire which
succeeded the Old Hittite Kingdom (*c*.1600 to *c*.1400BC).

Thirteen of the Hittite laws concerned offences in which death had been
caused; but although there are fifteen laws imposing the death penalty, not
one of these death penalties applies to a case where someone has died or
been killed. In this respect, the Hittite laws remind us of the laws of
Mesopotamia where the death penalty is not necessarily related to whether
the crime being punished had involved a death. The fifteen Hittite death
penalties are: for theft three laws, for sorcery three laws, incest six laws,
rejecting the judgement of the king one law; in two laws – one, theft where
the death penalty is listed as obsolete and one, sorcery, where the case is
referred to the king – the death penalty is presumably an option. There are
two laws imposing a penalty of mutilation: both apply to slaves – one is for
theft and one for arson. That contrasts with Hammurabi who had fifteen
penalties of mutilation – only one of them applying to a slave; and it might
contrast with the pre-Hammurabi laws whose surviving penalties do not
give a complete picture but do not include mutilation at all. There are seventeen laws about causing personal injury, all of whose penalties are financial, which is consistent with Hammurabi's main laws of personal injury
and contrasts only with his laws of talion. The Hittite laws contain no hint
of talion, and in this they contrast with Hammurabi.

Superficially the Hittite laws appear similar to those of Mesopotamia,
but a closer look reveals differences; while the possibility that the Hittite
laws may well be five hundred years later also suggests that they should
not be included in a study based on the laws of Sumer, Akkad and Babylon.

The middle Assyrian laws[7] probably date from the twelfth century BC
and are likely to be later than the surviving Hittite laws. There are ten
tablets containing one hundred and sixteen laws of which three tablets
contain ninety laws and the remaining seven, fewer than eight laws each.
Some of the laws are not decipherable. The laws deal among other things
with women, theft, marriage, inheritance. Some are so detailed that they
almost cease to have general application; some are distinguished by the
extreme violence of their penalties. They give a sometimes frightening picture of life in Assyria some six or seven hundred years later than Hammurabi. They do not illustrate the earlier world of Sumer, Akkad and
Babylon which culminated in Hammurabi in the eighteenth century BC.

In any society, the legal framework includes two kinds of law which are
equal in force but different in kind. One class of laws reflects and perpetu-

ates a society's continuing characteristics and ethical standards; the other enforces the shorter term policies of government. The two classes merge into each other at the edges but are distinct enough in the main. Sumer had laws about telling the truth (for example Ur-Nammu law 25 about perjury), but it also had a law laying down what must happen 'if an ox caused the loss of a straying ox' (Sumerian law fragment 10); the fragmented ending to that law says, simply, 'ox for ox'.

In the world of Sumer, Akkad and Babylon, law was conservative. It preserved, and was intended to preserve, the traditional framework of society. Adjustments were occasionally made if need arose such as the new laws made by Hammurabi when conflicting cultures had to be reconciled. The use of law to enforce change in accordance with a predetermined philosophy lay nearly four thousand years in the future.

Of our five collections of laws, the Sumerian fragment is a schoolboy's exercise rather than a fragment of an entire collection, and the choice of laws may well reflect a schoolboy's interests: of the ten laws copied two deal with causing a girl to miscarry, two with rape, three with rows between a son and his parents, one with losing a boat and two with a herdsman losing straying cattle. *Plus ca change* ... Of the remaining four codes two, Ur-Nammu and Lipit-Ishtar, were both laws of Sumerian cities and they are written in Sumerian; while two, Eshnunna and Hammurabi, were laws of cities in Akkad and are written in Akkadian. The cities of Eshnunna and Babylon were geographically not far apart and their surviving laws were fairly close in time; the two collections have, in places, a similarity of approach and some of their laws are identical, which suggests the possibility of an earlier common semitic/Akkadian tradition. Each of these four codes originally had a prologue and an epilogue in which the ethos of the

'Schoolboy, where did you go from earliest days?'
'I went to school.'
'What did you do in school?'
'I read my tablet, ate my lunch, prepared my tablet, wrote it, finished it. . .
. . .I spoke to my father of my hand copies, then read the tablet to him, and my father was pleased; truly I found favour with my father. . .'

In the ancient schools of Mesopotamia, the student would learn to write by copying tablets. Precise accuracy was the aim, and the curriculum may have taken some six years. This collection of ten Sumerian laws is an exercise, probably by an advanced student, both in handwriting and in law.

code was stated in unexceptionable and similar terms, highly flattering to the king's ego but not necessarily insincere. Traditional and picturesque curses were invoked against anyone violating the tablets.

Ur-Nammu, king of Ur, says in his prologue to the earliest collection of laws we have:[8]

> Then did Ur-Nammu, the mighty warrior, king of Ur, king of Sumer and Akkad, by the mighty Nanna lord of the city of Ur ... establish equity in the land. He banished malediction, violence and strife...
>
> ... The orphan was not delivered up to the rich man; the widow was not delivered up to the mighty man; the man of one shekel was not delivered up to the man of one mina ...

Law and order within a stable traditional framework was the foundation on which one of the most creative and progressive of all human societies was based. In an age of inter-city warfare, if a city were to survive its internal structure had to be defined and rigid so, over the years, the cities became socially stratified. Each individual had freedom within a prescribed sphere, and the laws reflected and reinforced a social organisation vital for survival. The definition of crime, the identification of offenders, the imposition of penalties which would above all be effective, and sometimes the allocation of different penalties to different social classes, including slaves, were the bases of their city laws. In Sumerian times laws were often surprisingly liberal, but by the time of Hammurabi, while the laws were much the same, many of the penalties had become almost inexplicably cruel.

In our journey through these old laws we shall take as our guide a fictitious Sumerian lawyer/scribe. We will call him Atu after the diviner (whom we will soon be meeting) named in the lawsuit brought by the slave Ninkuzu in the reign of king Shu-Sin of the city of Ur (c.2037–2029BC). Our Atu, by means which are not to be explained, can perceive the modern world, and from time to time he will be invited to tell us from his Sumerian standpoint his own opinion, both of our discussion and of what we have made of some of the principles first found in Sumer. For instance, Atu would smile and cock his head at the idea that individual freedom could be either the foundation or the objective of a civilised society. Prosperity and creativity, he would recall, had always flourished when order had prevailed while violence and crime were the products of unfettered freedom. But he would breathe more deeply and wear a characteristic frown when he pondered on the vastly greater numbers in our world and on the effect which enormous numbers must have on the ability to give weight to each individual's circumstances.

A LEGAL TABLET IN ITS ENVELOPE, from the Middle Babylonian period. Legal tablets were placed in clay envelopes for security or, possibly, to be transported.

CHAPTER 3

THE BURDEN OF PROOF

THE ANCIENT LAWS were concerned with justice not pedantry. The nature of justice was understood intuitively, though never defined on the tablets; and, of course, everyone knew what injustice was and that it threatened public order. Everyone also knew that justice was a balance in which truth was one, but not the only, element; so justice without truth was a fiction. They were particular about how the truth should be established and who should be responsible for establishing it. In principle, anyone who wanted a court to believe their word, must prove it; and that applied to prosecutor and accused, to plaintiff and defendant, and to witnesses. Occasionally, and disinheriting a son is an example, a law required that the court undertake its own enquiry into, say, a son's or a father's record, and no doubt there were many occasions when courts made enquiries even though the laws did not specifically require them to do so. Much of what took place in an ancient court would be familiar territory to a modern barrister, including the formal duty to seek the truth; but the systems separate when it comes to what the ancient world accepted as proof. In that world truth was sometimes held to have been established by means which a modern court might secretly envy, such as throwing an

THE LION GATE AT BOĞAZKÖY was one entrance to Hattusas, the ancient capital of the Hittites in modern Turkey. It is also a likely site for their law courts; the judges would often meet at the city gates.

accused into the river to see whether he drowned or not. That, in the end, illustrates how desperate they were to obtain the truth or, if truth were not available, an acceptable certainty. When deciding with whom the burden of proof must lie they were close to the modern world; when deciding what might be accepted as proof they were sometimes a long way away.

The principles underlying ancient laws are sometimes self-evident, but often they have to be inferred from the surviving laws, which leaves a greater margin for doubt; occasionally we have to interpret the laws and see, if we can, how a similar case was actually decided by a real court. Court records, known as *ditillas*, have often survived: they describe briefly the essential facts of a case with the names of the principal participants, and they give the judgement; they then list by name the principal court officials including the judges and, usually, the person acting as clerk; and they finish with a date in a form strange to us but caused by their lack of a fixed date in the past from which to identify their years. This is one court record:[1]

> Ninkuzu, daughter of Sur-Nanse, a servant of Atu the diviner, appeared before the court and declared:
>
> 'By the King's name, this is the position: Within two days I shall produce witnesses that Nasaba, a son of Atu, has freed me. If I do not produce them, let me be a maidservant to the heirs of Atu!'
>
> Because on the appointed day as per her oath by the King's name Ninkuzu did not produce witnesses to her having been freed, the maidservant was assigned to the heirs of Atu.
>
> Lu-uruka was the bailiff.
> Lu-digira, Sur-Istarana and Lu-digira were the judges.
> Year king Shu-Sin erected the lofty stela of Enlil.

Ninkuzu is (or was) the daughter of Sur-Nanse a slave of Atu the diviner. As the daughter of a slave she is the property of her parent's owner. Atu, her legal owner, has died and Ninkuzu now claims she has been freed by Nasaba, a son of Atu, who presumably had power to free her. Ninkuzu is not challenging the fact that she was until his death legally the slave of Atu, indeed she confirms it; so if she wishes to claim that a legally accepted situation has changed, the burden of proof rests with her and she must produce a prima-facie case which the heirs of Atu will have to answer. As her claim implies an accusation that the heirs of Atu have been holding her in slavery illegally, she is to that extent a prosecutor. Her claim that she has been freed by Nasaba can be established if she can produce witnesses who will swear that her claim is true; and the one witness whose evidence will carry most weight is, of course, Nasaba himself. The court agrees with her about what shall be held to constitute proof, in this case the production of witnesses, and allows her time to produce them. On the appointed day, Ninkuzu has not found witnesses, and Nasaba does not appear; so she loses her case. The court record does not go into detail, and does not need to: the statements that she had been required to produce witnesses and that she had not done so explain concisely why she lost her case.

We may speculate that perhaps the other heirs had objected to losing so valuable a property as an experienced slave and were manipulating the court by withholding the truth from it; or perhaps Ninkuzu had made up her story in the hope that the court would be easily fooled. Be that as it may, Ninkuzu is the accuser and the heirs of Atu are the accused; and the burden of proof rested in the third millennium BC where it would rest today – with the accuser. As Ninkuzu was not able to produce witnesses she lost her case, a very modern result; and posterity does not know where the truth lay – a perfectly contemporary situation.

The case of Sur-DUB.UMBISAG[2] is a little more difficult:

> Sur-DUB.UMBISAG swore by the king's life that by the new moon of the month of Eating the Malt he would produce the thief of Lu-Nanna's stolen sheep; and if he did not produce him he would be a thief.

> Before Sur-Ig.alima, son of Kagu; before Kagina, the messenger; and before Shesh-Sheshgu, the overseer.

> Month of the sowing, 14th day.
> Year the omen-kid chose the high priest of Inana.

> Seal: Sur-DUB.UMBISAG scribe, son of Utugu, chief of the weavers.

It was normal for the owner of cattle or sheep to hire a man to act as shepherd. It was also known for the shepherd to steal and sell animals, claiming that one or more of the (say) sheep in his charge had been seized by a wild animal and was therefore lost through no fault of his. There were lions in Sumer. But the lion does not eat the whole animal, bones and all, so where there was a kill there will have been a carcase. Hammurabi has the best formulation of ancient law in this predicament:

> If a visitation of god has occurred in a sheepfold or a lion has made a kill, the shepherd shall prove himself innocent in the presence of the god, but the owner of the sheepfold shall receive from him the animal stricken in the fold. (Hammurabi, law 266)

The words 'prove himself innocent' are literally correct but a shade misleading. The burden of proof actually lay with the prosecutor, Lu-Nanna, the owner of the sheep, as it would today. It was clearly Lu-Nanna who brought the case to court, not Sur-DUB.UMBISAG, the alleged thief. Lu-Nanna would have had to start his case by first establishing that he was in

THE ROYAL STANDARD OF UR. A third millennium BC representation of farm animals and produce, c.2600BC; an illustration of daily life in Sumer.

fact the owner of the sheep and that one animal had indeed been lost while in the care of Sur-DUB.UMBISAG. That would probably have required, first, a statement of the number of sheep that had been committed to Sur-DUB.UMBISAG's charge, probably supported by a receipt or witnesses; and, second, a statement similarly corroborated that that number of sheep minus one had been returned by Sur-DUB.UMBISAG at the end of his time as shepherd. That, if unrefuted, would be sufficient evidence to convict Sur-DUB.UMBISAG of theft and would therefore constitute a prima-facie case which the shepherd must answer. The existence of a procedure along these lines is attested by the laws of Hammurabi:

> If the professed owner of the lost property has not produced witnesses attesting to his lost property, since he was a cheat and started a false report, he shall be put to death. (Hammurabi, law 11)

The shepherd then as now would have to defend himself against a formal

43

accusation made before a court and supported by evidence sufficient to convict him; and in order to refute the evidence against him he would need contrary evidence to account for the missing animal. One form that contrary evidence could take would be a carcase; another might be witnesses. In the case of Sur-DUB.UMBISAG, who admitted loss of the animal, it was to be a witness in the form of the thief in person. If the accused had not been required to produce evidence in his defence, the dishonest shepherd would be paid for his stewardship, be paid again when he sold the stolen animal and would walk free from the court. Results of that kind are not unheard of today, and we have only to close our eyes to imagine our scribe Atu contemplating the release by our courts of established criminals and the conviction and imprisonment of honest citizens trying to defend themselves against those very criminals – allowed free to taunt them – to understand why he is silently raising one appalled eyebrow. But he will surely detect that the fault lies not with our judges but with the relationship, by now traditional, between our courts and the law. Perhaps, later, he may be persuaded to reflect on this himself.

Much is made of the fact that none of the ancient court records refers to any single written law, and the blanket inference is made that what we hold to be the rule of law, that is the rule of written law, was unknown in the ancient world. The case of Sur-DUB.UMBISAG makes it clear that the ancient courts were well aware of what the written laws said and in fact their judgements were generally in conformity with them. A law such as Hammurabi's law 266 will have been very old indeed, and it probably came down from the oral law which preceded the written. A court may well have been guided by the traditional oral law as much as by the more recent written laws. That a court would need to quote from the written law in order to give its judgement authority was a doctrine unknown in the ancient world; that would mean that the court's discretion had been replaced by a document, a development which still lay far in the future.

There is one point about Hammurabi's law 226 above. The words ' ... the shepherd shall prove himself innocent ... ' could be interpreted as evidence that an accused person was guilty until proved to be innocent. That is not a necessary interpretation, and it is not supported either by the court judgements or by the form of the laws. The confusion arises because, once the prosecution case has been made, the onus passes to the accused to defend himself against it; and at that stage he does indeed have to establish his innocence. A clear statement of this appears in Hammurabi:

> If a seignior accused another seignior and brought a charge of murder against him, but has not proved it, his accused shall be put to death. (Hammurabi, law 1)

That says nothing about whether the accused seignior was guilty in fact; it is concerned only that the charge against him must be proved.

The Sumerian law courts had four main methods of establishing the truth: hard evidence, witnesses, an oath before the god, and the river test.

HARD EVIDENCE

Hard evidence was of course ideal. The shepherd one animal short had a cast-iron defence if he could produce a carcase. Conversely, the prosecution had a cast-iron case if a thief was caught in the act:

> If a man entered the orchard of another man and was seized there for stealing, he shall pay ten shekels of silver. (Lipit-Ishtar, law 9)

But it was in the market-place that irreconcilable disputes arose. A man in possession of goods might claim he had bought them, while traders identified the goods as theirs and denied having sold them. So ancient law laid the onus of proof on the purchaser as this law from Eshnunna makes clear:

> If a man buys a slave, a slave-girl, an ox or any other valuable good but cannot legally establish the seller, he is a thief. (Eshnunna, law 40)

The penalty for being a thief is not stated in this law, but earlier laws in the Eshnunna code, laws 12 and 13, impose a fine of ten shekels of silver for theft by day and death for theft by night. Hammurabi also has a law requiring the purchaser to prove that he had bought goods in his possession, but with a harsher penalty:

> If a seignior had purchased or he received for safe-keeping either silver or gold or an ox or a sheep or an ass or any sort of thing from the hand of a seignior's son or a seignior's slave without witnesses and contracts, that seignior is a thief, he shall be put to death. (Hammurabi, law 7)

A seignior was a member of an upper class for whom Hammurabi's penalties were markedly more severe than for lower classes. In law 7, Hammurabi is clearly concerned with more than theft. The victims of this particular class of theft are both of subordinate status, one being the son and the other the slave of a seignior: so in this case the crime of theft is exacerbated by the additional crime of exploitation of the weak. Theft by itself was a crime that Hammurabi treated with great severity, and one for which the seignior regularly faced a death penalty, where less privileged citizens faced only fines. In Hammurabi's laws, what constituted a crime was the same for everyone but often the privileged classes faced a more severe penalty than those of lower status.

Now, here is Atu nodding agreement at Hammurabi's intention if not at his penalty because, in an enclosed city, thieves running free are a threat to public order and to society itself. He is grinning slightly because he can also see that after four thousand years we are still faced with the identical problem when a shopper comes out of a store with goods in his plastic bag but no receipt to prove he has not stolen them. Atu is also indicating with a resigned expression that unlike Hammurabi we do not convict our shopper of theft just because he cannot produce a receipt, and that our meticulous care permits both a more scrupulous individual justice and a high incidence of shoplifting. Atu is indicating that he is aware of the problem and envies our approach, but would like to enlarge on the difficulties which his world had to face and which we have largely overcome, if in the future he can find his full voice with which to do so . . .

WITNESSES

What matters about witnesses is that they tell the truth. That will be more likely if the consequences of not doing so are real:

> If a man appeared as a witness in a lawsuit, and was shown to be a perjurer, he must pay fifteen shekels of silver. (Ur-Nammu, law 25)

Fifteen shekels of silver was roughly three and three-quarter ounces. Refusal to testify was also a crime for which the penalty was real:

> If a man appeared as a witness in a lawsuit, but declined to testify on oath, he must make good as much as is involved in that lawsuit. (Ur-Nammu, law 26)

That a man might appear as a witness but refuse to testify suggests that the appearance of witnesses was not always voluntary and that they could

GOD OF JUSTICE AND THE SUN. From a cylinder seal, showing the sun-god Shamash holding a toothed saw, the symbol of the office of judge.

be subpoenaed. The modern crime is contempt of court, which transfers the conflict from one between the witness and one of the parties to the lawsuit to a conflict between a witness and the law. We will return to that. In the ancient court the conflict remained between the parties to the dispute, and the penalty for damage caused by a witness's refusal to testify was paid to the injured party as compensation for the injury caused by his silence. The principle of compensation for damage caused is clear.

As the law was not yet a legal entity involved in each case, financial penalties were normally paid as recompense to the injured party; when the law became a legal entity, it was the law that was injured, fines were paid to the state and an injured party might win his case but leave court without adequate, or even any, financial redress. We shall return to that as well.

THE OATH

But what about the witness whose evidence was uncorroborated? The simplest way was to rely on the oath, as in this law from the city of Eshnunna:

> If a man has no claim against another man, but nevertheless distrains another man's slave-girl, the owner of the slave-girl shall declare under oath: 'Thou hast no claim against me' and he shall pay him silver in full compensation for the slave-girl. (Eshnunna, law 22)

The oath was not just a matter of law, it was real. A later, but still Old Babylonian period, court record[3] concerns the sale of a house in the city of Susa, capital city of the country of Elam. Elam lay to the east of Sumer, was nearly as old and shared a similar culture. Elam and Sumer were traditional enemies, and Elam was one of those who destroyed Ur about 2000BC. The court record tells us that Abi-ili sold a house in Susa to Kuk-adar, but one of Abi-ili's sons challenged the sale and sued one of Kuk-adar's sons, Iqishuni. This extract gives the very serious accusation made by Abi-ili's son and tells how the problem was resolved:

> [the litigants] declared thus: 'Our father's house was not sold to your father; your tablet is forged.' Many men were present and, acting as a court, imposed upon Iqishuni the oath by the god. In the temple of Inanna Iqishuni pronounced the oath, saying: 'Thou, O Inanna, knowest that I did not fabricate a forged document, and that my father bequeathed this tablet to me.' Iqishuni having thus sworn, they cleared for him his title to the house.

There follow the names of witnesses and the formal decision that the judges cleared him for title to the house.

That is an original record of a simple declaration under oath made in the temple being accepted as decisive evidence in a court of law. That this record happens to come from Elam rather than Sumer makes no difference: the principle of the oath was clearly common throughout the region despite possible local variations in the content of some laws.

What kind of power lay behind such a simple oath that it could terrify a witness and convince a court? An oath before the god can be binding so long as you believe in the god; an oath on your honour is equally binding if you possess that quality; but neither will produce the truth in all circumstances. In the ancient world an oath before the god usually meant an oath sworn in the temple precinct or at the temple gate in the presence of a priest who probably knew the witness. So if the oath proved false there was a double penalty: the penalty for perjury laid down by law; and the arrival on your doorstep of a formally clad and grim-faced priest, equipped not only with the anger of the gods but with the more precise weapons of a priesthood who controlled most of the city economy, including its food supply and its labour force. The priest's visit may be a fiction, but the court judgements readily accessible seldom if ever mention witnesses who lied.

 'Yes, Atu ...'

He is trying to speak ... almost audible ... his grey, balding head is slowly shaking ... A strong face, intelligent eyes and a broad, humourous mouth ... his voice curiously high-pitched has a musical quality that conveys both clarity and authority ... his body seems slim rather than tall, and he is wearing a mantle draped around his shoulders.

'Please, Atu, can you tell us something?'

'... Yes, I have ... I can perceive ... clearly that your world is different from mine and yet ... Can you hear what I am trying to say ... ?'

'Yes, I can Atu. Please go on.'

'At last ... I was trying to say that I think we share the same basic principles ... I am not sure that what you have done with those principles is always quite what we would have done ...

... We both understand ... my ancient world surely understood that before justice can be done you have to get to the truth, and we both know how very difficult that can be ... but we were fortunate in a way because in our world religion was real, our priesthood had power as well as authority, and they were respected ... '

'Is that a look of pity in your eye Atu, because so many of our witnesses swear by a god they do not believe in, or affirm on their honour when they have no idea what that means?'

'... Sympathy certainly, but I am in no position to be patronising ... I think your profession of advocacy has ideals, and surely individual advocates have, but what they have done as a body has nearly destroyed justice

... law and justice are not always the same in spite of what some of your authorities would have you accept ... later, perhaps we can take that further ... but I think we got our principles right and our penalties often wrong, whereas you have your penalties not far from right but your principles have vanished ... And yes, I am sad that you have abandoned religion ... you have lost much there that you cannot well do without ...'

'If no one nowadays fears the priest, Atu, that is partly because our science has enabled us to explain so many mysteries that the unexplained is no longer inexplicable. Religion can survive defiance but not an explanation. Our science has not taken the mystery out of life but it has removed the area of remaining mystery to a territory so remote that ordinary minds cannot get there. People have not so much lost their faith as had it stolen from them, and they have lost their way because the only remaining mystery is: "why?": and that question they are content to leave unanswered as too remote to be relevant. The spiritual element in life which inspired you to give reverence to your temple and your priesthood is to us often a source of ridicule. Much that gave strength, colour, purpose and meaning to your societies is missing from ours, and our knowing that does not bring it back.'

'*... Your courts are happy to accept dubious evidence or the almost blatant suppression of the truth because they have no means themselves to reach out and find the truth, and without the means they deny the duty ... so what else can they do?'*

'You have a point, Atu. You can take pride in your intention to reach the truth and scorn our weakness in making no real effort to do so, but before you smile too broadly may we ask you to tell us about that river test we read so much of in your laws? Please, what have you to say about that?'

Atu has vanished.

THE RIVER ORDEAL

In extreme cases where corroboration was impossible the law prescribed the river test or ordeal. That consisted of being thrown into the river: if you survived you were innocent, and if you were guilty you did not survive ... so, either way, the case was brought to a conclusion.

> If a man accused the wife of a man of fornication, and the river ordeal proved her innocent, then the man who had accused her must pay one-third of a mina of silver. (Ur-Nammu, law 11)

or this:

> If a man had accused another man of [the offence is undecipherable] and he [the accuser] had him [the accused] brought to the river ordeal, and the river ordeal proved him innocent, then the man who brought him [the accuser] must pay him three shekels of silver. (Ur-Nammu, law 10)

Sometimes, and Hammurabi has laws on this, the river test was itself used as a punishment:

> If [a wife] was not careful, but was a gadabout, thus neglecting her house and humiliating her husband, they shall throw that woman into the water. (Hammurabi, law 143)

And Hammurabi who, for all his harshness, was not lacking in a sense of honour, also had this law:

> If the finger was pointed at the wife of a seignior because of another man, but she has not been caught while lying with the other man, she shall throw herself into the river for the sake of her husband.
>
> (Hammurabi, law 132)

The suspicion is, of course, that she had been lying with him. If that is a correct reading, this law illustrates Hammurabi's very modern dilemma: his devotion to truth as fundamental to justice is incompatible with the necessity to prove the case. Hammurabi's recourse is to appeal to ethical conduct, but by leaving it to the wife to throw herself into the river, rather than requiring the husband or the court to give her a push, he stops a hair's breadth short of compulsion and therefore of success. That does credit to his humanity as well as to his respect for procedure, but it means that he bequeathes to posterity a problem as well as a law.

To make any sense of the river test or ordeal you have to believe in it. You have to believe that the result of the ordeal reflected the intention of the gods rather than chance or having learnt to swim, that the gods really did know the truth and that their decisions were just. Today we have no such faith, and we sometimes doubt whether many people really did, even in the ancient world ...

Atu is stroking his forehead and there is a serious line around his mouth:

 '... I seem to recall that the submission of human problems for decision by the gods is a recourse far older than recorded history. A decision has to be made; it must be impartial, and it must be final ... those are the vital factors... An acceptable certainty is what we really seek though we call it the will of the gods. Whether a particular decision is right or wrong, either practically or even morally, cannot always be known at the time, so whether it is right or not is quite secondary ... though if it is clearly immoral it is obviously wrong ...'

'That is a dangerous philosophy, Atu, because it opens a high road to abuse, and then to an even more dangerous manipulation and disillusionment. Take the problem of war. The outcome of war is unpredictable. It is an example of man having so exhausted both his reason and his patience that in desperation he turns to the gods. Yes, even we in the modern world must admit that we go to war calling on God for justice and in the faith that God is on our side. So of course do our enemies, and we each know that the other is doing the same. We dare not contemplate the human predicament from a detached point of view: because our armies would never fight as they do if they had to believe that God is no more than another name for chance and that the outcome of all their sacrifices was merely luck. In peace it is different. Faced with a need for impartial decision, final and acceptable, in the sports of peace, we find it natural to toss a coin; but in a conflict between tribes, cities or nations where we meet the same need to seek the decision of the gods, the coin is too trivial and we insist on slaughter. Besides, war can be manipulated. In war, massive superiority in numbers or weapons will tilt the balance, but they do not offer certainty or justify a cause; so we still fear the gods and, nowadays, make or buy weapons more often than we fight with them. But if our calculations fail, as periodically they do, war follows; and then the decision of the gods has to be accepted, even in our world, because their decision involves the destruction of the means of resistance to it.'

'... *I think we always understood that...*'

'Indeed you did, Atu. And we also know that desperation for raw materials or power, the determination to win or die for the cause, the belief that participation in such a fight confers a status in this world, let alone the next, which is its own reward, the poetry of heroism, the thrill of danger, are motives which can make war seem desirable, though they may not directly lead to it. We have found that the outcome of war bears no relation to the worth of those who wage it or to the ideals for which it is waged. Nevertheless, in a crisis where a decision is vital, war, the life or death test, is still and frequently invoked.'

'*... I perceive that all too clearly ... I also perceive that even after four thousand years you have scarcely reduced the number of occasions on which you seek a divine decision, and that for all your science and technology you have still not abandoned the principle underlying the river test preserved for you by the scribes of Ur and Babylon ... the desperate submission of human conflict for decision by the gods.*'

'Atu! You have a twinkle in your eye.'

THE SEARCH FOR TRUTH

 'You have something to add, Atu?'

'*... Yes, I have... We thought we were talking about the burden of proof, but we now find that this whole discussion is really about the search for truth. In Sumer, the search for truth lay at the centre of our legal process. Witnesses, oaths and an appeal to the gods were the means we used to try and find it. But we could never be perfectly*

sure that we had succeeded, and when truth eluded us the vital importance of public order persuaded us to settle for certainty in its place ... '

'We also search for the truth, Atu, but we follow a different route. We have a profession of advocacy, with high ideals to be sure; but in the end advocacy means presenting a case. Though the advocate must not tell a lie, he has no duty to find and tell the truth. He presents the best case he can on the material given to him and within the law as he finds it. He has no means to investigate the basis of every statement made to him, nor does his duty toward one side in a conflict permit him to argue for the other or, indeed, for justice, unless he is sure that justice is on his side. Witnesses, as you know, Atu, can be formally held to the oath they swear and to the evidence they give under that oath, but that could not apply to our advocate; so we pit advocates against each other before twelve impartial referees, and expect truth to emerge from the dust.

You too, Atu, had laws which ensured that though the truth might be known, the court must not hear it unless it be proved. In a way, that is where it started; that is the knot we have not even yet untied. Even you could not dare to trust your courts with a known truth that could not be proved. Your records suggest that even in your world the next step was sometimes taken, and concealment from the court might occasionally have reinforced concealment in court. Dare we wonder whether in both our worlds certainty always was accepted as a substitute for truth? And yet ... the belief that certainty matters more than truth has propped up some of our most terrible tyrannies; but when the tyrannies have vanished and their memory has been condemned there remains the question whether, when truth is not to be found, certainty may be preferable to continuing doubt. In a world where security is the first consideration, in your world, Atu, what mattered most was that the judge must decide, the case must be disposed of and the conflict go away rather than hang around and fester. Ninkuzu came to your court legally a slave but contending that she was free; the court did not reach the truth, and she left it a slave for life. In our world, we are constantly reminded, by the example of judges who take that road, that a decision which defies the truth is the one that hangs around and festers. Truth is never just there, waiting to be discovered; it has to be worked for. I think that is beginning to dawn on us, though it emerges slowly through a fog of tradition. Perhaps we can stand more uncertainty than your world could, or maybe we are less prepared than you were to accept the unacceptable; but your problem is still with us. The real problem is not how to face the truth but how to face the problem of getting to it.'

'... Please, there is one point ... about your advocates ... You say, correctly, that they must not lie, and I think they do not. But do you really mean that they need not tell the truth? ...'

'That is a big point, Atu. We have said they have no means to investigate every statement they may make, so that giving them a duty to tell the truth may not be practicable. It is not that they fail to disclose a truth injurious to their case, but rather that the law itself is open to manipulation in a way that allows the advocate to procure for his client an advantageous injustice, a verdict that is untrue to the realities of the case, no matter what barrister or court may privately think. That is just one of the effects of allowing the written law to become the master of our courts, and that in turn was one of the effects of moving from an oral to a written law. You had no profession of advocacy, but you had scribes who specialised in law and gave legal advice for which they were, of course, paid ... That is not the same thing ...? Not quite, perhaps. But you are right, Atu, that you saw the law as a guide to the court, never as master, and still less as god.'

'... *True, my friend, we did not have a profession of advocacy. No advocate stood between our accused and the court, so our accused had to speak and answer in his own voice and the court judged him as they found him. Nor was our law so complex that the ordinary person could not understand it. The law was, and was meant to be, a guide to our part-time judges how they might use their sense and their discretion, but it did not bind them to a particular course, especially if the facts argued otherwise. Always our judges were expected to judge the particular case and the real individual who was before them. The rule of law emerged from their decisions as a natural outcome, as it had ever since our ancestors lived in caves and worked in stone. Our laws were precedents, but they could not dictate to the judge or deny him the use of his own sense; they could not defy the truth; they neither could, nor did, define justice, but our courts knew what justice was. Why have courts at all if they cannot decide the individual case? How do you call them courts of justice if justice is the one thing they sometimes cannot even try to do ...?*'

CAPTIVES IN MANACLES, probably off to a lifetime as slaves, the usual fate of prisoners of war and also of the main source of slaves.

CHAPTER 4

THE CONCEPT OF PROPERTY

ANCIENT LAW is permeated with property. The concept of physical property, that is property in things, is uncontentious, universal and even older than man. A dog with a bone has a sense of property. Ownership of physical property may not have been the first legal principle, but it is probably the principle from which our concepts of right and wrong arose. The only disputes about the concept of the ownership of physical property are about its extent and the penalties for its abuse.

By contrast, the concept of property in persons is controversial. The ownership of one person by another has a long history. It was, and is, the basis of the family. Under the name of slavery, it was the kick-start for technological advance, the power source of a pre-technological world. It raises but does not answer fundamental questions about the nature of Man and the purpose of life. It raises practical questions about employment and the distribution of social and political power. The mere suggestion of property in persons is enough to inflame both idealism and guilt until the noise becomes deafening.

No study of the ancient world can sidestep the concept of the ownership of persons, so we will start immediately with slavery and keep wives and children, or most of them, until the next chapter.

SLAVERY

There are degrees of slavery. It is a disturbing curiosity that the more cruel the form the more likely it is to be, at least relatively, modern. In Sumer, slavery seems to have been a minority status used mainly for service in the home or around the property. The great public works, such as maintaining the irrigation systems or the city walls, were undertaken by the forced, but paid labour, of free citizens. Conscription for survival or defence is probably older than the city and, though it raises ethical problems for the modern world in particular cases, the principle is still generally accepted and widely applied – and not only in a military context. It is not called slavery.

In Sumer, slaves were a minority, largely foreign and probably more women than men. Only a small number were Sumerian. The most common source of female slaves was Gutian girls captured from their homes in the Zagros mountains during raids launched for that purpose. That the Gutians nursed a hatred of Sumer and a longing to destroy it is presented as an inexplicable perversity in the Sumerian tablets. Twice the Gutians succeeded: they destroyed the dynasty of Agade and presided rather than ruled for maybe forty years before the third dynasty of Ur; and with the Elamites from the east and the Amorites from the west they brought the third dynasty of Ur to an end just before 2000BC.

A second and reliable source of slaves was prisoners of war. As the first fruit of any aggressive war aimed at raw materials, territory or power, prisoners were mostly men and all of working age. Slavery was the accepted lot of the captive, though from the law codes it is evident that some eventually found their way home:

> If a man has been made a prisoner during a raid or an invasion or if he has been carried off forcibly and stayed in a foreign country for a long time, and another man has taken his wife and she has born him a son – when he returns he shall get his wife back. (Eshnunna, law 29)

'Yes, Atu? All right, we know. In property terms that was not unfair, but today, as you can perceive, the final decision would most certainly involve, and in practice rest with, the wife. The property principle is still alive and well but, nowadays, it has its limitations. We will return to that.'

Let your mouth be restrained and your speech guarded;
That is a man's pride – let what you say be very precious.

From 'The Instructions of Shuruppak' c.2500BC. Translated by Robert D. Biggs.

Hammurabi's law is very similar:

> If, when a seignior was taken captive and there was not sufficient to live on in his house, his wife ... (has gone to another man and had children by him, when the husband returns) ... that woman shall return to her first husband, while the children shall go with their father. (Hammurabi, law 135)

A third, small and pathetic source of slaves was Sumerians or other natives of the cities who had fallen into debt and sold their wives or children into slavery as a means of paying it off. It was (slightly) less horrific than it sounds since their slavery was by law not permanent and their status as a result was different from that of other slaves. We will look at it more closely in the next chapter when we come to debt.

THE STATUS OF SLAVE

Of course slaves were useful but Sumer was not based on slavery. As slaves were mostly foreign they did not threaten either the economy or the social structure, so it was safe to allow them some rights. Even so, the slave was a slave, the property as well as the servant of his master, and his simple duty was to do what he was told. The ancient laws sometimes explicitly classed slaves along with animals and physical property, and referred to the slave as 'it':

> If the governor, the river commissioner or another official whoever it may be seizes a lost slave, a lost slave-girl, a lost ox, a lost donkey ... (From Eshnunna, law 50)

> A slave or slave-girl of Eshnunna ... shall not leave the gate of Eshnunna without its owner's permission. (From Eshnunna, law 51)

A property is valuable and productive only if it is carefully maintained and properly used, so slaves for whom a high price had been paid were not often mistreated by their owners. Mistreating another man's slave was, of course, to damage his property, and that was a crime for which compensation had

THE FREEING OF A SLAVE ON 12 JUNE 427 BC

On the 20th of Siwan, that is the 7th day of Phamenoth, the year 38 of King Artaxerxes — at that time, Meshullam son of Zakkur, a Jew of the fortress of Elephantine, of the detachment of Arpakhu, said to the woman Tapmut as she is called, his slave, who has on her right hand the marking 'Of Meshullam', as follows: I have taken kindly thought of you in my lifetime. I hereby declare you released at my death and likewise declare released the daughter Yehoyishma as she is called whom you have borne to me ... none has any right to mark you or to deliver you as a payment of money ...

And Tapmut and Yehoyishma declared: We shall serve you ... as long as you live; and when you die, we shall support your son Zakkur ... just as we shall have been doing for you while you were alive ...

From a papyrus at Elephantine, a Jewish colony on the Nile, translated and annotated by H.L. Ginsberg. The translator has noted that Tapmut had been married to Meshullam but, at the time of his death, was still his slave, as was their daughter. He left this document formally freeing both of them. Tapmut carried a brand marking her as his property; it is not stated whether, on gaining her freedom, she would (or could) have the brand removed.

to be paid. But the property principle cannot wholly explain the existence of laws against the physical maltreatment of slaves; there is a lingering sense of right and wrong in those laws as well, whatever the logic. Even so, in the earliest code a slave, in this case a woman, must know her place and control her temper:

> If a man's slave-woman, comparing herself to her mistress, speaks insolently to her or him, her mouth shall be scoured with one quart of salt. (Ur-Nammu, law 22)

Relations between a slave and her owner were sometimes a good deal closer than laws based on conflict would suggest:

> If a man married a wife and she bore him children and those children are living, and a slave also bore children for her master but the father granted freedom to the slave and her children, the children of the slave shall not divide the estate with the children of their former master. (Lipit-Ishtar, law 25)

So if a slave-girl had children by her owner she might be freed; and in that case her children too would be free but they would not inherit from her husband's estate. What is especially interesting in the context of slavery, whose image in the modern mind is derived from medieval abuse, is that the truly ancient laws from a past, often dismissed as primitive, provided for the marriage of a slave owner with a slave and, within the established ethos, tried to do justice both to the slave and to her children.

Children, both of whose parents were slaves, were not so lucky: they were the property not of their parents but of their parents' owner. That natural source of increase in the slave population was one of the more precious harvests of the ancient world. As fast as the slaves devised stratagems to save their children from a slave's life, the law followed with a crime and a penalty:

> If a slave-girl of the palace gives her son or her daughter to a muskenum for bringing him/her up, the palace may take back the son or the daughter whom she gave. (Eshnunna, law 34)

The term muskenum is not fully understood, but he was a free man of relatively low standing connected with the palace or the temple, whereas the seignior was a free man of higher rank. So it was risky to have a child brought up by a palace or temple official. Concealment might succeed for a time, but the child would still be a slave in law and liable to be seized if identified; and then the transition in a flash from the plans of freedom to the certainty of a lifetime of slavery would be too terrible for the child or parents even to risk having to contemplate. But many did risk it . . .

Hammurabi also had a law which confirmed by implication rather than directly that the children of a slave were the property of their parent's owner:

> If either a palace slave or a private citizen's slave married the daughter of a seignior and she has borne children, the owner of the slave may not lay claim to the children of the seignior's daughter for service. (Hammurabi, law 175)

A male slave has married the daughter of a seignior, and he has remained a slave, the property of a slave owner. So who owns their children? This law says that as the mother was the daughter of a seignior, the father's owner cannot claim ownership of his slave's children. So this law confirms by implication that under Hammurabi as well as Eshnunna a slave's children would in normal circumstances be the property of their parents' owner.

Adoption was another matter. The adopted child belonged to its adoptive parents, an aspect of the property principle we shall come to in Chapter 7. Meanwhile, there is one preliminary point that relates to slavery. If a slave's child were adopted in the city of Eshnunna, the slave's owner must be compensated for the loss:

> Also the adoptant of the child of a slave girl of the palace shall recompense the palace with its equivalent. (Eshnunna, law 35)

This law, and law 34 above, deal with open fostering or adoption, but if subterfuge were discovered one would expect the law to be more severe. In fact, the law can be interpreted equally as oddly humane or coldly calculating:

> If a slave-girl by subterfuge gives her child to another man's daughter, if its lord sees it when it has become older, he may seize it and take it back. (Eshnunna, law 33)

If the slave mother smuggles her child into another family and her owner sees the child and identifies it, her owner can claim the child as his own slave; but he may not actually take the child until it is old enough to be moved. That could be either humanity or prudence. The mother might have parted with her child either to try and save him from a life of slavery or to get him a different and presumably better owner. Whatever the reason, the property principle defined in law a slave's child as the property not of its mother but of its mother's owner, and thus secured for the slave owner the natural increase in that category of his livestock.

Sometimes a slave could buy his freedom:

> If a man's slave has compensated his slaveship to his master and it is confirmed that he has compensated his master twofold, that slave shall be freed. (Lipit-Ishtar, law 14)

That a slave might accumulate sufficient wealth to buy his freedom says something about a suppressed humanity in the status of slave in Sumer. It also says something about an enterprise economy in which a person, free or slave, could start with nothing and become comfortably off. It says something too about social mobility, that someone at the bottom of the social pyramid could cross class barriers and rise.

LOST PROPERTY

The slave might hide, or be hidden, but he could seldom escape from his legal definition as a slave. That was part of the burden of slavery, but it did not discourage slaves from trying. The more desperate ran away from their cities; others, accepting their status, tried to escape from a particular owner. Given the situation, the laws were not excessively severe, and they were certainly not blind:

> If a slave-woman or a male slave fled from the master's house and crossed beyond the territory of the city, and another man brought her/him back, the owner of the slave shall pay to the one who brought him back two shekels of silver. (Ur-Nammu, law 14)

Compare Hammurabi:

> If a seignior caught a fugitive male or female slave in the open and has taken him to his owner, the owner of the slave shall pay him two shekels of silver. (Hammurabi, law 17)

It is, incidentally, interesting that over the period of three hundred years spanned by these two laws, the monetary compensation for returning an ecaping slave should have remained unaltered. It was, of course, the duty of a seignior to return an escaping slave to his owner, and class solidarity will usually have ensured that the duty was performed when occasion arose. If it was not performed:

> If a seignior has harbored in his house either a fugitive male or female slave belonging to the state or to a private citizen and has not brought him forth at the summons of the police, that householder shall be put to death. (Hammurabi, law 16)

This is a case of a free man hiding a slave who has already escaped. But the slave is still the property of his owner, so the crime is theft for which Hammurabi's penalty is death. If a seignior actually helped a slave to escape from the city, we would expect Hammurabi to put that seignior to death: and we would be right (law 15). Helping a slave to escape would be to strike a blow against the whole social order inside the city and threaten the existence of the city itself; and that Hammurabi could not under any circumstances permit. But Hammurabi had one rather curious law about an escaped slave, which follows on from law 17 about the seignior who caught a fugitive slave:

> If that slave has not named his owner, he shall take him to the palace in order that his record may be investigated, and they shall return him to his owner. (Hammurabi, law 18)

This law illustrates the tight grip exercised by the literate bureaucrats and their interminable records over the lives of ordinary people. The palace would be the local administrative centre, and we may be sure that in its archives a tablet would rapidly be located with all relevant details inscribed on it; and the slave would then simply be taken home.

Throughout all these laws about escaping slaves there is not one that lays a penalty on the slave. The penalties are all on various members of the slave-owning class, either for theft, or for deceit in circumstances which imply a challenge to the state. Perhaps there was no need to prescribe the slave's penalty for escaping. The laws have plenty to say about maltreating another man's slave, or damaging his property, but they are silent about a slave owner maltreating his own slave, presumably relying on self-interest to prevent the owner from going so far as to ruin his own property. Hammurabi may have felt no need for a law in these circumstances.

If slaves could escape they could also be stolen. Stealing a slave was theft and the normal penalty, except with Hammurabi, was a fine. We have already seen part of this law from Eshnunna:

> If the governor, the river commissioner or another official ... seizes a lost slave ... and does not surrender it to Eshnunna but keeps it in his house, even though he may let pass only seven days, the palace shall prosecute him for theft. (Eshnunna, law 50)

Stealing a slave and hiding him for a short time may not have been too difficult; but keeping him permanently would have been another matter. Slaves were branded so as to identify their owner (an interesting early use of writing), so if the slave was to be kept, the brand mark would have to be removed (an early use of forgery):

> If a seignior deceived a brander so that he has cut off the slave mark of a slave not his own, they shall put that seignior to death and immure him at his gate; the brander shall swear, 'I did not cut it off knowingly', and then he shall go free. (Hammurabi, law 227)

Again, Hammurabi is particularly sensitive to a threat to the social order and to deception by those who are supposed to uphold it. This law also illustrates, yet again, the power of the oath in the ancient world.

SOME THOUGHTS ABOUT SLAVERY

 'Well, Atu? What have you to say about slavery? Of course, slavery was one of the main power sources of the pre-industrial age, and forced labour was another, in earlier times by far the greater. But forced labour was expensive, and no doubt hard to organise, while slaves were cheap and readily available, so from Sumer on for nearly four thousand years slavery tended to spread. It would be thousands of years before people could be replaced by machines, and when that happened society would face another kind of crisis. Nurtured as we have been on ideals of personal freedom and on the fact of freedom in our own lives, slavery seems to us to have been so appalling that is hard to look rationally at its underlying principles.'

'... *Well, yes, my friend, and it was appalling to us too ... the laws tell of slaves trying to escape, but they only hint at the majority who just did not dare ... But let us try for a moment to see it in the context of my world of Sumer ... It was accepted for thousands of years, long before slaves appeared, that people not only can be owned but that they need to be ... The ownership of people was only one aspect of a hierarchy of dependence which held communities together when life was fragile. Your conclusion that the ownership of people is wrong is very modern. The idea that you can belong without being owned is even newer, and I think that your legal systems are only just beginning to come to grips with its consequences for parents and children, in terms, for instance, of children taking their parents to court in a manner we would not only have considered perverse and unnatural but could not even have begun to envisage ... The use of law to break families apart, to destroy the natural links within the family and the essential authority of the parent over the child, by making illegal the only humane means by which authority can be enforced ... that would have been as repugnant in our eyes as slavery is in yours. In our world children who managed to stay alive were comparatively scarce and terribly precious; child abuse was hardly known. You have good reasons for what you sometimes do, though I think that my world would be hard to convince that destroying a family is a proper solution for social problems ... All right, save your breath ... yes, we did occasionally approve penalties which led to the destruction of the family, so I must be a little more cautious ...*'

'We will come back to that, Atu. We know that slavery is only one side of the coin of interdependence, and a later side at that. We also know that if there was a law against helping runaway slaves there must have been many who felt for, at least, particular slaves and were willing to try and save them. Where there is a law against something it must not only exist but be relatively common.'

'... *My friend, you rightly condemn slavery, but is not the other side of that coin forced labour ... ?*'

'A point, Atu. Directly forced labour is now rare. It is acceptable in war, and (more or less) for convicts in prison, and it may be about to become acceptable for those who cannot find employment. That is directly forced labour ... the indirect forcing of labour is among our most common techniques of management. Economic and social conditions nowadays can be, and are, manipulated so that labour finds itself compelled and ... yes Atu, you may say it without fear ...'

'... *Very well ... Is not the difference between slavery and the management of labour a difference of method rather than principle ...?*'

'We must be careful about this, Atu. The slaves have gone, but you are right that the element of indirect but real compulsion in the management of labour continues. Human labour must still be available where and when it can be productive, otherwise our whole society will collapse; and if a measure of indirect compulsion is needed to ensure that labour is made available, then we accept it for what it is, that is, management but not slavery. Slavery is, in part, the ownership of one person by another; that makes the slave, by definition, property. But there is another part as well. It is (or used to be) the nature of property that its owner can do with it what he will, and if the property happened to be a slave, the slave-owner had legal power to enforce his slave's obedience to any and every command he might be given. If slavery were being owned and nothing more, children would be slaves because they are owned by their parents. Yes I know, Atu ... we do now have laws as we have discussed that children belong with, but not to, their parents; but that also illustrates the increasing gap between some of our laws and the facts of nature, a subject we will be discussing much later. We shall be discussing families too, but in practice, whatever our new laws may say, the relationships inside the majority of our families are those of ownership, and normal children would be aghast if they were told that that security was to be taken away from them; and the expectations of society when children need care or discipline are also that the children are owned by their parents. But being owned does not make children slaves because the other elements of slavery which proceed from ownership are missing from the ownership of children. The ownership of children as a natural relationship is a different thing altogether from the ownership of adults which is not a natural relationship nowadays at all. In the same sort of way the subtle management of labour by manipulating economic and social pressures does not produce slavery, because the ownership element essential to slavery is missing. You ask, Atu, what are the limits of slavery? The answer has to be that slavery stops with the end both of the ownership of the person and of those other elements of slavery which derive from ownership. If both apply it is slavery; if only one applies it is not slavery.

'You said something, Atu? Indeed yes. I am sorry, I was wrong. Slavery has not even now entirely vanished ... that we must confess ...'

CYLINDER SEALS: *(left)* Akkadian serpentine cylinder seal depicting the goddess Ishtar in a presentation scene, *c.*2200BC; *(centre)* Babylonian amethyst cylinder seal with three lines of inscription: 'Ishtar Lamassi, daughter of Lushtammar, slave girl of Ninisina', perhaps c.1750BC; *(right)* Babylonian lapis lazuli cylinder seal showing a suppliant goddess in a presentation scene. It is remarkable that a slave girl should have a personalised cylinder to hang around her neck. The holes in the top are for the cord.

CHAPTER 5

THE FAMILY AS PROPERTY

T HERE IS A CHICKEN AND EGG QUESTION about the concept of the family. In the earliest times, wives were considered to be the property of their husbands and children the property of their parents. This concept of the family as property provided an intellectual framework simple enough for all within it to understand their place and functions, and it was close enough to reality to ensure acceptance. In a world with few social structures, the family provided a web of working relationships whose essential products were food and safety; and in the early cities, the family was the hard centre to which the state must look for the root of social order and long term survival. It is no wonder that the early legislators gave generous space to family law.

The chicken and egg question is this: was property the real basis of family relationships or merely a metaphor for a more profound pattern of dependence determined by nature? The importance of the question becomes clear when the property element is taken away. If the property relationship is the real basis of the family, let that be lost and the family loses its cohesion and, in effect, ceases to exist; but if property is only a way of visualising a pattern of relationships that in reality is profoundly a part of nature itself, then the

> To my brothers, speak;
> thus says A-GA-dahlugalma:
>
> We are about to go on a long journey,
> and may the just king, our king . . .
> Since journey will follow journey without halt,
> we shall not be able to take care of our mother.
> Before the sun sets, take good care to send to our
> quarter with a courier, 1 sila of salt, 1 sila gazi and
>   1 waist band.
> Our journey is a long one;
> it is urgent.

A letter found in an Old Babylonian school c.2000–1500BC, translated and annotated by Ali Fadhil Abdulwakid. An ordinary family, faced with an emergency, make arrangements for the care of their mother; and they are sufficiently well known locally for supplies sent to their quarter of the town to find them. The normal pressures of life and the responses to them do not change.

property element can be abandoned and the family will survive. The ancient world was clear that the family was real and rooted in nature; the modern world is not so sure. The idea of people, even young children, being seen as property, even in metaphor, has been ridiculed and the family as a result has been exposed to attack. Voices have been raised against the family in principle, seeing it as a constraint on the free growth of the individual; and some of these voices consciously intend to destroy the family altogether. This may be a reaction against ineffective families who cannot or will not educate their children, and so far it is a minority reaction. The majority of parents recognise still that the family is a growth of nature, a haven of reciprocal ownership in which the parents' ownership of their children is matched by the childrens' ownership of their parents – an intimate community whose members partly die if they are denied their roots.

In the ancient world, the family as property was both image and law. The law codified the fact of dependence and made it part of the fabric of society. A look at the family in the distant past, as reflected in some of the surviving laws, may lend perspective to a modern debate and understanding to a lasting predicament. But a measure of mental flexibility will be needed to try and see as from within what our ancestors were driving at with their property principle.

THE MARRIAGE PROCESS

For a start, marriage was a contract legalising a change in the ownership of property. A girl hitherto owned by her parents was transferred to the ownership of her husband, and the young man was required to compensate the girl's parents for their loss with gifts to a value agreed between him and the girl's father, or sometimes both her father and her mother. The bride price eventually agreed was clearly the result of considerable haggling, as it still is in those societies which retain the ancient laws. In later times, the marriage contract would be set down in a formal document but the bargain, and the bargaining, had hardly altered.

Under the marriage contract, whether written or not, the young wife in the ancient world would normally bring a dowry in the form of property, however modest, to her new family. The disposal of that dowry was also governed by laws, since in principle it was intended for the benefit of her children, and laws were needed to make sure that no one else got their hands on it. 'Her' children is what the laws prudently insisted on in a society that accepted more than one wife. The contract still exists, and we call it a marriage settlement.

The laws seldom mention either love or consent, because if there is love and consent laws are seldom, but not never, needed. The couple would not have reached the stage of betrothal, still less marriage, unless any reser-

vations the girl might have felt had been settled, or at least accommo-
dated. Family pressures, though informal, would always have been powerful
(as they still are), and as the girl's father made the contracts on behalf of
his daughter, pressure from within could clearly result in a girl's forced
marriage in practice. Even so, the tone of the laws and the absence of any
law about refusal suggest that it was at least officially acceptable for a girl
to be able to say 'no'... though not if she had once said 'yes', because to
choose was one thing but to change your mind was something else. That
challenged the nature of contract and its basis of trust and that was something very different. The laws are equally silent about the young man's
position in the matter of choice, but as he, rather than his father, made the
betrothal and marriage contracts with his prospective bride's father, it
may well be that he was free (more or less) in fact as well as in law. The
kind of marriage in which both partners are chosen by their families and
where the partners may even never have met, seems to have been the
product of a more modern world.

Marriage then as now was the culmination of a process. There were presumably as many subtle and informal stages among teenagers in the
ancient world as there are in the modern, but the first formal stage was
betrothal. The betrothal contract was sealed by the young man taking gifts
to his prospective father-in-law. In later times, these were in addition to
the bride price but they may have been the bride price in earlier times,
though custom could vary from place to place. A betrothed person had
entered into a contract recognised by law which carried a social status. It
also carried restrictions, backed by penalties, some of which bore on other
people. Betrothal was not irrevocable, but if either changed their mind it
was expensive. That too is a situation which has only recently altered.

BETROTHAL

The rules of betrothal were preserved orally and they are lost to us, so we
have to guess their nature from the few surviving laws governing breaches
of it, of which these are two:

> If a prospective son-in-law entered the house of his prospective father-
> in-law, but his father-in-law later gave his daughter to another man, the
> father-in-law shall return to the prospective son-in-law two-fold the
> amount of bridal presents he had brought. (Ur-Nammu, law 12)

> If a seignior had the betrothal-gift brought to the house of the prospec-
> tive father-in-law and paid the marriage price, and the father of the
> daughter has then said, 'I will not give my daughter to you,' he shall pay
> back double the full amount that was brought to him.
>
> (Hammurabi, law 160)

So it looks almost punitive if the girl changed her mind. But what happened if it was the young man whose intentions wavered?

> If a seignior who had the betrothal gift brought to the house of his prospective father-in-law and paid the marriage price, has then fallen in love with another woman and has said to his prospective father-in-law, 'I will not marry your daughter', the father of the daughter shall keep whatever was brought to him. (Hammurabi, law 159)

If an engaged girl changed her mind she had to pay back double the bride price, but if the man changed his mind he only lost his bride price once. Where is the justice in that? Perhaps the ancients were more canny than appears at first sight. The point is who had actually paid what? The bride price was paid by the man, so when he was at fault he lost what he had paid, a single cost and a single penalty; but the girl had received a bride price, so if she was at fault to pay it back would leave her where she started, in fact, paying nothing and with no penalty; while to pay it back double would actually have cost her one bride price only, the same cost or penalty for changing her mind as was incurred by the man for the same offence. So this law, which is older than Hammurabi and in legal terms almost certainly prehistoric, and which looks so unfair at first sight, is in fact an example of carefully thought out and perfectly equal treatment. We describe that law as probably prehistoric which can mean no earlier than just before the first laws were written; but it could equally be older, perhaps millennia older, and if so it may tell us something about the quality of justice in the distant past: and what it tells us is, at least, that in legal prehistory so often dismissed as primitive there was perfectly equal treatment between men and women who became engaged and then changed their mind. It also tells us how very careful were the early legal draughtsmen that their laws should say what they meant, and that they were sensitive to justice in its ancient, individual sense.

Jilting, or breach of promise of marriage, was part of our law until the middle of the last century when new techniques of contraception burst the whole betrothal system apart and almost destroyed it. Breach of promise was actionable, and damages were often awarded against the guilty party; so a young man had to be careful what he said to his girl-friend and she had to be equally careful how she replied. Those laws of ours were similar to the laws of Hammurabi and Ur-Nammu and probably went back deep into prehistory, but there are few now who would mourn their loss.

'Yes, Atu?'

'... I am sorry to interrupt ... but this is an excellent example of how your science has forced a change in some of your oldest laws to the benefit of your people. Our young would certainly have envied yours who enjoy a freedom we could not dream of. But ... there is one other thought going round in my mind, that in both our worlds the law used to look with equanimity on a marriage doomed to failure as a relationship ... and I am not sure that this was wholly wrong ... It seems to me, and with the needs of the children in mind, that we were bound to give more weight to their support system, that is the continuance of the family, than to anyone's mere happiness ... I think your system of social benefits has largely enabled you to reverse that, so that you can, and often do, put the happiness of the parents first ... No, no, I do not think you have necessarily taken a wrong step, because a family at war is no environment for young children ... It is just that your wealth has made it easier for you to support children outside the family ... but I am not sure that you have fully thought out the consequences for the children, or indeed for the family itself, of putting the parents first, or for society of bringing up children in what is, in historical fact, an unnatural environment ... I think what I mean is that the effects of weakening the family do not necessarily fall most heavily on the children immediately concerned, but on other children whose families might have held together, but for the example and the climate created by a too easy separation ...'*

A girl changing her mind was one thing, but a young man enticing his friend's fiancee was something different, and it was dealt with by similar but separate laws:

> If a son-in-law has entered the house of his prospective father-in-law and he made his betrothal but afterwards they made him go out of the house and they gave his wife to his companion, they shall present to him the betrothal gifts which he brought and that wife may not marry his companion. (Lipit-Ishtar, law 29)

> If a seignior had the betrothal gift brought to the house of his prospective father-in-law and paid the marriage price, and then a friend of his has so maligned him that his prospective father-in-law has said to the prospective husband, 'You may not marry my daughter,' he shall pay back double the full amount that was brought to him, but his friend may not marry his intended wife. (Hammurabi, law 161)

The betrothal contract was meant to be binding, so any breach was serious and the penalty heavy. Even so, it is remarkable that where a girl is responsible for breaking the contract Lipit-Ishtar is satisfied that she simply return the betrothal price without suffering any real financial penalty, and they go back to square one; but he does add the embargo that she shall not marry her new young man. Hammurabi's case is slightly different in that his rival has maligned him, and it is his malice that has caused the girl, or her father, to change her mind. In these circumstances, Hammurabi makes the girl pay twice so she does suffer a financial penalty, and she too is forbidden to marry her new suitor whose malice was responsible for her change of mind.

The possiblity that the partners might find themselves committed to a marriage doomed to failure could not override the need to abide by your word. These laws are not cases of simple change of mind where no commitment has been made and all is fair in love and war; that could be, and probably was, dealt with by social sanctions when contemporary convention was overstepped. These are cases where the couple have already bound themselves by a legal contract backed by finance. There is a feeling that after the contract has been made, a proposed change of mind becomes a test of sincerity as well as of marriage as a commitment, while the property principle lurking in the background contributes an underlying tone of theft and a hint of the penalties attaching to that crime ...

'... And what else,' murmurs Atu, 'lies behind your modern social sanctions on the occasions when they are applied ... ?'

In Atu's world the girl's father paid the penalty if his daughter abandoned her commitment, but in those days the poacher did not walk off with his prize.

MARRIAGE

Marriage was the final commitment by which a couple were bound to each other in a new status of man and wife; and it marked the maturity and the ownership within which the couple's children would be born and brought up. The laws governing marriage laid down with a clarity no doubt intended to be unnerving that marriage was a contract, and that nothing short of a contract could produce a marriage:

> If a man takes another man's daughter without asking the permission of her father and her mother and concludes no formal marriage contract with her father and her mother, even though she may live in his house for a year, she is not a housewife. (Eshnunna, law 27)

> If a seignior acquired a wife, but did not draw up the contracts for her, that woman is no wife. (Hammurabi, law 128)

AN ORDINARY COUPLE who are fond of each other, from the second millennium BC. This may have had magical implications.

The law had to be particular about the status of wife because legal ownership was involved; and without a contract of marriage, ownership of a girl could not be transferred in law from her father to another man. The formal marriage contract still exists, but in the modern world it is concerned with the disposal of property rather than of persons whose disposal or status is regulated by law but no longer by a separate contract. But the substance of a marriage contract continues, and the principle of ownership, though no longer acknowledged, has probably not changed essentially since the stone age: except that in ancient times ownership and the dependence that implied was always formal but not always real while today it is often real but no longer formal. So long as a marriage proceeds harmoniously laws do not matter: laws for the conduct of a happy marriage did not exist in the ancient world any more than they do now. Laws are about conflict, and of this in the ancient world there was also a reasonable supply:

> ... if he concludes a formal contract with her father and her mother and cohabits with her, she is a housewife. When she is caught with another man, she shall die, she shall not get away alive.
>
> (from Eshnunna, law 28)

> If the wife of a man, by employing her charms, followed after another man and he slept with her, they shall slay that woman, but that male shall be set free. (Ur-Nammu, law 4)

Hammurabi had this law:

> If the wife of a seignior has been caught while lying with another man, they shall bind them and throw them into the water. If the husband of the woman wishes to spare his wife, then the king in turn may spare his subject. (Hammurabi, law 129)

All three laws impose the death penalty on the wife if she commits adultery, but their treatment of the man differs. Eshnunna's law 28 says nothing, which does not mean that the man escaped scot free but that so few of the Eshnunna laws have survived that we cannot tell his fate. The Eshnunna laws are not so neatly arranged as Hammurabi's (though they are arranged), and Eshnunna' law 29, for instance, deals with a soldier taken prisoner by the enemy. Ur-Nammu's law 4 concerns a wife who was deliberately enticing her partner, so Ur-Nammu's specific sentence of death for the woman and freedom for the man is not inconsistent with the ancient view of these things. In Hammurabi's law 129 we can almost hear his impatience; he deals summarily with both and no nonsense in his mind about circumstances, and thus exhibits an almost modern sense of equality which not all modern opinion would necessarily agree with. But he does leave a chink of discretion open to the husband; he may pardon his wife but, if he does, of course the king must pardon the other man or he would leave open to the furious husband a high road to murder.

The severity of all these laws which probably have their roots deep in prehistory must tell us something about the vital importance of families in what was still a precarious society. For instance, of the twenty-three surviving laws of Ur-Nammu this is the only one that carries the death penalty.

In the ancient world if a wife slept with a man other than her husband, let alone set out to seduce him, that must have been a treachery so profound as to constitute an attack not only against everything society stood for but against what it relied on for its very existence. It was also an assault against the property principle which in the later, though not in the earlier, laws would by itself justify a death sentence. But why should the woman always be blamed? Why should man, the aggressor unless shown to be otherwise, ever escape scot free if he goes along with a relationship for which woman, the victim of male domination, is punished? Hammurabi, left to himself, did not let the man escape. By now it is clear that the very ancient laws were not generally prejudiced or capricious, so it may be well to visualise one or two of the constraints of life in the early cities as they may have appeared to the people living in them who, however, accepted them as normal.

The ancient city states were islands of remarkable culture surrounded by jealous and uncivilised hordes waiting to enter the city gates and destroy them; and what threatened the city had to be fought. In Sumer and Akkad the most threatening of the infiltrating intruders because of their numbers and persistence were the 'Martu', 'people of the west', groups of desert nomads hoping to settle in fatter lands whose name has come down to us as 'Amorites'. They had their own culture of course, but to the city dwellers they were an alien and persistent menace. That fear was realised when the Martu helped to destroy Sumer, and then they did settle especially in the cities of Asshur and Babylon which became capitals respectively of the Amorite regions of Assyria and Babylonia: king Hammurabi was an Amorite.

The security of the family was the city's second line of defence and the basis of its continuance, so the laws defended the family with the same ferocity as the people would defend the city walls. The fact that infidelity was probably the effect of something deeper, and that the problem might be curable with sympathy and insight, could be allowed no weight: what threatened the family must be stopped ruthlessly in its tracks, because a soft centre could kill the city from within.

The laws have plenty to say about rape, and we will come to that. But the laws above deal with illegal sex where the woman is a consenting participant if not the initiator, and they unite in placing the blame, or some of it, on the woman. None of these laws exonerates the woman, while one does exonerate the man. The reasoning is probably simple: if the woman had not consented (let alone provoked) sex, the crime would have been rape and the laws against rape would have applied; so as she did consent in all these cases, she was indisputably at fault whether the man was also blamed or not. That view basically blames the woman for an act in which the man is by nature the active agent, and it is increasingly rejected by the modern world ... one moment ... Atu ...?

 '... I think you are being a little simple ... I am ... I have perceived a tendency in your world, as well as in your reactions to our world, to discount the overwhelming power of the male sex urge which is the result, you say, of the male's continuous manufacture of sperm? You have scientists who may wish to correct me, but you know what I mean ... that men more frequently, and more fiercely than women have a quite overpowering need for sex which cannot be contained forever and, if aroused beyond a certain point, can no longer be held back. This is a fact of nature for which men cannot be held responsible. Generally they dislike it, even fear it: but they have to recognise it and live with it, and the laws are there to prevent them from harming others. In this respect, women are different from men. Because their urge is different, overwhelming no doubt but less dominant, women do not feel what drives a man and sometimes cannot

recognise it ... often they do not even know about it ... though there are
plenty of women whose experience has taught them all that and more about
men ... Many women expect the man to know his own limits and live
within them, and they cannot be blamed for that; but sometimes they forget
their own power to arouse and suppose that a man can go on resisting for-
ever ... but in that they are wrong. A few men are indeed born with the
power to resist indefinitely; but they are exceptional, and perhaps lucky. So
all that most men can do is try to see danger at a distance and prepare to
avoid it. That is where morality comes in, not in the sex drive itself nor in
the need to asssuage it. And ... yes ... I do think that laws which ignore the
facts of nature end up by destroying people, and even society ...'

A SECOND WIFE

In the ancient world, if a man took a second wife he must continue to support his first wife:

> If a man has turned his face away from his first wife ... but she has not
> gone out of the house, his wife which he married as his favourite is a
> second wife; he shall continue to support his first wife.
>
> (Lipit-Ishtar, law 28)

This is not a case of taking an additional wife and remaining equally affectionate to each; it is emotionally abandoning the first wife and giving all
his affection to the second. Even then in the ancient world the man was
expected to continue to support his first wife. Whose duty could it be to
support her if her husband did not? For the man there was of course an
alternative to marriage:

> If a man's wife has not borne him children but a harlot from the public
> square has borne him children, he shall provide grain, oil and clothing-
> for that harlot; the children which the harlot has borne him shall be his
> heirs, and as long as his wife lives the harlot shall not live in the house
> with his wife. (Lipit-Ishtar. law 27)

Of course the oldest profession was older than Sumer, and even in Sumer
the public square was already a cliche for the place where a man might
look for its practitioners... But this case is slightly different. If the wife
cannot have children, it was acceptable that the husband might take a
harlot who would provide him with heirs. and though she would not dis-
place his wife in her house, he would have to support her.

'Atu, yes?'

'... And, please ... how does this differ from artificial insemination and surrogate parenthood ...? We had the same problem as you but even more acutely, because our heirs were our security in old age. We had no pensions. You also are now discovering at last that all your clever financial manipulations come down in the end to this fact which we never questioned: that it is only the young who can really support the old. We coped by using the harlot, and then taking her and her child into the family without displacing the primary wife. I understand your difficulty about more than one wife and your reasons for having adopted that policy, but your way means that a mother surrenders her child, and that the child is either brought up on a lie or on a rather terrible truth... Artificial insemination of the wife is, of course, easier to accept because the child knows and keeps the mother who gave it birth ... and the rest is theory ...'

If his wife were barren, the harlot's children would be acceptable heirs, and no problem. But suppose the wife were not barren and the couple had children, so it was not a harlot but a second wife who made her appearance followed by a second family?

> If the second wife whom he had married bore him children, the dowry which she brought from her father's house belongs to her children, but the children of his first wife and the children of his second wife shall divide equally the property of their father. (Lipit-Ishtar, law 24)

So the children of his first wife do suffer loss when a second wife appears and has children; but they keep their share of their mother's dowry, as do the children of the second wife keep their shares of her dowry. All the children share equally in the property of their father and though the first wife's children may feel some sense of loss it is no greater than their elder brothers or sisters will have felt at their arrival.

What happened if the second wife was a slave?

> If a man married a wife and she bore him children and those children are living, and a slave also bore children for her master but the father granted freedom to the slave and her children, the children of the slave shall not divide the estate with the children of their former master. (Lipit-Ishtar, law 25)

This law says something about the nature of slavery in the very ancient world, that a man could marry a slave and she and their children could be accepted into the family, no matter that there were some limits. But the limits were not based on social class distinction so much as on a fair division of property. The slave and their children (this law says nothing about pre-existing children so we assume she was a virgin on marriage) are released from slavery and they get their freedom. Compared with that, nothing else can have mattered very much. The slave's children though free in the home were different from the children of the first wife in that they did not inherit any share in the estate of their father. Was that justice? No it was not. At least, not in modern terms. The now free children of the slave are not treated equally with the children of the first and born free wife as are the children of a second and free wife in Lipit-Ishtar law 24 above. They are still discriminated against. But granted slavery, the slave's children had much to be thankful for, so perhaps we need not be too pedantic on their behalf . . .

The tone of these laws about marriage is one of care for persons and for common sense and, within the principles and circumstances of the age which included slavery, to do justice to all. But marriage is not, unfortunately, the whole of the scene.

DIVORCE

Marriage was part of the natural order of life. Therefore it did not always work. So divorce was provided for. The few surviving laws tell us some of the grounds for divorce and we can infer others; but then as now most, but not all, the formal grounds for divorce were effects rather than causes. Divorce was relatively expensive for the husband:

> If a man divorces his primary wife, he must pay her one mina of silver.
> (Ur-Nammu, law 6)

A mina of silver was a small fortune. It was about 480 grams or just over one lb. This law also tells us that there were, and necessarily, two grades of wife. The primary wife was the first wife a man married and therefore she was already in charge of the house and the mother of any children before the second wife arrived. It would be unreasonable to demote her from that position in her home and expect domestic harmony. The laws do not say whether there was a limit on the number of wives a man might have, but they do not actually mention more than two. The divorce payment was made to the wife whom the husband was divorcing and it was clearly meant to enable her to live without his support. Our divorce laws, apart from costs, make the same provision.

> If the wife whom the husband was divorcing was not the primary wife but a former widow, he must pay her one-half mina. (Ur-Nammu, law 7)

This may reflect an ancient practice that a close male relative, usually her brother, is bound to marry a widow left stranded by a husband's death. Such a marriage was intended to provide support for the widow and define

Zukania,
should he [Ahhu-ayabi] forsake her,
one mana of silver he shall pay.
Ahhu-ayabi, should she deny him,
from the pinnacle he may throw her.
As long as Innabatum [Zukania's mother] lives,
Ahhu-ayabi shall support her...

From the marriage contract of Ahhu-ayabi and Zukania during the reign of Hammurabi's son, Samsu-iluna who ruled Babylon 1749–1712BC:

This contract, translated by Theophilus G. Pinches, is close to what the laws of Hammurabi had laid down for the husband and the wife: law 139 decreed that if a husband divorced his wife and there had been no marriage price, he must pay her one mina (mana) of silver as a divorce settlement; law 129 decreed, in effect, that if a wife were caught with another man, both would be thrown into the river unless the husband asked the king to spare them. But Hammurabi did not precisely lay down that a widow must be supported by her daughter and son-in-law, since law 180 implies that she should have been given life interest in a portion of her father's estate.

its source. This law also seems to assume that the former widow already had some capital from her previous marriage. But there is this little sting:

If however the man had slept with the widow without there having been any marriage contract, he need not pay her any silver.

(Ur-Nammu, law 8)

So far there is no mention of children, for whose sake the whole edifice of marriage is held to exist. Hammurabi makes it plain that children were indeed the purpose of marriage:

If a seignior wishes to divorce his wife who did not bear him children, he shall give her money to the full amount of her marriage price and he shall also make good to her the dowry which she brought from her father's house and then he may divorce her. (Hammurabi, law 138)

That inability to bear children was grounds on which a husband might divorce his wife fills our modern world with ...

'Atu, what on earth ...? No, this was not building up to a typical man's disparagement of women, or to an anti-feminist harangue ...'
'... Do observe, please ... the delicacy with which Hammurabi does not say or even hint whether the cause of the lack of children lay with the wife or with the husband. He leaves that entirely open.

We had not your means of deciding these things. Hammurabi preserves for you our law which ensured an equitable settlement within the property principle. The husband has to give the wife the full value of her bride price. He has already paid that price to his wife's father, and he does not get it back; so he now has to make a fresh additional payment to his wife of money and goods to the value which he has already agreed should be set upon her. Is that unfair to the woman? So she departs with a sufficient independence for herself. Now, please, turn your eyes to that dowry. You have noticed correctly in one of your earlier comments that it was intended for the children of her marriage. Yes, her marriage; the 'her' is important. See how precisely Hammurabi disposes of that dowry by making a separate issue of the husband's legal obligation to return it to his wife on their divorce so that she shall retain under her control the provision which she and her family had made for any future children of hers. Does this sound to you as though Hammurabi was implying that fault must lie with the woman if she had no children with one man, that he makes that man return to her the means to provide for her children in future with another man?'

'What about the woman herself?'

'*. . . She has been set free from a husband with whom she has not been able to have children, and she has proper provision for a future marriage and for any children she may produce . . . Is that unfair treatment . . . ?'*

There were of course other grounds for divorce:

> If a seignior's wife who was living in the house of the seignior, has made up her mind to leave in order that she may engage in business, thus neglecting her house and humiliating her husband, they shall prove it against her; and if her husband has then decided on her divorce, he may divorce her, with nothing to be given her as her divorce settlement upon her departure. If her husband has not decided on her divorce, her husband may marry another woma with the former woman living in the house of her husband like a maidservant. (Hammurabi, law 141)

The working wife who neglected her home was already a problem four thousand years ago. But Hammurabi's working wife was not in quite the same position as so many of today's women. She had herself decided to engage in business and to leave home during the day as a consequence (the phrase 'leave home' must mean during the day only); and she knew this would mean neglecting her house and humilating her husband. She was not under pressure to leave home for a job or a second income without which her husband and family would find it hard to survive. Nor did her neglect depend on the word of her husband alone; it had to be proved against her. If she were proved to be in the wrong, then she could be divorced without compensation; or, if her husband did not divorce her, he could marry again and his first wife would be demoted to the status of servant in her own house. One moment ...

'Yes, Atu, again ... ?'

'... *Indeed yes ... the importance we gave to the family meant that husband and wife had different priorities. In our world the wife's first duty was to care for her family; the man's first duty was to provide for his family. Neither city nor family could survive if the wife* tried to exercise the same priorities as her husband or the husband the same priorities as his wife. I see ... your desire to treat women and men as though they were the same as being against nature, against the facts. Does it not lead increasingly to rejection of even the idea of family ...?'

'That is partly true, Atu, but I do not think it is increasing. The majority of people even today do not reject the family, but they do think that women on whom the incessant burden of child rearing falls deserve a better chance to experience wider challenges than they have had ever since your creation of cities produced the man's world. We are groping for ways to achieve this, and do not pretend to have succeeded yet. Hammurabi's law may have been fair if the family came first, but it was hard on the women, and in this case it was after all the man who decided to divorce ...'

'... *Ah yes, the decision to divorce rested usually though not always with the man, and I admire the way in which you have given women equality in that. But that is a slightly different point ...*'

Atu's musical voice grows stronger,

'... *Please observe that it was Hammurabi's woman, not the man, who made the original decision to engage in business, and the woman would suffer no penalty if neglect were not proved against her ...*'

This is only one of the cases in which the woman, not the man, had power to decide an issue which affected them both.'

'Atu, could you please look very carefully at Hammurabi's next law?'

If a woman so hated her husband that she has declared, "You may not have me," her record shall be investigated at her city council, and if she was careful and was not at fault, even though her husband had been going out and disparaging her greatly, that woman, without incurring any blame at all, may take her dowry and go off to her father's house. (Hammurabi, law 142)

'... *You see, my friend ... it was not only the man who could divorce his wife. In Hammurabi's laws the wife could sometimes divorce her husband, and she could do so without specific grounds; her own statement of personal incom-*

patibility was enough if it withstood investigation and she was not, for instance, involved with another man. In this case the husband would have to return her dowry to her; but he would not have to pay her the value of her bride price. The husband has already paid that to his wife's father and she will be returning to her father's house. Also, it is the wife who is initiating the divorce, not the husband. So, as you would put it 'within the customs of our age' the couple part on reasonable financial terms. The fact that the wife could divorce her husband was a feature of our world; please, try to be fair . . .'

'Thank you, Atu.'

And there are two more features we will bear in mind. That by the time of Hammurabi in the early eighteenth century BC there were already city councils, which are not explicitly mentioned in earlier laws; and these councils would investigate social, rather than criminal, cases coming before the courts in much the same way as social service departments still do today. It is not always appreciated that the principle of a social service investigation and report is certainly four thousand years old and that a procedure of that kind may well go back to the stone age.

In these divorce laws we have inferred that the interests of children were given a high priority. At last, in the city of Eshnunna, we can see how high:

If a man divorces his wife after having made her bear children and takes another wife, he shall be driven from his house and from whatever he owns and may go after him who will accept him. (Eshnunna, law 59)

Atu is nodding and there is the beginning of a smile around his lips.

CHAPTER 6

CHILDREN

CHILDREN POP UP all over the laws, and there are even a few we
shall meet in person; but mostly, we will have to be content with a
less exciting glance at how the laws saw and safeguarded their
interests. Children were the most precious of all the possessions of the
ancient world; they were loved, they were valued, they were taught – the
lucky ones at school (though they would not always have agreed with that)
and the less fortunate at home. But they were expected to behave. A few
laws set the limits beyond which they could not go, and those limits were
clearly marked with the most terrible punishments. Within those limits
there were no laws directly restricting their behaviour, though we know
from other sources that behaviour was the province of parents and teachers and that physical punishment was used. Nowadays, a strict regime can
offend the sensibilities of adults but, short of brutality, it seldom harms
children. They like the assurance of firm guidance and would rather know
in advance where they will stand so they may decide for themselves
whether a risk is worth it. But above all, children recognise and value fair-
ness. Let Hammurabi tell us about the favourite eldest son:

> If a seignior, upon presenting a field, orchard or house to his first-born,
> who is the favourite in his eye, wrote a sealed document for him, when
> the brothers divide after the father has gone to his fate, he shall keep
> the present which the father gave him, but otherwise they shall share
> equally in the goods of the paternal estate. (Hammurabi, law 165)

The father is allowed to favour his first-born son, but there are limits. If he
gives him a substantial present then that gift must be attested at law by
means of a document bearing a seal, so that none thereafter may challenge
it. But that gift apart, when it comes to dividing their father's estate, all
the sons share equally, and then there is no special privilege for the eldest.

We have seen the principle of equal sharing well stated by Lipit-Ishtar
in his law 24, where a husband with two wives has died. The children keep
the dowry brought by their respective mothers but all share equally in the
property of their father. Hammurabi's law has a slightly different setting
but the same result:

> If, when a seignior acquired a wife and she bore him children, that
> woman has gone to her fate and after her death he has then married
> another woman and she has borne children, when later the father has
> gone to his fate, the children shall not divide according to mothers; they
> shall take the dowries of their respective mothers and then divide
> equally the goods of the paternal estate. (Hammurabi, law 167)

ROYAL FAMILY AND CHILDREN. Not many pictures of children have survived. This royal family from Lagash are celebrating the building of a temple.

Children owned and, on her death, shared their mother's dowry, so the husband's children by his first wife would not expect to share the dowry of his second wife. The basis for all the sons' sharing equally the father's property is stated: they have the same father and they are all equally his sons.

The special needs of the youngest son were not overlooked. The youngest was the most likely to be unmarried when the father died. The married sons will already have had a bride price from their father, but if the father died before the youngest son married and the whole estate were then to be divided among his sons, the unmarried son could find it impossible to obtain money for a bride price:

> If a seignior, upon acquiring wives for the sons that he got, did not acquire a wife for his youngest son, when the brothers divide after the

father has gone to his fate, to their youngest brother who did not acquire a wife, to him in addition to his share they shall assign money enough for the marriage-price from the goods of the paternal estate and thus enable him to acquire a wife. (Hammurabi, law 166)

This principle would probably apply to any sons too young to marry when their father died. It is interesting to speculate whether it would also apply to any unmarried son whatever his age. It is conceivable that sons would be expected to marry as soon as they were old enough to do so, and that if they chose not to marry at that time they would have to bear the consequences and sacrifice a bride price; but there is no law to confirm this.

To our world it seems strange that among the surviving ancient laws there are none about child abuse. Perhaps right and wrong in relation to children may have been so well understood, and the sanctions so ancient and so familiar, that they were retained in oral form even when new laws began to be written, because to write the obvious was superfluous. On the other hand, in an age when children were truly valued they may have faced fewer dangers or, when families were more tightly knit, perhaps the home was generally able to protect them so that laws were not needed. The possibility that physical child abuse may have been rare is reinforced by the thought that if ancient laws arose from court judgements in real cases, the absence of laws about physical child abuse may tell us that there were few serious cases of it. The tone of the generality of their surviving laws does not suggest that child abuse would have been defined differently in ancient times. Laws guarding children from some other dangers have been written down:

If a widow, whose children are minors, has made up her mind to enter the house of another, she may not enter without the consent of the judges; when she wishes to enter the house of another, the judges shall investigate the condition of her former husband's estate and they shall entrust her former husband's estate to her later husband and that woman and they shall have them deposit a tablet to the effect that they will look after the estate and also rear the young children, without ever selling the household goods, since the purchaser who purchases the household goods of a widow's children shall forfeit his money, with the goods reverting to their owner. (Hammurabi, law 177)

In the prologue to his law code, Hammurabi wrote:

In order that the strong might not oppress the weak, that justice might be dealt the orphan and the widow ... I wrote my precious words on my stela ...

Law 177 is one of the laws in which Hammurabi does what he says and protects the widow and the orphan. First, the decision to re-marry must of

> ### Then he said to his son:
>
> Let not thy heart be puffed-up because of thy knowledge; be not confident because thou art a wise man. Take counsel with the ignorant as well as the wise. The full limits of skill cannot be attained, and there is no skilled man equipped to his full advantage. Good speech is more hidden than the emerald, but it may be found with maidservants at the grindstones...
>
> From 'The Instruction of the Vizier Ptah-Hotep of Egypt', around 2450BC, translated by John A. Wilson. Excavation is revealing that the whole area of the ancient Middle East, and beyond into Iran, was enlightened by what was virtually a common culture from at least the middle of the third millennium BC. Of course there were regional variations; but as a quotation from ancient Egypt would not have been out of place in ancient Mesopotamia, it need not be so in a modern study of the region.

course rest initially with the widow, but if she has children who are minors she cannot carry out her intention without the consent of the judges. Before giving their consent the judges have themselves to investigate, not the suitability of the new marriage but, with that sharp realism typical of Hammurabi, the condition of the former husband's estate. The point is that the former husband's estate belongs ultimately, as we have seen, to his children. If the judges are satisfied, they will then entrust that estate to the widow and her new husband. But entrusting is not enough; the widow and her husband must deposit a tablet setting out precisely what that estate consisted of and formally undertaking not to sell anything from it. Finally, this law reminds everyone of the penalties for buying goods which belong to a widow's children.

This law demonstrates yet again that the judges had a duty to investigate and be sure personally that they had got as near to the truth as possible. And there is a wider point. These laws are framed with particular circumstances in mind which probably occurred in actual cases, but they are not confined to those circumstances.

 ... Atu '... he is trying to say something ... louder ...
'... I have been trying to make clear ... a point you have alluded to once or twice. It concerns the relationship between the law and the judges. There is a feeling in some of your comments that the concept of the rule of law requires that the law bind the judges as master of

the court ... We did not think that way ... I hope you will allow me a little time later on to say more, but I would like to come in here with a preliminary comment ... Some of your wise men, and wise women too, will insist on saying that because we in Sumer and the ancient world expressed ourselves in terms of particular instances we had no grasp of universal principle. Please let me say clearly that nothing could ever be further from the truth. This law makes plain the general principles by which the former husband's property shall be safeguarded for his children; and it does so by setting out the actual circumstances in which the key decisions were taken. The principles are universal; that is why a law embodying them exists. But the form in which they are to be applied in future will naturally depend on the facts of the particular case. That is the task of the judges. The judges are the ones who have been chosen and appointed to do it, and it is only they using their sense and their discretion who can do it. The law has to state the actual circumstances out of which the decisions arose so that the principles it embodies can be properly understood and used correctly. You will notice that to be properly understood was not, in our world, the same as to be expressed in writing. We knew, and knew with clarity, that if you try to lay down too much in your law, you destroy justice: but you destroy truth first. That is all for the present ...'

Here is something else that is universal:

> If a seignior has stolen the young son of another seignior, he shall be put to death. (Hammurabi, law 14)

That at least is clear. The maximum penalty permitted by law shall be applied without question to the kidnapper of a child. The child has not died, so it is not murder. The child is not harmed, so it is not injury. There has been no loss. We do not need to invent reasons why the child may have been kidnapped; Hammurabi does not. Plain and simple: kidnapping a child attracts the maximum penalty of the law. Even Atu is not bothering to come in ...

But there is another danger, unpredictable, insidious, often unavoidable, which came dressed in such everyday clothes that it might not be recognised until too late. Debt. Debt was and is theft, but within debt there was and is a distinction. The distinction is the intention to steal. If there was an intention to steal then it was called theft in the ancient world. There is no actual law saying this but it can be reasonably inferred from, perhaps, two laws. First, a fraudulent claim:

> If a trader borrowed money from a merchant and has then disputed the fact with his merchant, that merchant in the presence of god and

witnesses shall prove that the trader borrowed the money and the trader shall pay to the merchant threefold the full amount of the money that he borrowed. (Hammurabi, law 106)

The trader has borrowed money from a wholesaler and then denied his debt. The detail does not actually say that he borrowed on interest, but it would be strange if he had not. The threefold penalty covers repayment of the loan, payment of any interest due, and then an element of punishment. The element of punishment reflects his false denial of the debt or, in other words, his intention to steal. The second example is from Lipit-Ishtar:

If the master of an estate or the mistress of an estate has defaulted on the tax of the estate and a stranger has borne it, for three years he the owner may not be evicted. Afterwards the man who bore the tax of the estate shall possess the estate and the former owner of the estate shall not raise any claim. (Lipit-Ishtar, law 18)

The owner has defaulted on his tax and is, therefore, in debt. That debt has been paid by a third person. The owner is not immediately accused of fraud, but the question whether he may be deliberately defaulting on his tax and therefore intending to steal is left open. The judges decide the issue by putting it to the test. In the first instance it is assumed that the owner has no intention to steal, so he is given three years to clear his debt during which he may remain in possession of his estate. If he does not clear his debt in three years, an intention to steal is assumed and his estate goes to the third party. The tax will have been assessed on the basis of the expected yield of the estate, so it is likely that the reason for non-payment would have been the owner's other financial liabilities. The owner could, of course, have said this, acknowledged that he could not pay his tax and put his estate on the market; but he has not done that, so an assumption that he intended to 'try and get away with it', in other words to steal seems fair. Three years is a reasonable time limit, and if he has not settled his debt by then, or made other moves to render a court case unnec-essary the assumption that he is dishonest is likely to be correct. The rights and wrongs of the stranger's position are open to debate; for him,

One should not buy an ass who brays too much.
One should not locate a cultivated field on a roadway.

From 'The Instructions of Shuruppak to his Son Ziusudra' (Akkadian 'Utnapushtu'), translated by Robert D. Biggs from Sumerian tablets of c.2500BC. It is one of the oldest surviving examples of Sumerian literature.

payment of the tax due on the estate could have been a shrewd invest-ment, perhaps based on knowledge, which would enable him to acquire an estate for the price of only three years' tax. What matters for our more lim-ited purpose is that the issue in this case turned on whether or not there was an intention to steal; and that the court went to considerable lengths to establish the probable truth by imposing a practical test over a period of three years.

Debts were sometimes settled direct between citizens by a method which would not commend itself to every modern legal system. If a debtor defaulted it was legitimate for the creditor to seize members of the debtor's family, or his slaves, and hold them until the debt was settled. There are no laws saying this directly, but there are several laying down penalties for distraining someone in error, which probably means either falsely claiming to be owed money or failing to establish the validity of a claim:

> If a man has no claim against another man, but nevertheless distrains the other man's slave-girl, the owner of the slave-girl shall declare under oath: 'Thou hast no claim against me' and he shall pay him silver in full compensation for the slave-girl. (Eshnunna, law 22)

So if the subject of this law, a free man of any rank, had had a valid claim, it would have been legal for him to distrain his debtor's slave. It is not clear whether the full compensation was the value of the slave-girl, or merely the value of the time for which she had been distrained. If the slave-girl had died while illegally distrained, two slave-girls would have been required in compensation (Eshnunna, law 23). But if the subject of law 22 above were to be so foolish as to distrain unjustifiably the wife or child of a Muskenum, who might be rendered 'a free man of fairly junior standing', and if that wife or child were then to die while under wrongful distraint then, as Eshnunna law 24 so neatly puts it: 'The distrainer who distrained shall die'. We assume again that if the claim had been valid, then it would have been legal to distrain the wife or child of the debtor. Hammurabi has similar laws (113–116) but, in one case (116), a very dif-ferent penalty that we shall come to in due course when we discuss the law of talion.

Sometimes debt meant that money had run out and a whole family faced destitution. The parents may not have been clever managers, but they need not have been dishonest. So who bore the weight of that ...?

> If an obligation came due against a seignior and he sold the services of his wife, his son, or his daughter, or he has been bound over to service, they shall work in the house of their purchaser or obligee for three years, with their freedom re-established in the fourth year. (Hammurabi, law 117)

In case of debt, the wife, the children, the whole family could be sold into slavery; but it was only slavery of a sort. We have seen that the essence of slavery was that the slave was the property of his owner. This law says that the debtor had sold the services of his family or that he had bound himself over to service, while the purchaser bought their services; but it says nothing about the ownership of their persons. So the stark horror of their condition is relieved by knowledge that their slavery would not be total or last for ever. At the end of three years they would be free again. But they would be slaves while they were working off the family debt. How the children, for instance, would be treated while they were household slaves we do not know; but they are unlikely to have been treated as family guests. Life as a slave must have shattered their self-confidence and left its mark forever on their lives. Did social status mean less in the ancient world than it does now? The evidence suggests that if anything class distinction and social status meant more . . .

'Excuse me. . .'
'Yes, Atu.'
'. . . I am sorry to interrupt . . . but people who became slaves to pay their debts were still people, and you are right that with their freedom guaranteed after three years they were not in the same category as other slaves. They worked as slaves in the status of slave but they were not wholly the property of their masters. We recognised that even those born to slavery were people and we gave them at least some rights. And that,' murmurs Atu 'is quite a distinction from what used to happen in your world not that long ago and even, I believe, very occasionally still does . . .?'

The ancient world was a disciplined society, but the people who made it so were normal, ordinary people. So what was the ultimate sanction used against rebellious youth?

> If a seignior, having made up his mind to disinherit his son, has said to the judges, 'I wish to disinherit my son,' the judges shall investigate his record, and if the son did not incur wrong grave enough to be disinherited, the father may not disinherit his son. (Hammurabi, law 168)

The decision whether or not to disinherit a son lay with the parents but it could not be exercised without the permission of the judges. Once again, the judges are required by law themselves to investigate before making a judgement. The law does not make it clear whether they were to investigate the son's record or the father's, but in practice they could hardly do either without investigating both. They then take over from the father his own power to judge whether what his son has done is serious enough to justify an extreme punishment. Even in these early laws, so often described as primitive, it was illegal for a father to impose an extreme punishment on his son, and if he tried to do so he would find that he too had to submit to the indignity of an enquiry and justify himself to the court. The law finally lays down explicitly that if in the court's judgement the son's conduct did not warrant it, the father may not disinherit his son. Whether the judges made their enquiries personally, or by asking city councils, or their officials, to make enquiries, and report, we do not know; but if it was officials, they must have reported to the judges in much the same way as social service departments today make enquiries in social cases and report to the courts. In case this particular son, or any like him, might have nursed ideas about serious defiance, there is a second law:

> If he has incurred wrong against his father grave enough to be disinherited, they shall let him off the first time; if he has incurred grave wrong a second time, the father may disinherit his son. (Hammurabi, law 169)

If the judges decide that the son's behaviour warrants disinheritance, they must let him off the first time; but if it happens a second time, the father may disinherit his son; so, in ancient Babylon no errant son could complain that he had not been given a chance. Finally, there is a delightfully delicate touch over parental responsibility in circumstances where the family cannot cope. The judges have no hesitation about relieving the father of his power to decide in principle; but when it comes to taking action, responsibility has to be returned to the father or the family will be destroyed. If the son has repeated his offence after a warning and therefore in knowledge of the consequences and in defiance not only of his family but of the court as well, the judges may then give permission for him to be disinherited; but that is where they stop. They give permission for the father to disinherit his son, but they leave it to the father actually to do it. So even within the final judgement there is still another interval and a last opportunity for father and son to reach agreement; then, if disinheritance takes place it means that that final opportunity has been lost. The judges do not suspend the family by taking upon themselves the function of the father; responsibility for action rests with, and is handed back to, the father, and it is he who actually does the disinheriting. Even in disinheritance the family authority remains in place and the family continues to that extent intact.

A small collection of Sumerian laws was listed among our sources for ancient law codes. It was probably a schoolboy's exercise. So we now have two youths we can almost meet, the rebellious son whose relationship with his father we have just observed and who did not arouse our uncritical sympathy, and now an earlier Sumerian teenager whose fate was so terrible that we can hardly remember he once enjoyed a sense of humour at all.

This tablet was written in the very early second millennium; but some of the laws transcribed are especially interesting. This is what the Sumerians thought about disinheriting a rebellious son:

> If a son has said to his father and to his mother: 'You are not my father; you are not my mother,' he forfeits his heir's rights to house, field, orchard, slaves, and any other property, and they may sell him into slavery for money at full value. (Sumerian collection, law 4)

It comes as a surprise that the earlier Sumerian law should impose a penalty harsher than that of Hammurabi. The Sumerian law supposes that the initiative has come from the son who has rebelled against his family. Before that final stage was reached, there must have been many a confrontation between father and son, until the son had to choose either to obey or lose his whole world and become a slave forever. That such a sanction should be placed in the hands of the head of a family is a measure of the vital importance which the Sumerians attached to family cohesion and to the discipline which that involved. Here is an older discipline that Hammurabi did not invent, and one harsh penalty he did not copy. Again, there is a second law:

> If his father and his mother say: 'You are not our son,' they will forfeit the estate. (Sumerian collection, law 5)

Here, also, is the ancient principle of equality before the law. The parents have a position of authority, the son a duty of obedience; but they come equally before the court, and if either offends against the law he will suffer the penalty that is prescribed for all equally. Within the family, the law expresses and enforces a bond of reciprocal duty to each other, and it enforces that bond with fierce penalties to match the ferocity of family passions. A law of that kind was clearly needed to keep families together and children safe in the ancient cities.

There is a further aspect of these laws which needs to be noticed. Power to activate the ultimate sanction against a rebellious son, expulsion from the family and reduction to slavery, was placed by the Sumerians in the hands of the son himself. The parents could not expel him from the home because if they did they would lose the home; then all their sons, including the son they had just expelled, would inherit it. But if the son himself refused the family discipline and denied his parents then he could lose both his home and his inheritance and end up a slave. It was not a question of who was right and who was wrong; at the end of the day it was the son's duty to adapt. By placing responsibility for activating the ultimate sanction, and therefore for the existence of order in the home, on the children the Sumerians were in fact being very subtle – and rather modern.

A SCHOOL EXERCISE BOOK
from *c*.2000–1500BC.
Top: the teachers' example
Bottom: on the reverse, the
pupil's not very successful effort.

'... *Modern* ...', Atu is struggling, '... *but you do not give your children responsibility at all ... You have annihilated all real sanctions so you have lost control over the determined and unruly youngster who doesn't care. Well, why should he care? He can defy you all with impunity, and let a law abiding citizen lay so much as a finger on him and your judges will have that citizen in prison, and the law and the ruffian will laugh together ... so now ... yes, you are beginning to be appalled at the consequences of what you call freedom ... but you will not put it right just by imposing sanctions ... there is a whole attitude here ...*'

CHAPTER 7

ADOPTION

ADOPTION MEANS CHILDREN, and the laws governing adoption reveal a society's attitude towards them. Adoption forces any society to define responsibility for its children, and to confront the controversial principle that children are property. The questions were, and in essence still are, who owns the child, and whose duty is it to maintain him? In the ancient world the negative answer was that the child was not owned by – nor was his maintenance the duty of – the city. But the city did have a duty to answer the question, and the outlines of the answer can be discerned in the very few of their remaining laws. These tread the ground of the adoption process with decision and humanity, but when it comes to enforcing the adoption laws there is a cold cruelty which does not fit. So there is a mystery that will have to be faced eventually.

Meanwhile, there is a stylistic dilemma when discussing adopted children in general. In the laws of Hammurabi they are all masculine, but there is one law of Eshnunna, law 34, that refers equally to a son or a daughter of a slave-girl being given for adoption. 'He or she' is unwieldy, 'it' is insulting and 'they' is wrong; so we shall continue to use the generic form, which is the same as the masculine, where the alternatives to doing so are misleading. Let a law of Hammurabi set the tone for our discussion of adoption with a ruling about the permanence of the adoption of a boy:

> If a seignior adopted a boy in his own name and has reared him, that foster child may never be reclaimed. (Hammurabi, law 185)

This law does not say that an adopted boy may never be reclaimed; it says he may never be reclaimed once he has been reared by his adoptive parents. So the law implies that in the early years of an adoption a change of mind was possible, and that would certainly be consistent with Hammurabi's humanity. There were circumstances even in later years in which the adopted son could himself decide to return to his natural parents, and those we shall come to; but in later years the natural parents themselves have no right at all to reclaim him.

We have seen that in the ancient world families were close and children were owned, so what kind of predicament could lead to a child being adopted?

Adoption, in any age, supposes two conditions: people who want to adopt, and children available to be adopted. The most common reason for wanting to adopt a child, again possibly in any age, was a married couple who could not have children of their own. A childless couple might seek to adopt a son to carry on the husband's business or craft, to inherit the estate, and to provide a family who would give them at least a part of the essence of continuity; and adoption would calm the perpetual worry of the ancient world by providing children and grandchildren to care for them in their old age. Probably the most common source of children available for adoption in ancient times was younger sons of a large family for whom adoption was an opportunity for training in a craft or ownership of a business unlikely to be available to them if they stayed at home.

In the ancient world adoption was generally a local affair. The adopted son would not have to move far. One law, Hammurabi law 193, suggests that he ought not to know who his natural parents were ('if ... he found out his natural parentage...'), and he certainly could not visit them; but other laws, Hammurabi 189 and 190 for instance, give circumstances when an adopted son 'may return to his father's house', so it is likely that many adopted children will have known who their natural parents were in fact. On the other hand, the natural parents could watch his progress from a distance and keep themselves informed if not in touch. Adoption did not always have to be the total and final break it later became.

Adoption was, of course, a contract and, though the laws do not refer to it, the contract was usually in writing and kept carefully. The contract

Speak to Isme-Dagan: Thus Ishhi-Addu your brother. Right now, just to relieve my feelings, I must speak about this matter which should not be spoken about. You are a great king; you made me a request for two horses, and I had them conducted to you. But you sent me 20 minas of tin! Without any formal agreement with me you have not gone wanting what you requested, and yet you sent me this bit of tin! Had you simply not sent me anything, by the name of the god of my father my feelings would not have been hurt. The price of these horses over here by us in Qatna was six hundred shekels of silver, yet you sent me twenty minas of tin! What will the one who hears thus say? Will he not vilify us?

From a letter from the king of Qatna in Syria to Isme-Dagan, king of Assyria, c.1780–1741BC, translated by William L. Moran. The letter is contemporary with King Hammurabi of Babylon; it was found in Mari, and may have caused a diplomatic incident. The phrase 'your brother' was appropriate as a greeting between kings of equal status, but the king of Qatna seems to be using it to suggest that he was the equal of the king of Assyria. No doubt the insult perceived by being rewarded with tin was intended to remind Ishhi-Addu that they were not equal.

would typically lay down the duties of the adoptive parents towards their adopted son and also his duties towards them. If an adopted son returned to his natural parents that was nearly always a sign of a breach of the adoption contract by one side or the other. That the son was not a party to the contract in the first place did not mean that he was not bound by its terms; he had had no say in his birth but was, like everyone else, bound by duties to his parents arising from his birth; and those duties did not materially change when adoptive parents arrived on the scene and replaced his natural parents.

> If a member of the artisan class took a son as a foster child and has taught him his handicraft, he may never be reclaimed.
>
> (Hammurabi, law 188)

In Sumer and Babylon artisan was a social class. So it was in Europe until not so long ago; these things are far older than our history books tell us. The reason for the adoption in this case may well in fact have been that the artisan and his wife, unable to have a son of their own, wanted to obtain a son to serve as the artisan's apprentice and carry on not only his craft but his business within the craft. The vital component of such an apprenticeship may well have been time rather than money: years given to training an apprentice cannot be replaced. Loss of the adopted son after his training had been completed would be a shattering blow to the artisan whose security in old age would vanish with the apprentice, and it would give the natural parents an earning asset they had done nothing to deserve.

'Ah ... Atu ...?'

'... Yes, please ... I would just like to point out before the wrong climate is created that, although they may seem detached and inhuman, laws based on the principles of property and contract can have advantages. I fancy you would never bind an adopted child, or indeed a natural child either, in the way we did; but with all your wealth you can afford to provide for your elderly parents so that your children can live free lives. You have done what we could not do, and I admire you for it. In our world the children, whether natural or adopted, had to care for their elderly parents; and the city's function was limited to ensuring that they did so. The means by which we did our duty to the elderly were adherence to the property principle, legally enforced duties, and contracts binding on the young. Am I wrong in perceiving that something of the same principle has survived into your world since the money which you devote to caring for those of your elderly who are not well off comes from taxation levied under laws which are binding on all; so that, although your young are individually free, they are still collectively forced to provide ... ?'

Of course there is another side to this particular coin:

> If he has not taught him his handicraft, that foster child may return to his father's house. (Hammurabi, law 189)

If the artisan fails to fulfil the terms of his contract to teach his adopted son his craft, that son may walk out and go back to his natural parents. We have noticed that the initiative for return rested not with the natural parents but with the boy himself. That allows the boy who feels affection for his adoptive parents, or perhaps fear of his natural parents, to stay with his adoptive family even though he is not being trained in the family craft and the contract for his adoption is not being fulfilled.

The distinction between fostering and adoption was obviously understood as this law about fostering from the city of Eshnunna illustrates:

> If a man gives his son away for having him nursed and brought up, but does not give the nurse rations of barley, oil and wood for three years, he shall pay her ten minas of silver for bringing up his son and shall take back his son. (Eshnunna, law 32)

Clearly this is fostering, not adoption. Giving his son away to have him nursed and brought up could, of course, suggest adoption; but by placing him with a nurse rather than with a family, by giving the father a duty to provide for his maintenance, and by the absence of any mention of adoptive parents, this law makes it clear that long term fostering was intended. Perhaps there are advantages in not always making too sharp a distinction in these matters. Three years seems a generous period of grace in which to allow a father to default on his maintenance payments, but the penalty for default is interesting. If the father fails to support his son he pays a huge financial compensation to the nurse and gets his son back. The law does not tell us which of those two was considered to be the more severe penalty.

The adopted son became part of the family of his adoptive parents:

> If a seignior has not counted among his sons the boy that he adopted and reared, that foster child may return to his father's house.
>
> (Hammurabi, law 190)

This is another occasion on which an adopted son may walk out and return to his natural parents, but again the decision rests with him. This case concerns inheritance, and it tells us that if the adopted son is not properly provided for he may go back to his original home. The law protected the adopted son against injustice from his adoptive parents but, as we shall see, he had to behave himself.

Suppose a childless couple had adopted a son but then produced children of their own, what happened then about the adopted boy?

If a seignior, who adopted a boy and reared him, set up a family of his own, has later acquired children and so made up his mind to cut off the foster child, that son shall not go off empty-handed; his foster father shall give him from his goods his one-third patrimony and then he shall go off, since he may not give him any of the field, orchard or house.

(Hammurabi, law 191)

These two laws, Hammurabi 190 and 191, describe different circumstances but they try to produce an equally balanced justice: that the adopted son must be treated fairly. Law 190 makes it clear that there were already sons of the family before the parents adopted, so the adoptive father has to provide for his adoptive son along with his other sons, and if he does not, the adopted son may leave; but the immediate inference that the adopted son must be treated the same as the natural sons turns out to be premature. In law 191 there were no other sons initially but they appeared later, and that produces a complication: the adopted son is supplanted by the natural sons in his adoptive father's affections. It then emerges that the adopted son could not inherit land, orchard or buildings if there were natural sons of the family, so in that case his inheritance had to be taken from the other property of the estate. As there were no natural sons at the time of his adoption, he had a legitimate expectation that he would inherit both land and property, and that expectation has now been disappointed. By this time the adopted son is grown up, so the last part of the law is no longer dealing with a child. The adopted son has to be given his one-third value of the estate, which suggests that his adoptive parents had produced two natural sons of their own, but he must then leave because life would be impossible if he stayed. It is disturbing that the arrival of natural children could have the effect of depriving the adopted oldest son of his home as well as of his legitimate expectations; but law 191 is another occasion when Hammurabi takes account of both emotional and financial realities and offers as fair a solution as he can. That solution would not be considered fair in the modern world where the adopted boy should be treated as a full member of the family and equal in all respects to the other children whether already there when he was adopted or subsequent arrivals. But in the ancient world, genetic descent was considered to confer an identity and authenticity which adoption could not confer; and it is not even now entirely certain that they were wholly wrong in fact. But the genetic principle could neither be questioned nor overruled at that time, and within that principle Hammurabi's solution was as balanced as he could make it.

Just as we are feeling rather pleased to make allowances for the darker facets of an early and precarious civilisation, and especially in the presence of laws whose intentions are humane, we are confronted out of

> Of ramparted Uruk the wall he built,
> Of hallowed Eanna, the pure sanctuary.
> Behold its outer wall, whose cornice is like copper,
> Peer at the inner wall, which none can equal.
>
> From the 'Epic of Gilgamesh', probably an eyewitness description of the city of Uruk
> with its double wall. Eanna was the temple of Inanna, the city god of Uruk.

nowhere with a horror for which no allowances of any kind are possible; and the horror is made worse by being set in the context of the adoption of children. A boy has been adopted by a member of one or other of two privileged classes, a palace servant or a priest, and there has clearly been a family row:

> If the adopted son of a chamberlain or the adopted son of a votary has said to his foster father or his foster mother, 'You are not my father', 'You are not my mother', they shall cut out his tongue.
>
> (Hammurabi, law 192)

By formally denying his adoptive parents, the boy has tried to dissolve the adoption by himself. That was a defiance of the rule of law which always provoked Hammurabi to the most violent penalties. We saw earlier in the Sumerian collection of laws that a boy who denied his natural parents could be sold 'into slavery for money at full value' and that slavery, or at least the fear of it, was the ultimate sanction against rebellious youth, the final means of keeping the family together. The adopted child was a full member of the family and, though in some respects of a different status, he was subject to the same sanctions as natural children. Slavery as an ultimate penalty was bad enough, but Hammurabi adds to a cruel tradition a new horror of his own. To the question was this barbarity real or was it just raising the threshold of fear because fear of slavery had proved insufficient, we have to say we do not know but we will be discussing the problem in some detail. Here we may reflect that even in the earliest of cities their rulers must have understood that if the family failed, the weight of poverty would pull the city down; and if the law failed, disorder would destroy it. But there is one even greater horror:

> If the adopted son of a chamberlain or the adopted son of a votary found out his parentage and came to hate his foster father and his foster mother and so has gone off to his paternal home, they shall pluck out his eye. (Hammurabi, law 193)

The greater horror is not the loss of an eye as opposed to the loss of the tongue, but that the first law could appeal to the vital importance of self-control under unbearable stress and to public policy, while the second contradicts the natural operation of the most human of all instincts, love for one's natural parents. We are left with the feeling that it is just because love of natural parents, or at least the longing for them, is so profound an element in human nature that the laws of adoption had to be defended by an ultimate penalty that would truly terrify . . .

'Yes, please help us, Atu . . . we were half hoping . . .'
'*. . . I am sorry to butt in . . . There is another point, and we were certainly aware of it. Adoption, however well intentioned, is as you say a defiance of the instinct of love and longing for one's parents upon which stable human society has always been built. Our laws of adoption were necessarily terrible because in the end they had to enforce defiance of the very instinct which our other laws were intended to promote. There lay the contradiction. And that same contradiction is forever at the heart of the adoption process, and only some failure or tragedy can make adoption acceptable . . .*

. . . Of course there is no justifying these penalties, and their existence is not excused by the fact that they were seldom if ever carried out. But mutilation had not always been practised, so these penalties speak of a change that had been creeping over our world for three hundred years . . . You are going to talk about this later and I hope you will allow me the occasional word . . . but in the meantime the question to ponder is not what considerations of class or office or convenience made such penalties acceptable to us, but what had happened to Hammurabi? Hammurabi was the most delicately humane of all our rulers and yet . . . he could be the most pitilessly cruel . . . that is the mystery you will have to turn to in the end . . .

. . . And please . . . just what are your laws for children and adoption about if it is not the ownership of children? The distinction you make, or at least imply, between the ownership and the guardianship of children does not stand up. Your laws set limits on what the natural or adoptive parents can do with their children, but within those limits, no matter how you play with clever words, your children, like ours, are envisaged as being owned. Your children are lucky: even when quite young they can, if things go wrong, say who they would or would not like to live with; but they all need, and also want, the certainty of being owned by someone, of knowing who they are and where they fit. But I can perceive that some of your young people live in insitutions, or have families with what some of you call 'a modern outlook', where they are usually well guarded and looked after . . . some certainly prosper, but some feel the emptiness of freedom and it is you who call them

rootless ... Some of your people try to destroy the very concept of the owner-ship of children ... and complain when the children emerge lost ...

... Apart from our sanctions and your lack of them, the situation of an adopted child has changed little since my day ... and earlier. Adoption is always the result of a personal or social failure and gives rise to a second failure of its own; and all any of us could ever do about it was try the best we could for the children according to our lights. We stressed the child's inner sense of security and gave it discipline, an ordered life and the knowl-edge that it belonged; you stress that your children must be free to grow in their own way and their lives lack what we knew as shape or form. We both produced originality, we both had rootless young; but some of you have abandoned in principle what we knew to be the means of filling their void which was the terrible emptiness of being owned by no one and belonging nowhere ...'

CHAPTER 8

RAPE AND THE FAMILY

THE REASON for associating rape with the family will become apparent, but there will be nothing of child abuse. The laws about rape add little to our knowledge of the crime, but they reveal much about the thinking and structure of ancient society and, in particular, about how duties operated within the family. They are based, as we would expect, upon the property principle, and within that on the concept of theft. So the first question is 'what has been stolen?', and the second 'who was the owner?' Within the very early period there are only five surviving laws about rape, and as each describes a different situation they will appear in date order: that is the approximate date order of the tablets concerned which may not of course be the real date order of the actual laws. The earliest law of rape comes from the laws of Ur-Nammu, *c.*2100 BC:

> If a man proceeded by force and deflowered the virgin slave-woman of another man, that man must pay five shekels of silver.
>
> (Ur-Nammu, law 5)

To the question what has been stolen, the reply is clearly a slave's virginity; but to the second question, who owned it, the answer is not obvious. Within the principles of slavery, the slave belonged entirely to her master so her virginity was his property; and it may be that the theft of the slave's virginity was theft from the master of a quality in his slave that he had intended for himself and of which he has now been deprived. That possibility is compatible with the fine of five shekels of silver (approximately 40 grammes or 1.212 ounces) which compares with some of Ur-Nammu's other penalties: for false accusation three shekels, for personal injury causing loss of a limb (possibly a foot) ten shekels, for causing a severed nose forty shekels, or two shekels for a tooth. Equally, the penalty of five shekels may simply reflect damage to another man's property; or it may be recognition that rape is a crime and though the victim be a slave a real penalty must be imposed. This one law about the rape of a slave woman provides no basis on which to decide between these possibilities. The second law comes from the city of Eshnunna:

> If a man gives bride money for another man's daughter, but another man seizes her forcibly without asking the permission of her father and her mother and deprives her of her virginity, it is a capital offence and he shall die. (Eshnunna, law 26)

All those involved in this case are free citizens. It would be nice to think

The land became wide, the people became numerous,
The land bellowed like wild oxen.
The god was disturbed by their uproar.
Enlil heard their clamour
And said to the great gods:
'Oppressive has become the clamour of mankind.
By their uproar they prevent sleep'.

Opening words of the epic 'Atrahasis', written about 1700BC, translated by E. A. Speiser. Atrahasis means 'exceeding wise'. The epic is a flood story and Atrahasis is not unlike Noah.

Enlil was god of the air and affairs of earth and, by this period, the supreme god. His initial reaction to the uproar caused by mankind was to try to starve them into silence by drought and famine, but he later decided on a flood. One of the gods, Enki (Akkadian Ea), god of wisdom and of the waters beneath the earth, forewarned mankind through the wall of a reed hut in these words:

The task which I am about to tell thee
Guard thou well:
Wall, hearken to me,
Reed-hut, guard well all my words!
Destroy the house, build a ship,
Renounce the worldly goods,
Keep the soul alive!

that the death penalty for rape reflected the ancient world's abhorrence of that crime. Rape was a crime in the ancient world and they did abhor it, but that does not fully explain the character of the laws against it. If the laws had been intended to reflect no more than social abhorrence of the crime and the proper punishment of the offender, the victim's circumstances would not be relevant to the crime itself, though they might be relevant to the penalty. It is a condition of this particular law that the bride price has been paid and the victim is formally betrothed. Betrothal, as we have seen, was a contract by which ownership of a woman would be transferred in the future from her father to her future husband and, as betrothal is a significant element in the case, property would seem to be at the bottom of it. There are two possible ways of looking at this law: that rape was a personal injury to a free woman for which restitution must be made; or that rape was theft from her future husband of a valuable quality in his betrothed that been destroyed for ever and could not be replaced. As the penalty is not restitution but death, it is the second which, regrettably, seems really to be the concern of this law.

The city of Eshnunna had two laws imposing the death penalty for theft by night (though not by day), theft from a field (law 12) and from a house (law 13); it was death for a wife who committed adultery (law 28); for undetailed capital offences tried by the state (law 48); and two laws where death had been caused, wrongful distraint where the captive had died (law 24) and collapse of a wall known to be dangerous which had killed a free man (law 58): so death for raping a betrothed virgin (law 26) does not stand out as eccentric in the laws of Eshnunna.

As an aside, it is interesting that in Eshnunna permission to marry had to be sought not from the father alone but from the father and mother together.

Two of the laws on our schoolboy's exercise tablet deal with rape. This is the young man whose ten chosen laws seemed to illuminate both his teenage interests and his sense of humour, and so to introduce into our rather staid discussion an element of life and sanity still there after very nearly four thousand years. What these two laws have to say about the circumstances of a terrible crime, incidentally throws a unique light on relationships within the family and on the duties which members of a family were held at law to owe to each other:

> If a man deflowered the daughter of a free citizen in the street, her father and her mother not having known that she was in the street, and she then says to her father and her mother: 'was raped' her father and her mother may give her to him forcibly as a wife.
>
> (Sumerian collection, law 7)

Again, both the rapist and his victim are free citizens so the special status of a slave does not arise. The rape happens in a public place, and the key factor is whether the victim's father and mother had known she was out. If they had known, they would have been responsible for her safety. In this case, as the girl went out without her parents' knowledge she is herself partly responsible for what happened to her; but as her parents did not prevent her from going out a share of the penalty must also fall on them. The girl establishes that she was not acting as a prostitute by swearing an oath that she was raped, but that does not end the matter. She has lost her virginity, and she may in addition have become pregnant; so her potential bride price which would have been the property of her father, has been reduced, and perhaps annihilated. That is one loss to her family. A second is that if she cannot now find a husband her family will have to support her for the rest of her life. The judges then decide on an extraordinarily neat solution: her father and mother are empowered to decide whether to compel the rapist to marry her and, of course, her to marry the rapist. If they take that course, the parents lose their bride price as a penalty for neglect; the daughter marries the rapist as a penalty for defying the discipline of her home; and the rapist marries his victim, a life-long penalty for rape. Rough justice all round, but it illustrates the dangers of city life in the ancient world and the vital role of the family in providing security.

> 'Something . . . I know what you are about to say, Atu . . .'
> *'Do I have to say it, then? . . . All right . . . are the dangers in your cities less than they were in ours ... and were our judgements always so very inferior to yours ... ?'*

We will allow Atu that one, and turn to the second of these two laws:

> If a man deflowered the daughter of a free citizen in the street, her father and her mother having known she was in the street but the man who deflowered her denied that he knew her to be of the free citizen class and, standing at the temple gate, swore an oath to this effect, he shall be freed. (Sumerian collection, law 8)

As the victim's father and mother knew their daughter was out in public they were responsible for her safety; and even though she may not have been blameless, they have clearly failed in their duty of care. This victim's family will have suffered the same twofold loss as the family above, but as they were at fault they must bear the loss and live with the consequences. So far as the rapist is concerned, if he can establish that he did not know she was a free citizen he can go free; and he does that by swearing an oath at the temple gate. An inference that it was no crime to rape a slave would of course be over-hasty. We have seen that under Ur-Nammu's law 5 above, raping a virgin slave in the city of Ur was theft of her virginity which was the property of her owner; and that Ur-Nammu's penalty for that theft was a fine of five shekels of silver. We do not know from which city this law was copied, or whether a law similar to that of Ur-Nammu might also have applied to this case. Even so, the rapist is almost certainly asked to establish that he did not know that his victim was a free citizen so that the court could decide whether he had committed a crime; it is interesting that his intention seems to have been the deciding factor. If he knew that his victim was a free citizen, he must be charged with rape, but if he did not know it, and intention was crucial, he must go free. He could not, of course, be charged with raping a slave since on this occasion a slave had not been raped.

This law also illustrates that a formal oath could be sworn at the temple gate, and that an oath so sworn was normally accepted as evidence. Our fifth law comes from Hammurabi:

If a seignior bound the betrothed wife of another seignior, who had had no intercourse with a male and was still living in her father's house, and he has lain in her bosom and they have caught him, that seignior shall be put to death, while that woman shall go free. (Hammurabi, law 130)

This victim is a free citizen and innocent, and the rapist is caught in the act. The fact that she is a virgin is important, and that indicates that the crime was theft. So, with Hammurabi as in the city of Eshnunna, it is death.

Rape was a crime, but because essential human relationships were based on the concept of property rape was seen in the context of the ownership of women, the ownership of slaves and the ownership of virginity. It was the pervasive concept of ownership that prevented rape from being seen, or at least acknowledged, as above all a criminal assault against the person, because a woman was not in law a fully independent person but a part of someone else's property, and that is how she was treated ...

 ' ...I think ... maybe ... I will get in first this time before you become patronising about our principle of property. We did not treat people merely as though they were property: they were in fact property, they were owned, they knew their owners and in a world without your police or security structures they knew where they belonged, they knew the names of those responsible for their safety and knew that generally they could breathe by day and sleep at night. ... I am sorry ... you were about to say ... ?'

'I was about to say that your laws on rape seem remarkably fair to all parties except the women and the slaves. What would you say about that, Atu?'

' ...Nothing ... well ... thank you ... of course you are right about the slaves, and my only defence is that we could see no alternative. About the women I am less sure ... Yes, considered by themselves and according to your modern lights our laws on rape were indefensible. But I think we need to look at the position of women as a whole, and at the consequences of their position, in each of our worlds. Women can, and could, live more or less as men, and in our world sometimes they did; but if they lived as women, they had to accept that for much of their time at least their lives must be different. Meanwhile I would just reflect that no one can defy nature without both suffering and causing damage, and that your concepts of freedom and equality are not always consistent with nature ...'

'Please, let us enlarge this a little, Atu. I think we need to talk of the family as a whole, and whether your concept of the family as property and our concept of the family as equal and free individuals are really incompatible with each other or whether they are just different ways of looking at the same situation.'

' ...My friend ... I do not think they are just different ways of looking at

the same thing; they are more than that, the differences are real. The bond that makes a family, in both our worlds, the bond that matters, is owner-ship: 'my child', 'my mother', 'my husband', 'my wife', 'my brother', do not just indicate a relationship in which we happen, incidentally, to stand to each other, as you might say 'my car'; these words identify an organic unity, an entity made up of the persons included in it. The relationship is not hier-archical or patronising; it is reciprocal ownership, and it is the product of the normal working of nature. The concept of family gives to each the iden-tity of the whole, it enlarges life and is creative in two senses; it replaces loneliness with self-confidence and is the foundation of the future ...

... You talk about favouritism ... yes of course family members favoured each other, it is what families are for, but the charge of nepotism relates only to public affairs. In my world, and in yours too in affairs considered to be private, family membership was a respected basis for entry to business, pro-fession or craft. We expected a man to provide a future career for his sons and they were in turn expected to follow their fathers unless they had rea-son to do otherwise. For daughters whose career was marriage and mother-hood, husbands must be found; and if future husbands produced a bride price from the resources of their family the bride's father was expected to produce a dowry from the resources of his. Now your world has got to the point when it has to distinguish between the private and the public spheres. In the private sphere, including private businesses, the tradition of family succession is often treasured; while the same attitude in public affairs is condemned as nepotism and is an offence. But the real offence is not, as your people so often say, that you favoured members of your family but that you disadvantaged those who are not members of your family to whom, in public affairs, you owed a duty of impartiality. In our world, family influ-ence always counted, both in commerce and in our scribal communities, because those not within the family network could not have obtained the knowledge of writing or other qualifications expected of new entrants. The difference is that we did not consider that to be wrong ...'

'Are you saying, Atu, that we have made ourselves a difficulty which you did not have? We acknowledge the family to be the setting in which chil-dren learn the ethics of life, and when children fail we blame the family as often as not. So are you saying that our family of basically independent individuals dilutes the essential bond, until the family on which we rely for our social standards is rendered powerless if not meaningless?'

'*... Yes, I think so ... You find the constraints of family stifling so you break out of it and seek freedom. You then bond in the bigger society rather than the smaller, and in one way you are right: we can only really commu-nicate with our own generation, and they are outside the family, especially when there is only one wife ...*'

'In our modern world, yes, it is our own generation rather than our family that provides the framework of support and control in which we live our lives. Is that what you mean, Atu?'

'...*Perhaps we are slightly at cross purpose on this ... We, of course, understood that both the family and the bigger society are needed, but we insisted that the bigger must not be allowed to destroy the smaller and that the family was the more important of the two ... My world was very creative in one way, but it was all terribly precarious. You have cruel and destructive wars, more cruel than ours generally; but you do not have barbarians at your gates because there are no more barbarians and you have got rid of your walls. Within your cities you have precarious areas, but your civilisation is deep rooted and wide spread; ours was a thin film on the surface of a barbarian ocean. Both you and we could destroy individual cities and survive; but when we destroyed all our cities, as we did once, the advance of civilisation stopped in its tracks and then receded somewhat, but not all the way; and it was two hundred years before a great king started us moving again. If you destroyed all your cities the same might happen to you, but you have so many cities and you can see the danger, and so far you have avoided the worst ...*

... Our old cities were just large enough to spark a cultural leap, and a whole empire was like a city writ large; it generated advances that individual cities could not. Our empires were created by war followed by oppression and often by immense destruction but, like all empires, they became areas of peace until the imperial will faltered and somebody seized arms. But so long as they lasted, our empires were huge regions of peace within which cities could develop their own crafts, industries, trade and the beginnings of science over long periods of time...

... You have built on our vision in this and are now, in effect, one world wide city. Your telling phrase "the global village" is already more than half right, and what you have made has for centuries been almost too big for even you to destroy. With us, safety had to come first and that meant ensuring social cohesion. Our city societies were rigidly stratified with each individual having a function, especially the slaves. Each life was restricted to a defined sphere, but each belonged and each had a purpose. Those of you who have been through wars will be able to imagine what life inside our cities felt like: it was a little like your barrack room, cramped and lacking privacy, but safe, purposeful, a bonded cohesion, curiously respectful, and exhilarating. Our families were microcosms of our cities: bonded, purposeful, full of respect so long as obedience and respect were given, but harsh when they were not. This was the framework within which civilisation started, just as it had been the framework within which our ancestors had lived. We, like they, saw personal freedom and equality as deceptive; to us, they were the enemy within...'

'That is a fair picture, Atu, but did you ever ask yourselves what your civilisation was for ... what your cities and your infant industries were really aiming to achieve...?'

' ... *Not really, no. We valued our cities because of what they had enabled us to escape from: the life of the nomad and the tent, of constant movement and the search for food such as we saw among the desert Martu, your Amorites, who were forever infiltrating and threatening our cities; or the life of the village with its plantings and harvests and its full storage bins, but its monotonous round of exhausting labour, its little crafts and narrow repetitive lives such as we knew in our neighbours, the Gutians of the Zagros mountains. We knew what awaited us if our cities failed, and we valued them above all as a means of escape. We felt no need to identify particular aims ... perhaps you would like to identify the aims of your cities...?'*

'A point, Atu. But to return to the family. With all your discipline, your closeness and your so very well defined classes and functions, did not your young sometimes feel suffocated? Did they not just occasionally want to burst out and be themselves?'

'*... Frequently ... and you are right that the narrow and precise ways we defined our laws reflected the narrow and precise ways we defined so much in our lives. But as a result, our cities did last for over two thousand years while our best brains brought us to the edge of science. You have ten times the numbers we had, you enjoy the leisure and security of a scientific age, you can manage pain, you command nature and are even beginning to respect it, and you have seen through the gods (or think you have) and installed the laws of reason and personal freedom in their place; and the consequences are fulfilled lives and a threat to the planet. I do not think you are wrong; on the contrary, I envy you. It is what we would have done had we been able ... in a sense ... you are the continuation of us so, somehow it is what we too have done ... I just hope that your personal freedom and individual growth survive if they destroy the security which nurtures them, and the family as an institution withers...'*

CHAPTER 9

WOMEN ACCORDING TO THE LAWS

THE LAWS about family, children, adoption and rape have been full of women, but a perspective on woman's place in society requires that women be given a chapter to themselves. It is one thing to glimpse women as part of another topic, but something else to extract from scattered references a sensible picture of their status and their lives.

The status of 'woman' cannot be discussed separately from that of 'man'; they are inter-dependent, and both 'man' and 'woman' are stereotypes. Before discussion can start, stereotypes for 'man' and 'woman' must be chosen because there is no way of knowing what were their actual stereotypes in the ancient world.

Stereotypes colour our understanding of the ideas they summarise; so a modern choice of the stereotypes for man and woman could distort our understanding if applied to the ancient world; but distortion can be reduced if the bases on which they have been constructed are acknowledged. Distinction between men and women according personal qualities has often been tried: for example, man has been said to be the more logical and analytical, while woman with her deeper experience of the realities of life

When on high the heaven had not been named,
Firm ground below had not been called by name,
Naught but primordial Apsu, their begetter,
And Mummu-Tiamat, she who bore them all,
Their waters commingling as a single body;
No reed hut had been matted, no marsh land had appeared,
When no gods whatever had been brought into being,
Uncalled by name, their destinies undetermined –
Then was it that the gods were formed within them.
Lahmu and Lahamu were brought forth, by name
they were called.

From the Creation Epic (translated by E.A. Speiser). The Apsu was universal water under the earth, the abode of the god Enki, god of wisdom. Mummu-Tiamat was the universal mother. The gods thereafter were created by being named; Lahmu and Lahamu, associated with Enki, were first. Mankind was fashioned later, out of the blood of one of the gods who had rebelled, to undertake the labour previously done by gods who were thus set free.

109

is thought to bring a practical and more realistic judgement to people and events. But 'a logical mind' or similar qualities are no more exclusive to man than 'sound judgement' is to a woman; and while personal qualities may to some extent reflect experiences of life, they do not come only from those experiences which one gender has and the other does not; so personal qualities are not a basis on which serious masculine and feminine stereotypes can be constructed.

An alternative might be to look at what men and women are supposed to do; 'supposed', because what they actually do may be another matter entirely. In the old days it was what they had to do by pressure of expectation and the facts of nature, and these continue to underlie the perceived differences between male and female roles. Man is still seen in stereotype as owner and provider with woman as organiser and manager, man as authority and woman in the background as the effective power; and those images could come from as long ago as the earliest cities of the fourth millennium BC and possibly, even, from the Stone Age. The modern contribution to those stereotypes is not that they are altered but that each can be fulfilled by either gender. Early myths of a mother goddess as creator of mankind, as opposed to the now traditional God the Father, suggest that in the world before cities, the roles of woman and man may have been closer to each other than they later became. It was cities that first took man's work away from the homestead, and placed both man and his work

My queen, the Annuna, the great gods,
Fled before you like fluttering bats,
Could not stand before your awesome face,
Could not approach your awesome forehead.
Who can soothe your angry heart!

From the 'Hymnal Prayer of Enheduanna: The Adoration of Inanna of Ur', written by (or attributed to) Enheduanna, daughter of King Sargon of Akkad, about 2300BC. She was chief priestess (en-priest) of the temple of Nanna, god of the moon and city god of Ur. Her position would be more 'Archbishop of Canterbury' than 'Pope'. Translation by S. N. Kramer.

Undoubtedly Enheduanna was capable of writing this hymn which casts various lights on the status of women in Ur society in the second half of the third millennium BC. The picture of the goddess Inanna is forbidding, but Enheduanna herself can be gentle:

I, Enheduanna will offer supplications to her,
My tears, like sweet drinks,
Will I proffer to the holy Inanna, I will greet her in peace . . .

ENHEDUANNA. One of the few portraits of a known person. This is Enheduanna, daughter of Sargon of Agade who became high priestess of Nanna, the patron god of Ur. *c.*2300BC.

in the shop, the office or the storehouse; so the existence of the man's world as distinct from the woman's may, like the invention of writing, be one of the more enduring legacies of the first cities.

Conventional distinctions between what men and women were supposed to do emerge from their laws, but these stereotypes never prevented individuals from defying opinion and crossing the line. For instance, the man's world did not discourage at least one fearsome lady who appears in the Sumerian King List, four dynasties before and probably earlier than King Sargon of Agade, perhaps sometime during the first half of the third millennium BC:

> In Kish, Ku-Bau, the innkeeper, she who made firm the foundations of Kish, reigned 100 years as 'king'.[1]

So, we read of early times when a woman innkeeper could rise to become 'king' in spite of any established role models and, in a long reign whose figures are not understood, 'made firm the foundations' of her city. Nor is the modern world entirely devoid of similar characters.

And what of King Sargon of Agade's daughter, Enheduanna? That powerful high priestess of Nanna, patron god of the city of Ur, was appointed by her father probably around 2300BC to one of the supreme offices in

Sumer and her name survives as poetess as well as religious leader. Ku-Bau held office in a man's world, which may explain the inverted commas around 'king' used in the translation; while Enheduanna exercised power as a woman in a woman's world. It is Enheduanna's name that is the better known, and her office may well have been the older.

Stereotypes of man and woman that are meant to be applied to the ancient world are better based upon a reading of their laws than on any attempt to ascribe personal qualities to physical gender. The line separating the expected role of man from that of woman indicated an existing norm. But in the ancient world it did not exclude the able and the bold any more than it does in the modern, though in many of the worlds in between it excluded strictly. The freedom to choose which world you will live in is far from new.

Perhaps Hammurabi's business lady took too much for granted (Hammurabi, law 141) . She was the wife of a seignior living with her husband, and she decided to engage in business; but this resulted in her neglecting her home and humiliating him. The court's immediate judgement was that the case against her must be proved; but if it was proved, and if the husband wanted a divorce, he could have it and pay no divorce settlement. If he did not want divorce, he could marry a second wife, and the business lady could remain at home in the status of servant, which might or might not mean the status of slave. Here was a head-on clash between a woman's right to choose and the needs of her family, and there could never have been a moment's doubt which side Hammurabi would take in that conflict. But there must have been some reason why that case was singled out as a precedent to be carved on stone and displayed in public . One reason may have been the general message that a free lady with no family may engage in business; but if she has husband or children, family must come first, and then she may engage in business for only so long as her family have no reason to complain that they are being neglected.

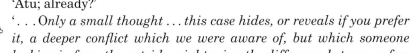 'Atu; already?'

'. . . *Only a small thought . . . this case hides, or reveals if you prefer it, a deeper conflict which we were aware of, but which someone looking in from the outside might miss: the difference between a free person and a free choice. Individuals have always been physically able to choose freely. That is part of human nature. But if they chose unwisely in our world they had to be constrained by social pressures and ultimately by laws so that they did not damage the societies they lived in. We have already recognised that in our cities all had obligations, and those of a man were different from those of a woman. We had few means of enforcement to ensure that obligations were met; what we called police were*

really guards, or agents for making arrests. The weight of civil order rested on the family and the discipline of its internal hierarchy; and also on the reasonable expectation that private individuals would accept their obligations. With us, personal freedom was always subordinate to public need.

... Defence and food depended on the continuous maintenance of city walls and irrigation canals, so the forced but paid labour that such maintenance required, which so appals you, was accepted by us as a part of life. The doctrine of unfettered freedom had to await the discovery of a power source other than human labour, and even now when you have power in plenty you still find that unfettered freedom is an aspiration more often than a reality, and not always a blessing at that ... '

Another departure from the apparent norm that man owned and woman managed is found in this pre-Hammurabi law:

> If the master of an estate or the mistress of an estate has defaulted on the tax of the estate . . . (from Lipit-Ishtar, law 18)

Here is woman in the world before Hammurabi, not just owning an estate but managing it as well, a woman held liable to pay the tax arising on the estate and being penalised identically with men if she should fail. And, incidentally, tax inspectors four thousand years ago were even then not intimidated by social status; and if women were the gentler sex they were not necessarily the weaker.

Many of the earliest laws involve women equally with men in a context where conventional modern opinion might expect to find only the man. The master or the mistress of an estate are not the only example: in the city of Eshnunna, a young couple who tried to marry without bothering with the formalities found (Eshnunna, law 27) that the man was required to obtain permission from the girl's mother as well as from her father, and that without a contract freely signed by both her parents she could not become a wife. No doubt the popular image of a mother-in-law has its roots in the stone age, and Eshnunna' law 27 will have done little to modify it. The daughter who ventured into the street without telling her parents and found herself facing the consequences of having been raped, was reminded that she should have obtained permission to be out of her home from both her mother and her father (Sumerian laws 7/8). These laws, one Akkadian from Eshnunna (27) and the other Sumerian (7/8), not only confirm woman's power in the home but, surprisingly, give that power the force of law.

In both these cases, though the man was instigator and perhaps the more guilty of the two, the law is so worded that the penalty seems to fall on the woman. In the first, the law says '. . . even though she may live in his house for a year, she is not a housewife'. The law does not say that he is not her husband though that must follow. In the second case, Sumerian law 7 says '. . . her father and mother may give her to him forcibly as a wife'; while Sumerian law says, only, that if the accused man can establish his innocence of rape, '. . . he shall be freed.' It is not easy to see the reason why the laws should have been worded so as to seem to penalise the woman when both man and woman were guilty except in terms, previously mentioned, of an imperious sex urge which propels men with a force quite different from anything experienced by women. If the ancient laws were in fact recognising the existence of such a force, then a man could not be held wholly responsible for the consequences of an imbalance in nature; and the imbalance of nature precedes the imbalance in the law. The man is never wholly innocent of rape, but the laws seem to imply that, unless she is forced by violence, the primary guilt rests on the woman.

Today that would be condemned as discrimination, unequal treatment typical of man's injustice to women; and the fact that the inequality arose in nature before it was reflected in law would not excuse the law from criticism for reinforcing it. The modern world is reluctant to accept that man is so impotent in face of the sex urge, yet it cannot easily dismiss the outcry when the facts of a particular case suggest that a man has been aroused beyond the limit of self-control. A proper balance between nature and civilised behaviour is as elusive as ever.

The impact of the laws of adultery is not always predictable. None of Lipit-Ishtar's laws of adultery have survived and our Sumerian schoolboy had not (perhaps) progressed so far, but Ur-Nammu's wife who enticed another man to sleep with her, suffered death herself while her partner went free (Ur-Nammu, law 4). The husband (Ur-Nammu, law 8) who married a former widow who was not his primary wife and then wanted to divorce her, could send her packing with no compensation, provided he had slept with her adulterously before marriage, but must compensate her with half a mina of silver if he had not. In Eshnunna, it was quite simply death for the adulterous wife (law 28). Hammurabi in four laws, threw one

Give food to eat, beer to drink,
Grant what is requested, provide for and treat with honour.
At this one's god takes pleasure.
It is pleasing to Shamash, who will repay him with favour.
Do good things, be kind all your days.

From 'The Instructions of Shuruppak'. The phrase 'one's god' refers to the Sumerian personal god, who was not one of the great gods of the pantheon but a personification of individual conscience who had access to the great gods. Shamash was the Akkadian name for the Sumerian sun god Utu.

THIS LADY would surely have been capable of running an inn, though her actual occupation is unknown. *c.*1800BC.

adulterous wife as well as her partner into the Euphrates unless the husband wished to spare her, in which case her partner would also be spared (Hammurabi, law 129}; a second seignior's wife accused by her husband could take an oath by the god that she was innocent and return home, though to what reception law 131 does not say; a third seignior's wife suspected of adultery but not caught in the act was required to throw herself into the river for her husband's sake (Hammurabi, law 132) – which implies a measure of scepticism about her innocence that is at variance with what appears to have been the judgement of the court; while a fourth

115

wife who murdered her husband for the sake of another man was impaled on stakes, (Hammurabi, law 153}.

The question remains: why, in all but one of these laws (Ur-Nammu, law 8), does the penalty fall on the woman rather than the man? In every case the woman must have consented to intercourse, because if she had not consented it would not have been adultery but rape. So, whatever the man's contribution to adultery may have been, it was certain that the woman at any rate had to be wrong. Hammurabi's insistence on treating both adulterers the same (law 129) has an unusual, but refreshingly modern ring about it; while the other ancient laws seem to assume a temptation that women can resist when men cannot.

The wife who enticed her partner was clearly guilty while, in ancient eyes, the man was not. The former widow, who cohabited with a married man before their marriage, deserved no compensation if divorced; but had she waited until after their marriage she would have been blameless and have deserved her half mina of silver. For the man it was no crime to marry a second wife and a resort to a trial period is not, apparently, quite so very modern as is sometimes thought. Of Hammurabi's four errant wives, the first was treated no more severely than her partner; the second swore an oath that she was innocent and went free; the third's guilt could not be proved but her innocence was not believed, and the fourth murdered her husband for the sake of another man and suffered an agonising death penalty – though whether for murder or for adultery is hard to disentangle.

> Gilgamesh, whither rovest thou?
> The life thou pursuest thou shalt not find.
> When the gods created mankind,
> Death for mankind they set aside,
> Life in their own hands retaining . . .
> . . . Let thy garments be sparkling fresh,
> Thy head be washed; bathe thou in water.
> Pay heed to the little one that holds onto thy hand,
> Let thy spouse delight in thy bosom!
> For this is the task of mankind!

Enkidu has died, and Gilgamesh goes on alone and disconsolate to find (Akkadian) Utnapishtim ('Ziusudra' in Sumerian) who has the secret of eternal life. He meets an ale-wife, Siduri, who can direct him to 'Utnapishtim the Faraway'. Siduri is dismayed at his appearance, and suggests, in effect, that he should not indulge in self-pity.

Today, it still is a woman's duty to resist, so the ancient world did not differ from the modern about the woman; but it did differ about the man. If a married man slept with a girl who consented, it was never rape; but today he is guilty of adultery whether she is married or not. And for once, Hammurabi would probably have agreed with the modern world.

Even a casual look at the ancient laws makes it impossible to present a woman's life in Hammurabi's Babylon, or in the earlier world of the third millennium BC, as one of downtrodden exploitation, near slavery to husband and children or second-class citizenship in either her home or her city. On the other hand, a woman's life was not supposed to be identical with that of a man. Women could choose to live in the man's world if they wanted to, as did Ku-Bau or Hammurabi's business wife. But if they did, they lost the privileges and probably much of the power that the conventional woman exercised over husband and family, a loss that may or may not have been compensated by the more public rewards of the man's world.

The contentious conflict between the identical and the equal is already looming over the horizon, but slightly before its time because we shall have plenty to say about those and other concepts in another chapter. Here we must state, for the moment dogmatically, that the ancient world separated what the modern world so often combines and, in combining, confuses. People do not have to be identical in order to be equal. Men and women can be different and lead different lives with different priorities and obligations, and still be of equal status. If individuals had to be identical in order to be equal, either equality or individuality would be impossible.

It was the differences between man and woman which gave ancient woman her advantages. It was the differences which were valued because they made people special, defined them as individuals, gave them status and their lives a purpose; it was differences that formed a complex framework in which the mass of individuals could live full lives, have careers and achieve at all levels.

A little imagination can suggest something of what the life of a woman might have been. Like all people and especially all children, the young girl was owned; she was the property of her parents ...

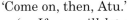 'Come on, then, Atu.'
'...If you will let me ... but please ... you must first try to distance yourself ... for a moment only ... from your belief in personal independence and individual freedom. Independence and freedom are of course fundamental to your image of yourselves; they are the basis of your self-respect. Without your independence you do not exist and without freedom you cannot grow ... So it is difficult to ask that you detach yourselves from the conventions of your age and try to see yourselves in a

different and alien perspective ... but if you can hold that detachment for just a few short minutes ... please ... ask yourselves in the tiniest voice you have how far your belief is, actually, true ... and if it is true for you, whether it is necessarily true for everyone and for all time. For instance, your great thinkers of two hundred years ago are as close to you now as are your present contemporaries compared with the time span that separates your world from mine; and it was they who really taught you to speak in terms of social principles. One of them thought it obvious that man is born free ... well ... is he? ... We did not share the various philosophies that you have built upon the answer to that question. In our world, people were not born free; we were all somebody's property, and that was how we liked it. Slavery was an abuse of the property principle, not an example of it; but it was a necessary abuse without which our society would have developed more slowly and less fully, and you might not have today's technology at all. Examples of our property principle were the family which you still, just, keep, or social hierarchy with its obligations, or the status of employee with its mutual economic advantages, which you also keep. Being property meant belonging, and it is a fact of nature that everyone needs to belong somewhere ... Because our children were property, they knew where they belonged; and because they knew they belonged they had the confidence to grow up and be strong ... '

'Inside the family, boys and girls were equally children, but to some extent they lived different lives: they were trained to the different duties of men and women. Little girls do not expect to play boys' games, and small boys view with horror the thought of having to play girls' games ... '

'... My friend .... please .... it was not only that. In fact, young boys and girls played happily together for much of the time, as they still do ... No, the big differences arose from the structure of society and the different functions of men and women within it ... The boys had ultimately to be given a bride price sufficient to allow them to get wives, so their families were always saving for the boys' future ... yes ... you are right, the girls had to have a dowry, but that was not so large. The boys were expensive, but they would remain on the fields or around the farm, or most of them would; they were the family's future and the support for their parents in old age. The girls were not so expensive and they would go away where their husbands took them, but for the girls the family received a bride price ... so the girls were a very special asset inside the family and great care was taken over their upbringing and training ... the family that exploited its daughters would end up poor ... '

The laws say little about the adoption of girls. It was boys who were adopted, perhaps when there were too many sons for the land and, at the same time, couples around who had land or a trade but no sons to follow them and care for them when old. The adoption of boys could make good sense: training and a career for the boys, a solution to overcrowding for their parents and their homes, security for a childless couple otherwise facing an empty future. Girls stayed with their parents until they married, and missed the adventure of leaving home to tears of separation and sighs of relief. And the dowry they would get when they married would stay with them because by law it was meant for the eventual support of their children. Girls never left the web of ownership which grew with their lives: being owned by their parents then by their husband, bringing the bride price to their parents' home and taking from that home the dowry which would go on to their children who, in turn, they would own. The ancient world cared for its women and kept its future safe, for thousands of years; and if that was patronising, the women knew the realities of power where it mattered, and enjoyed the status and respect that society gave them.

The teenage girl did not have to panic about young men she had never seen, visiting her father secretly; or older men coming to the house who she did not even know: she decided for herself whether she would marry a particular suitor or not. And it was the young man who had chosen her and whom she had accepted who came to her home to negotiate with her mother as well as her father for the betrothal or bride price he would pay the family when he married her and took her away. She would move from the security of her parents' home to the equal security of the home of her chosen husband, and her ownership would be transferred from the one to the other, not by oral custom, but by written contract, signed and witnessed, which she could keep. And with her would go the dowry for the security of her children.

Perhaps it was not always quite like that; but then nothing is. Even so, something along those lines is what the laws suggest. The possibility that marriages might have been arranged in fact and enforced by irresistible family pressure cannot be discounted; that happens today even in societies that would fiercely deny any such thing. But there is no evidence that the arranged marriage was normal, any more than it is normal in many African societies, for instance, which still keep their ancient laws.

The laws do tell of failed marriage. Divorce, like marriage, was a matter of law that involved property. It involved the physical property of an estate, and the human property of a wife and possibly children. That a woman could divorce her husband if she had good cause underlines her status as a person, and makes it plain that in the ancient world to be owned was not necessarily to be demeaned.

The laws also tell of women owning property and managing its affairs equally with men; and they were consulted, when the time came, over the

AN ORDINARY SUMERIAN WOMAN. But some things do not change: a middle-aged housewife looking content. *c.*2500BC.

marriages of their children who in some cities at least were required by law to obtain the consent of their mother equally with that of their father. And no doubt women engaged in all the normal activities of life as the independent personalities they undoubtedly were. Today's women would probably have found this most ancient of worlds to be refreshingly modern in its practices and outlook: the dark period in the status of women was the middle ages, not the ancient world.

It is no longer fashionable to look back to a golden age when the world was stable and problems did not exist. Modern orthodoxy requires a tale of progress, with occasional reverses maybe, but on the whole a picture of achievement, of solid gain to offset the loss of physical space. Without progress as consolation, the modern world's image of itself would be dazzling but empty. Progress involves change, so change must be provoked for the sake of the future: at least, that is often the logic. The idea that progress can take place within a stable society is foreign to modern orthodoxy, but the balance which that implies was one of the most precious secrets of the ancient world which they practised in their cities and preserved in their laws. In the specific field of women's status in society, a look backwards into the distant past can be disconcerting because the progress achieved by the modern world is sometimes a little hard to discern.

CHAPTER 10

CRUELTY UNDER THE LAW

THE NATURE OF CRUELTY

We have seen, casually and in passing, a couple of horrors on which we chose not to linger: one adopted son who had his tongue cut out for trying to end his adoption by himself, and another who discovered his natural parents and ran back to them in disillusion only to find that the law required that he must now lose one of his eyes. The time has come when we must peer, however reluctantly, into the chamber these horrors came from.

Any punishment can be represented as cruel; and in a sense it is. Fear of punishment has to be the foundation of social order because public spiritedness will override self-interest only occasionally. In very ancient times, communities were small, people knew each other and punishment was generally mild. The death penalty existed and must occasionally have been carried out, but probably more for crimes which threatened the community than for revenge. In very ancient times, each life was needed.

The earliest recorded death penalty is Ur-Nammu's law 4: the wife who seduced a man other than her husband, for which the wife suffered death and the man she seduced walked free. That would not appeal to the modern feminist, but it was a crime that threatened the family and therefore the stability of society.

The death penalty is still widely used, and not only in cases where death has been caused: the traitor and the dissident still court death in many countries. The death penalty by itself is not generally considered to be cruel: where it has been abolished, it is mainly for fear that the wrong people are being executed. Countries which still have the death penalty and also a conscience have elaborate appeal processes which can last ten years. After the final appeal has been rejected the sentence will be carried out even though execution ten years later is widely held to be not only a form of cruelty in itself but an irrelevance. The death penalty can also become cruel if the method of execution causes unnecessary suffering so that a form of torture is added to the penalty itself. That may gratify a few people but it does not seem to deter criminals.

Mutilation is another matter. Our two adopted sons were by no means alone; they had thirteen companions who were condemned to physical mutilation in ways which fill us with a peculiar horror. They are listed in Table 6. Among the ancient laws we are considering, the penalty of mutilation is recorded only in Hammurabi. We cannot be certain that the earlier laws did not include mutilation, but if they did the laws imposing it have

THE HEADDRESS TELLS US IT IS THE HEAD OF A KING. It could be Hammurabi, king of Babylon but no one can be quite sure; it is a portrait of a remarkably sensitive person and this fits what is known of Hammurabi's character – particularly from some of his social wars.

not so far been found. Even in Hammurabi, the penalty of mutilation sits uncomfortably with his pervading sense of moderation and fair play, so we suspect that mutilation may have been introduced from some source outside the ancient traditions of Sumer and Akkad. We will be considering that possibility.

Another element in our early laws which appears only in Hammurabi and which is also likely to have come from outside the city tradition of Mesopotamia is the principle of retaliation or talion. Talion differs from restitution in that it replaces the principle that damage must be made good by the contrary principle that for damage caused equivalent damage shall be inflicted. Talion will be considered in some detail in Chapter 11.

It is possible to debate whether the death penalty is in principle cruel, or even necessary; but there can be no doubt about the cruelty of mutilation, or about the injustice of condemning to death persons agreed to be innocent as happened under the logical extreme of talion in Hammurabi. It is doubtful whether the extreme of talion, condemning the innocent to death, survives anywhere in the modern world; but it remains a disturbing fact that the cruelty of mutilation still persists in some countries where it produces societies distinguished for their civil peace and orderliness, at little public expense. The thought of mutilation terrifies with a peculiar revulsion, but for the fear of mutilation to be effective it must be, and is, inflicted.

Hammurabi is distinguished from his recorded predecessors by the harshness of many of his penalties. The twin cruelties of mutilation and the execution of the innocent are recorded for the first time in surviving history in his laws; yet, the main body of Hammurabi's laws are characterised by moderation and what we shall call a careful justice. An explanation of this apparent inconsistency will be proposed (probably not for the first time) in Chapter 11 which will, incidentally, argue that Hammurabi faced a more complex problem and was an even greater person than is generally realised.

First, the death penalty as it appears in the ancient laws.

THE DEATH PENALTY

None of the surviving laws of Lipit-Ishtar or of the small Sumerian collection imposed the death penalty. That does not mean that there were no death penalties under Lipit-Ishtar's laws but only that if there were they have not survived; it may also mean that our Sumerian schoolboy was not sufficiently interested in the death penalty to choose for his exercise a law imposing it. Although the laws of Hammurabi are almost complete, the earlier collections of laws are so fragmentary that reliable figures cannot be derived from them; but, while statisticians are asked to look the other way, a table giving the proportion of surviving laws which impose the death penalty can be quite interesting:

Table 1

A ROUGH IMPRESSION OF THE USE OF THE DEATH PENALTY

	Number of decipherable laws	Death penalties	
Ur-Nammu	23	1	4%
Sumerian collection	10	–	–
Eshnunna	59	7	12%
Lipit-Ishtar	22	–	–
Hammurabi	259	28	11%

In most of these collections the laws are grouped by broad subject such as theft, marriage, personal injury, etc; but the grouping is not consistent, is occasionally surprising and is never by penalty. In Eshnunna, for instance, stealing a boat is grouped with laws about boats not with laws about theft; while in Hammurabi, both law 1 and law 230 carry the death penalty, with death spread fairly evenly in between. As the death penalty is found more or less at random throughout a collection of laws, it might not be unreasonable to expect that, though the collections are of different sizes, a particular percentage of death penalties among the surviving laws may reflect a similar percentage of death penalties in the original. Conversely, that a marked difference in the percentages from one collection to another might reflect a real difference in its use. At any rate, these highly precarious figures, Ur-Nammu with one law or 4% of all his laws carrying the death penalty, Eshnunna with 7 laws or 12% and Hammurabi with 27 laws and 10% carrying death, at least do not contradict the impression that the laws of the city of Eshnunna and of Hammurabi of Babylon – close together in both time and place – seem to form a Semitic/Akkadian group with a greater use of the death penalty. What the figures do not suggest is the reason why. We shall return to that.

Before looking in detail at the kinds of crime which attracted the death penalty, it will be interesting to separate within the total of death penalties the number of crimes which had involved death from the number of those which had not:

Table 2

DEATH PENALTIES ACCORDING TO WHETHER OR NOT
THE CRIME HAD INVOLVED DEATH

	Decipherable laws	Death was caused	No death	Death penalties
Ur-Nammu	23	– (0%)	1 (4%)	1 (4%)
Eshnunna	59	2 (3%)	5 (8%)	7 (12%)
Hammurabi	258	5 (2%)	22 (8%)	27 (10%)

In Hammurabi law 97 the death penalty is clear, but, as the crime is undecipherable, that law has not been included in this or subsequent tables.

The larger proportion of death penalties under Eshnunna and Hammurabi than under Ur-Nammu (statistically this is a precarious thought to entertain) is not accounted for by the death penalty for crimes which had themselves involved a death. The figures for the death penalty for causing death – Ur-Nammu 0%, Eshnunna 3%, Hammurabi 2% – are close enough to be consistent with each other, do not contradict our shaky hypothesis that the random distribution of death penalties may give consistent proportions across collections of different sizes, and show none of the distinguishing severity we have associated with a possible Semitic/Akkadian tradition. These figures may even go so far as to challenge the occasional dismissal of the earliest laws as being based on the principle of revenge. In fact, they invite the very guarded but opposite comment that the death penalty for crimes in which death had occurred might well have been fairly consistent throughout Sumer and Akkad in prehistoric times and these laws could reflect a prehistoric tradition that was far more moderate and 'modern' than some of its successors. What does stand out is the larger number and proportion of death penalties under both Eshnunna and Hammurabi for crimes in which death had *not* occurred: Ur-Nammu 4%, Eshnunna 8% and Hammurabi 8%. In these cases where death had *not* occurred, some principle other than precise restitution seems to be at work, and in Hammurabi and Eshnunna that principle appears to be twice as frequent as in Ur-Nammu. That, too, we will come to.

The thirty-five kinds of crime for which the death penalty was imposed, omitting Hammurabi law 97, are listed in Table 3 below:

Table 3

THE THIRTY-FIVE KINDS OF CRIME CARRYING THE DEATH PENALTY

(a) The seven crimes which had involved death and which carried the death penalty. As there happens to be only one surviving law per category, each law in this section is identified by its number.

UR-NAMMU
None

ESHNUNNA
24   Causing death of a wrongly distrained wife or child.
58   Owner of a building ignores warning, house collapses and kills a free man; capital offence, jurisdiction of the king.

HAMMURABI
116   Causing death of distrained son of a seignior – seignior's son to die.
153   Wife kills husband because of another man.
210   Seignior striking pregnant woman who dies; if daughter of seignior, his daughter dies.
229   Collapse of building kills owner, the builder to die.
230   Collapse of building kills owner's son, builder's son to die.

(b) The twenty-eight crimes which had not involved death but for which the death penalty was imposed.

	No. of laws	Total
UR-NAMMU		
Wife seducing another man	1	1
ESHNUNNA		
Theft by night	2	
Rape of betrothed virgin	1	
Wife committing adultery	1	
Serious injury	1	5

HAMMURABI

The fact that in three of these laws, Hammurabi laws 116, 210, and 230, the death penalty was imposed on a person who had not caused the original death and so far as these laws were concerned was wholly innocent of any crime, will be considered later as one aspect of talion. These three laws, together with law 229, are also listed in Table 7.

	No. of laws
False accusation	3
Theft	10
Perjury	1
Kidnapping a child	1
Draft dodging	2
Military officer wronging private soldier	1
Woman wine seller failing to arrest outlaws in her shop	1
Nun taking a drink in a pub	1
Raping the betrothed virgin daughter of a freeman	1
Incest	1

The figure which catches the eye is Hammurabi's ten laws imposing the death penalty for theft. But that is deceptive because Eshnunna has two such laws, making 3 per cent of all its surviving laws while Hammurabi's ten is only 4 per cent; so there is no great contrast between Eshnunna and Hammurabi where the death penalty for theft is concerned. There might, of course, be a contrast between the theft laws in Eshnunna and Hammurabi taken together and the laws of theft in the other collections but, unfortunately, none of Ur-Nammu's and only one of Lipit Ishtar's laws against theft have survived (law 9, stealing from an orchard, penalty ten shekels of silver), so we do not know whether they had the death penalty for theft or not. The impression that Hammurabi's laws introduced a new harsh regime cannot rest on the surviving death penalties for theft.

It might rest on Hammurabi's death penalties for all crimes together, but if so his 'death rate' at 10 per cent of his laws was below Eshnunna's at 12 per cent, and these compare with what is really a guessed 4 per cent based on a single surviving law from Ur-Nammu. Figures like these might support a slightly more severe reputation for a Semitic/Akkadian tradition but they are no basis on which to erect a reputation for cruelty in Hammurabi alone, especially since the death penalty is not necessarily considered to be cruel. Neither Hammurabi's death penalties for theft nor his death penalties overall can account for his reputation for cruelty; so we will have to turn elsewhere.

There are two clues: the first is those two adopted sons of whom one lost his tongue and the other his eye for rashly following a natural and laudable instinct, though neither lost his life; and the other is those three laws we hardly dared to notice which imposed the death penalty on persons who were known to be wholly innocent. We have suggested that Hammurabi introduced a vein of terrible severity into a legal system whose roots lay in an ancient and simple justice, and we must now ask whether that charge might arise from the inclusion, within his collection, of laws of an altogether different kind and which had nothing to do with the death penalty as such. That will soon be investigated. But when searching through Hammurabi's other laws and trying to fit them into a rational pattern it will be necessary to adopt a rough definition of cruelty. As a general guide, cruelty may be taken to include both mutilation and punishing a person for a crime of which he is known to be innocent.

There are a few thoughts about the thirty-five crimes that attracted the death penalty in the other collections of laws under discussion. Some of these death penalties appear harsh; yet they stand distinct from the extremes of cruelty it will soon be necessary to face.

Two principles will surely be agreed: first, that all crime is an attack against society but that not all attacks are equally dangerous; and second, that society, in the name of the greater number, has a duty to defend itself. No one can be certain of the reasons behind the laws which formed the ancient legal systems, but any attempt to make sense of the societies they served requires that some guesses be made. It seems, for instance, that in the ancient cities, crime that threatened the basis of society had to be controlled at all costs; and so it seems to have been a belief that the easier the crime the more severe the penalty needed to control it. By contrast, in the modern world, the harsher penalties are attached to the more repugnant crimes regardless of how easy or difficult they may be to commit. Theft, for example, undermined the property principle and threatened all activities and institutions built upon property; and that meant the larger part of city society. Theft can be easy to commit while the identity of the thief can be difficult to prove; so it is no surprise that in certain cases theft attracted the death penalty in the ancient world. It is only relatively recently that it ceased to attract that penalty in Europe. But there are, on today's view, more serious crimes than theft: for instance, a seignior who kills an aristocrat in a brawl. Perhaps that killing was not considered to threaten the system because Hammurabi's penalty was a fine of just half a mina (law 207).

'Atu ... welcome, and please come in ... '

'... Yes, I'm sorry to intrude ... but you have not remarked on the curiosity that for all our wide use of the death penalty and our supposed cruelty we had no law against murder ... nothing which said Thou shalt not kill ... I think this does call for comment, because the answer sheds light on our different ways of thinking. Our laws all illustrated specific circumstances, and we had laws describing circumstances in which people had been killed; some carried the death penalty while others, and Hammurabi's brawling seignior is an example, did not. In each law the penalty was made to fit the particular circumstances. To us a single universal law made no sense: we could see individuals and their lives and we could see examples, but we could not see universality. So our laws started from representative particulars and led to the creation of examples including penalties based on those particulars, while your laws seem so often to do things in reverse, to start from generalities and proceed towards the particular which, of course, the law can never quite reach. You would be expected, therefore, to leave detailed judgement to the judge and his court, and that would be fine but you do not do it; you phrase your laws so as to deny your judge the discretion he needs if he is to exercise the detailed judgement you require of him, and the result ... I'm sorry ... perhaps this is another problem we must come back to later ...'

It has been observed more than once that the ancient cities were precarious and had to prevent disorder at almost any cost. In practical terms that meant death for those whose conduct threatened the system. According to the surviving laws that included helping escaped slaves (Hammurabi law 15), the wine seller failing to arrest thugs in her shop (Hammurabi law 109), and the nun (poor soul!) taking a drink in the pub (Hammurabi law 110) who presumably threatened the priestly hierarchy.

The person who makes a false accusation undermines the reputation of a blameless citizen and so threatens public order. Hammurabi has three laws about false accusation which carry the death penalty: false accusation of murder (law 1), false accusation in any case involving life (law 3), and where the owner of lost property starts a false report that it has been stolen (law 11). Those falsely accused must have legal redress, but even the devastating effects a false accusation can have hardly warrant...

'Ah, Atu ... again, yes please...'

'... I must ... just mention what you seem to be about to sidestep, that in your world, and in ours too, one frequent scene of false accusation is the courts of law themselves, where false accusation is very public and can do so much damage ... That problem disturbs me. A false accusation, direct or by innuendo, can be the unavoidable consequence of an enquiry necessary to the search for truth, or it can be used as a tactic to intimidate a witness. So the tactic of false accusation can be used with devastating effect under the pretext of being necessary to truth and therefore justice ... I think we should not lose sight of that difficulty ... and we will need to return to it ... But all our laws were based on cases brought to court. We did not have laws about damage to reputation in the world at large where no specific accusation was made in a court, a safeguard which you rightly have and use; so our laws had to be extra strict to protect the innocent, to preserve public respect for our legal system and because, as you have mentioned, our societies were never rich enough to withstand more than a superficial level of conflict ...'

Rape, seduction, adultery, incest and kidnap of a child threaten the family and therefore the state. It is no surprise that family law should have formed the second largest section of the laws of a city, after the laws about commerce and its affairs; and for all the pressures of modern life there would be few who say they had their priorities wrong. That the death penalty has vanished sooner than the problems that gave rise to it is not a criticism of the modern world: death terminates problems but does not solve them. And our world has at last embarked on the endless, but not necessarily fruitless, search for solutions to family tensions which the ancient world largely confined inside the family where they had arisen; and it did so by using the family hierarchy as the principal legal instrument of social discipline. They knew that if they destroyed that hierarchy, and with it the authority of the family, they would destroy their civilisation ...

The three military crimes carrying the death penalty are interesting. Draft dodging (Hammurabi laws 26 and 33) endangers security, and with Hammurabi we are millennia away from allowing the individual conscience to defy the state. We are not told what the officer did who wronged the private soldier (Hammurabi law 34), but respect for the individual soldier and a more severe penalty for the powerful and the privileged are entirely consistent with Hammurabi's thinking.

That perjury and causing serious injury should appear as threats to the state for which death was the proper penalty causes no surprise. Serious injury speaks for itself; while the acceptance by almost any modern court anywhere in the world of that aid to dubious advocacy, that you must not lie but need not tell the truth, is contrast enough with the ancient view that truth matters and that those who would deceive the court deserve to die.

Of the seven crimes which involved death, three have already been noted within Table 3 because they condemned the innocent (Hammurabi laws 116, 210 and 230); they must wait for the next chapter because they need more than just a mention. The other four, the man from Eshnunna who caused the death of a wrongly distrained wife or child (Eshnunna 24), Eshnunna's builder who ignored a formal warning and whose house fell and killed a free man (Eshnunna 58), Hammurabi's wife who killed her husband because of another man (Hammurabi 153), and the builder in Babylon whose house was so shaky that it collapsed and killed its owner (Hammurabi 229) ... Atu is gazing impassively into space ... so perhaps we can save our sympathy for when we shall be needing it in full measure.

Now, a glance at one of the most pervasive legal principles of all time, a principle simple enough to have come from the stone age and useful enough to inform a wide range of legal and political thinking today: the principle of precise compensation for damage caused.

JUSTICE AS RESTORING A BALANCE

The principle that damage to person or things must be made good by the individual who caused it may well be an offspring of the concept of property. Certainly in the oldest surviving laws we have a glimpse of the pervasive concepts of property and ownership, and of the principle of restoring a balance. That principle underlies the majority of modern legal systems, embodies the everyday concept of what justice ought to be, and produces the kind of non-threatening law that people are happy with and can understand.

If that were all, there would be little left to say. But we have already seen that it is not all, because Hammurabi embedded in his non-threatening, normal laws some laws of an entirely different stamp; and he presented them all together without differentiation as though the two kinds of law belonged with each other and they all fitted. The reason why he had to do that will emerge in due course ... or at least, what will emerge in due course is one possible reason why we might think he had to do that, because we have no means of knowing what in fact his reasons may have been. An attempt to explain these laws is permissible, but it must be preceded by an attempt to understand. The attempt to understand Hammurabi's more unusual laws must involve not only laws, but at least a glance at what seem to have been some of the social and political problems of the city of Babylon and of Hammurabi's dynasty within it. But even Hammurabi's most cruel laws can be presented as another aspect of the principle of balance. Here we will discuss cruelty in the laws of Hammurabi; talion will be considered in detail in Chapter 11.

Hammurabi's more cruel laws do not all concern personal injury, but that is the field in which they stand out most clearly; so we list all personal injury laws from all our collections. Even a casual glance will then reveal where the discrepancies lie and enable us to assemble groups of laws that hang together and consider them as a unit.

Three of our collections of laws contain laws of personal injury: Ur-Nammu, Eshnunna and Hammurabi. Of the other two, the remains of the Lipit Ishtar collection contain no personal injury laws, while our Sumerian schoolboy appears to have found the whole subject no more interesting than he found the death penalty. The surviving personal injury laws in our three collections are best tabulated individually, but they are separated into pre-Hammurabi and Hammurabi so as to illustrate the new principles which Hammurabi introduced. The surviving personal injury laws of Ur-Nammu and Eshnunna are relatively few in number and are listed in numerical order as they occur:

Table 4

THE OFFENCE OF CAUSING PERSONAL INJURY
IN PRE-HAMMURABI LAWS

		Penalty
UR-NAMMU		
15	Foot cut off	10 shekels
16	Limb smashed (as the limb is not identified and the penalty is the highest of all, it may have been the penis)	1 Mina
17	Severed nose (with a copper knife)	⅔ Mina
18	(Both injury and penalty undecipherable)	
19	Tooth knocked out	2 shekels
LIPIT ISHTAR		
No personal injury laws survive.		
ESHNUNNA		
42	Severing the nose (by biting)	1 mina
	For an eye	1 mina
	For a tooth	½ mina
	For an ear	½ mina
	For a slap in the face	10 shekels
43	For a finger	⅔ mina
44	Throwing a man to the floor and breaking his hand	½ mina
45	Breaking a foot	½ mina
46	Assaults and breaks (limb and penalty undecipherable)	
47	Hit a man accidentally	10 shekels
48	In addition, cases involving ⅔ mina to 1 mina must come to court. Capital cases go to the king.	

In the surviving pre-Hammurabi laws of personal injury there are no distinctions of social class and no mutilation; the penalty is always imposed upon the person found guilty of the crime, and in the detailed generality of these laws it is always a fine. The exception is Eshnunna law 48 which provides for a category of capital crime that has to be referred to the king. The damage caused by severe personal injury cannot be repaired, and in these laws it is given a monetary value which allows compensation to be paid and the social balance be restored. In the ancient world, value was expressed in terms of the weight of metal, and in these laws the following scale of weights of silver applies:

> 60 shekels = 1 mina
>
> 60 mina   = 1 talent

(1 talent is about 500 grams, or about 1 lb weight. The monetary unit most common in these laws is 1 mina of silver or about 8.3 grams)*

The act of fixing a price for each injury makes the laws universal: all are treated the same and all know in advance the penalty they will suffer or the compensation they will receive if the accused is found guilty by the court. Once compensation has been paid the balance is restored and conflict can cease. In these matters, the more ancient laws are curiously modern.

The laws of Ur-Nammu and of Eshnunna are about one hundred and twenty-five years apart so, as an aside, it is interesting to compare the monetary penalties they impose for the three crimes they have in common:

	Ur-Nammu	*Eshnunna*
Tooth	2 shekels	$\frac{1}{2}$ mina
Foot	10 shekels	$\frac{1}{2}$ mina
Nose	$\frac{2}{3}$ mina	1 mina

Bearing in mind that 60 shekels make a mina, Ur-Nammu's tooth was cheap, no more than one-fifth of the value of his foot. In Eshnunna a tooth and a foot were valued the same, which seems to make the foot cheap. In both sets of law the nose was valued more highly than the foot, which may reflect the threat to health of impaired breathing, or possibly even vanity. The higher monetary penalties in Eshnunna compared with Ur-Nammu may, at a guess, reflect a century and a half of inflation as well as some adjustment to relative values, though the data do not allow figures to be calculated.

Even in the abrasive field of personal injury these two sets of early laws convey the moderation and rational restraint we have come to expect of an ancient and civilised city world; but as we pass to Hammurabi there arises, in part, a very different mood.

*Based on S.N. Kramer *The Sumerians*, p.107

With Hammurabi we enter a different kind of world altogether. His twenty-six laws of personal injury are numerous enough to gain from being arranged not in the numerical order in which they appear on his pillar but according to whether their penalty is a fine; or mutilation, death or a killing of the innocent; and within those two categories we group the laws roughly according to social class and the kind of assault. Even a brief glance at the laws and their penalties so arranged will be quite enough to make our meaning clear. Here they are:

Table 5

TWENTY-SIX LAWS OF PERSONAL INJURY
IN THE LAWS OF HAMMURABI

(a) Fifteen laws whose penalty is a fine

	Seignior injures seignior of equal rank	
203	Seignior strikes seignior of equal rank	1 mina
	Seignior injures commoner	
198	Seignior destroys eye of commoner	1 mina
201	Seignior destroys tooth of commoner	½ mina
	Seignior injures seignior's slave	
199	Seignior destroys eye or breaks bone of seignior's slave	½ slave's value
	Commoner injures commoner	
204	Commoner strikes cheek of commoner	10 shekels
	Seigniors involved in brawling	
206	Seignior strikes seignior in brawl and causes injury	oath it was accidental pay for the doctor
207	if that seignior dies and he was an aristocrat	½ mina
208	if a commoner	⅓ mina
	Seignior strikes a man's daughter causing miscarriage	
209	Seignior strikes seignior's daughter causing miscarriage for the foetus	10 shekels
211	Seignior strikes commoner's daughter causing miscarriage	5 shekels
212	if she dies	½ mina
213	Seignior strikes seignior's female slave causing miscarriage	2 shekels
214	if she dies	⅓ mina

133

The careless doctor

219	operating on a commoner's slave causing his death	make good slave for slave
220	destroyed the slave's eye	½ slave's value in silver

(b) Eleven laws whose penalty is mutilation, death or killing the innocent

Violence within the family

195	Son strikes his father	cut off his hand

Seignior injures seignior superior to him

202	Seignior strikes cheek of seignior superior to him	60 strokes with oxtail whip in assembly

Seignior injures seignior of equal rank

116	Seignior caused death of distrained son of another seignior:	seignior's son to die
196	Seignior destroys seignior's eye	destroy his eye
197	Seignior destroys seignor's bone	destroy his bone
200	Seignior destroy's seignior's tooth	destroy his tooth

Seignior strikes a man's daughter causing miscarriage

210	Seignior strikes seignior's daughter causing miscarriage; if the daughter dies	death for his daughter

The careless doctor

218	A physician operating on a seignior caused his death or destroyed his eye	cut off his hand

The careless builder

229	Builder of house for seignior ... house collapses, kills owner:	the builder to die
230	Builder of house for seignior ... house collapses, kills owner's son:	builder's son to die

A slave causes injury

205	Seignior's slave strikes cheek of aristocrat	cut off his ear

---

Even at first glance it is clear that something new is happening in Hammurabi's personal injury laws. The fifteen laws in section (a) whose penalty is a fine have penalties that are compatible with what would be expected under the pre-Hammurabi laws of Sumer and Akkad. The commoner's eye under Hammurabi (Hammurabi 198) costs one mina, the same as anyone's eye under Eshnunna (Eshnunna 42). Hammurabi's commoner's tooth (201) at half a mina is the same as anyone's tooth in

A REPRESENTATION OF HAMMURABI carved around 1760BC. It was made for a city governor under Zimri Rim, king of Mari, an almost exact contemporary of Hammurabi. This fragment was probably found at Sippar, one of the oldest cities of Sumer, south of modern Baghdad.

Eshnunna (42) and compares with two shekels for a tooth under Ur-Nammu (Ur-Nammu 19). Hammurabi's ten shekels for a commoner striking a commoner's cheek (204) is the same penalty as Eshnunna (42).

But the description of circumstance in Hammurabi's fifteen laws in section (a) goes far beyond the mere naming of the injury in the pre-Hammurabi laws: for the first time social class is crucial to the nature of the penalty. In law 209 Hammurabi's seignior strikes a seignior's daughter causing a miscarriage while in law 211 the seignior does the same to a commoner's daughter, and the penalties are different.

A brief and preliminary glance at the eleven laws in (b) of Table 5, whose penalty is mutilation, death or killing the innocent, produces a sense of outrage that anyone should dare even to try to present Hammurabi as a humane and civilised king. The fact that these penalties can all be found somewhere in the modern world makes no difference: if this was Hammurabi's contribution to order in the city of Babylon, it was a barbarity and he was a monster.

And yet, what we cannot excuse we might just try to explain, even though detailed evidence is usually lacking. The laws themselves can tell us quite a lot; while the attempt to understand what persuaded an otherwise humane and intelligent king getting on for five thousand years ago not only to adopt a policy of cruelty but to publish it in his laws might have some small interest if not relevance to several aspects of the modern world.

These eleven laws in section (b) can be re-grouped so that those which are based on the principle of retaliation can be considered as one unit, and those whose penalty involves mutilation can be considered as another unit. Three of the laws in section (b) fall into both categories; and there are additional laws whose penalty is mutilation but whose crime did not involve personal injury and which do not, therefore, appear in Table 5 at all. For this reason, mutilation and retaliation will be considered separately, mutilation based on a special Table 6 and retaliation based on a special Table 7. Thus all the laws in section (b) will be discussed, three of them from two points of view.

One specific reaction to Table 5 must certainly be surprise that social class distinctions should be given such weight. Of the twenty-six laws in Table 5, seventeen apply only to the seignior, a free man of standing who ranked below an 'aristocrat' but above a 'commoner'; two apply to a commoner only, three to a doctor, two to a builder and one each to a son striking his father (195) and a seignior's slave (205).

A further surprise is how class was treated. We are used to linking the word 'class' with privilege: a special standard of living, a special social status, a special status before the law. All those existed in Hammurabi's

Babylon, except that the special status before the law meant that the errant seignior faced a privileged severity rather than leniency: 60 strokes with an oxtail whip in public for a seignior striking his senior (202) speaks of an aristocracy required to behave and an authority that knows how to make it do so. And there is a further surprise that the penalty should be influenced by the social status of the victim: the most severe penalties being reserved for the seignior injuring someone equal or superior to himself. The seignior who injured an equal's eye and suffered the penalty of losing his own (196), was fined one mina when he injured a commoner's eye (198) and if it was a slave's eye he paid half the slave's value (199), to the slave's owner not to the slave himself.

So much for a seignior injuring his juniors; but what happened if the commoner or slave caused the injury? Two laws hint at the answer: the commoner who struck another commoner paid ten shekels (204), while the slave who struck an aristocrat lost an ear (205).

These laws tell of a structured society, full of rank and privilege, but one that worked; a society where those who caused injury paid for it and all but slaves received compensation according to their status. A military hierarchy anywhere in the world could be described in very similar terms even today, and though the ancient world can still be found if we look for it, we prefer to govern our civilian affairs rather differently when we can. And we obtain rather different results.

When discussing discipline in the family we have already noticed with horror the son having his hand cut off for striking his father (195); but here, in context, he is not alone. Hammurabi's concern for order only started with the family; it went on from there to pervade the whole class structure of society. Anyone in a position of trust who threatened the chain of obedience in the form of the duties owed to those above him and received from those below him, struck at the sinews binding the whole together. Such a man imperilled both city and empire, and the oxtail whip seems almost a matter of course.

When dealing with injury inflicted by a seignior upon one of equal rank, a nice balance of retaliation is struck. Here is the earliest surviving record of 'an eye for an eye and a tooth for a tooth' (196, 197, 200) which ruled much of the ancient Near East and entered the legal sections of the Bible. The old principle of compensation for damage caused is abandoned and in its place is installed a tally of precise revenge. The victim has exchanged reasonable compensation for a right to get even, while from the several modern societies which have retained these principles it can be inferred that Hammurabi will probably have produced order where a more liberal justice does not. This is the perceived highlight of Hammurabi's legacy to the modern world. His humanity, his care for the weak, his instinct for common justice are all

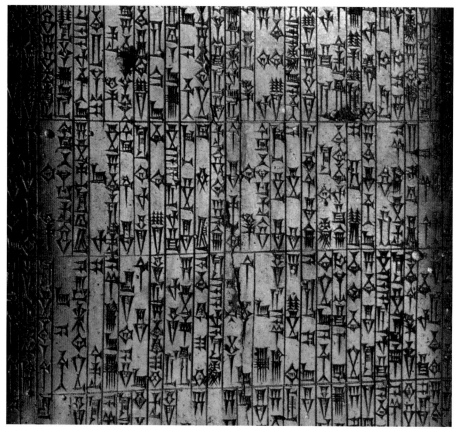

THE LAWS OF HAMMURABI were engraved in, what even then was, an archaic format, presumably to give them the authority of tradition (which many of them actually had). They are written in columns from the right but have to be read as if rotated anti-clockwise, in lines from the left.

ignored, because 'an eye for an eye' paints a more vivid picture in the mind. But whether Hammurabi was the originator or the inheritor of the tradition of precise retaliation as carried to its logical conclusion, will soon be considered. What is invariably overlooked is that revenge was not a general principle of Hammurabi's laws, but was restricted to cases of injury committed by a relatively senior free man against another of equal or superior rank.

If a seignior injured a commoner the penalty was a fine: not an eye for an eye but a mina for an eye (198); and for a tooth it was half a mina (201). We have observed that these penalties are identical with those in Eshnunna; and while this restores in part the feeling of a distinct Akkadian legal tradition, it highlights Hammurabi's departure from that tradition in the case of injury between upper class citizens; and in doing so it raises the question 'Why?' We shall attempt to answer that question in Chapter 11.

We have seen that if a seignior injured a slave he paid the slave owner one-half of the slave's value (199); and in that resort to the property principle Hammurabi was being entirely traditional.

When a commoner struck another commoner, Hammurabi's ten shekel penalty was again the same as in Eshnunna: it looks as though Hammurabi may have been sticking to tradition when he could.

If a slave injured an aristocrat (205) he suffered the same penalty, losing an ear, as a slave who denied his master (282). Hammurabi had a keen eye for a threat to society.

Seigniors brawling were less of a threat, so principles of simple justice could prevail. The seignior causing the injury must take an oath that it was accidental and, a delightfully modern touch, he must pay the doctor's bill (206). If the injured seignior dies, and if he was an aristocrat, the penalty is a mere half mina (207), the value of a commoner's tooth (201). So that is what Hammurabi thought of aristocrats who allowed themselves to be drawn into a brawl. If the dead man had been a commoner, the penalty was one-third of a mina (208), just double the penalty for striking a commoner's cheek (204). It is interesting that in Hammurabi's Babylon a seignior was not necessarily an aristocrat though he could be one (207).

The penalty for striking a pregnant girl and causing her to miscarry is not so easy to understand. If the girl is of the seignior class the penalty is just ten shekels for the foetus (209), if a commoner five shekels (211) and if a slave two shekels (213). The extraordinarily low value placed upon unborn children contrasts with Hammurabi's concern for the children who lived; even if it is the mother's grief he is measuring, he is still doing so in terms of the child who died. But if the girl struck by the seignior dies from her blow, the penalty comes as a shock: if she was a seignior's daughter then the daughter of the seignior who struck her must die (210), and that is not, as we shall see, an irrelevance but an example of retaliation and punishing the innocent which we will consider in some detail. But if she was a commoner, the penalty for killing her was half a mina (212), and if a slave a third of a mina (214). So why might the life of a seignior's daughter require the life of the daughter of the seignior who killed her while the life of a commoner's daughter (212) was worth no more than his tooth (201)?

Hammurabi had a way with the problem of medical error. The poor physician who killed or blinded a seignior was rendered safe by losing a hand (218). If he killed a slave he got away with buying the slave's owner a replacement (219); and if he blinded a slave the damage was assessed at half the slave's value paid in silver (220).

In case anyone may think that Hammurabi imposed mutilation only where personal injury had been deliberately caused, let Table 6 be produced, which consolidates Hammurabi's use of mutilation, and includes eight further laws in which he imposes mutilation for offences in which either personal injury had *not* occurred or it had occurred accidentally or incidentally:

Table 6

THE PENALTY OF MUTILATION
IN THE LAWS OF HAMMURABI

(a) Eight laws which appear for the first time in this Table where NO personal injury occurred, or it was accidental or incidental

127	Seignior accuses nun or wife of another man and cannot prove it	cut off half his hair
192	Adopted son of chamberlain or votary denies foster parents	cut off his tongue
193	Adopted son of chamberlain or votary discovered his parentage, hated his foster parents and returned him	pluck out his eye
194	Seignior gave son to nurse, son died in care; if nurse contacts for another son without knowing her history	cut off her breast*
226	A brander cut off the slave mark from another man's slave without permission	cut off his hand†
253	A seignior hired to oversee another seignior's field, found to have stolen seed or fodder	cut off his hand.
256	If that seignior could not fulfil his obligation to cultivate the field	drag him through the field with oxen
282	A male slave denied his master	cut off his ear

(b) Seven laws which have already appeared in Table 5, personal injury in the laws of Hammurabi

195	Son strikes his father	cut off his hand
202	Seignior strikes cheek of seignior superior to him	60 strokes with oxtail whip in assembly
196	Seignior destroys seignior's eye	destroy his eye
197	Seignior destroys seignior's bone	destroy his bone
200	Seignior destroys seignior's tooth	destroy his tooth
205	Seignior's slave strikes cheek of aristocrat	cut off his ear
218	A physician operating on a seignior caused his death or destroyed his eyes	cut off his hand.

---

* Law 194 is not listed in Table 5, personal injury, because the nurse was not accused over the death of the son in her care but of having concealed his death from a subsequent client.
† In law 226 the personal injury is incidental to an act of theft.

The false accusation (law 127) must surely be sexual: the penalty of merely losing half his hair might not be inconsistent with Hammurabi's three other laws of false accusation (laws 1, 2 and 3) whose penalty was death, because the circumstances described in each of those laws show that they each might have cost a life. The two adopted sons (192 and 193) who lost respectively a tongue and an eye are now old friends. The careless wet nurse who failed to acknowledge that a child had died in her care and as a consequence lost one of her breasts (194) arouses sympathy, but not too much; the brander caught trying to steal a slave (226) and the seignior with his hand in the till (253) who for the same crime lose a hand each must have known the risk, gambled and lost, so few tears for them; but there are tears for the seignior who could not fulfil his contract to cultivate a field and found himself being dragged through it behind a team of oxen (256); and tears also for the slave who tried to sack his owner and lost an ear (282).

In all these laws there is a measure of 'making the punishment fit the crime', but there is nothing particularly eccentric about that. They do not punish the innocent. Modern, innovative law reform is moving towards penalties that are more relevant both to the offence and the offender, and thus in the direction of penalties that were normal four thousand years ago – though without realising, or at least acknowledging, the tradition to which they are returning...

Cruelty under the law suggests insecurity and desperation. In the most ancient cities of Sumer and Akkad, when the city of Babylon was as yet insignificant, the threat of attack came mainly from other cities, so their internal structure was tight rather than harsh. The death penalty was rare and mutilation under the law unknown. Hammurabi's fifteen penalties of mutilation tell of a more modern world, not of the laws of the ancient cities. Mutilation was not a minor adjustment to an earlier tradition, but a major departure from it introducing an entirely new principle.

An entirely new principle is not overstating it. The first sign of that principle was the arrival of a new source of fear. Fear of crime was older than the city and, if the continuity apparent in the earliest laws is an indication, the earliest cities did not greatly affect the traditional nature or scale of crime within them. The old laws continued to work. But with the arrival of Hammurabi's immediate ancestors, the social structure of Babylon did change; and that change produced a new scale of fear. A fear that needs mutilation to control it suggests, in the light of our knowledge of Hammurabi's priorities, that it was probably fear for the continued existence of the city itself. In the next chapter, the probability is examined that the cause of that fear may have been the city aristocracy running wild among a population and culture to which they did not really belong; and the needle point of that is that Hammurabi himself was one of them. It will also become apparent that mutilation was not the only exotic cruelty that Hammurabi introduced with his laws.

Here, it is enough to note that some new factor had arisen that had not existed in previous ages, a factor that struck such terror into the rulers of Babylon and its growing empire that desperate measures were called for. That is understandable. But there is a further problem: that these measures not only took root but pervaded the whole western world for nearly five thousand years, and in some measure they still do; and that suggests that the widening scale of public enterprise and government may have had something to do with it.

So the question 'what is Hammurabi doing?' is now real and must be faced. On other fields Hammurabi largely consolidates and reflects the laws traditional in both Sumer and Akkad, and he does so with a moderation, a compassion, a sanity which tell of a truly great king. So why should he now, with no sign of a precedent in the surviving earlier laws, suddenly resort to mutilation in its cruellest form in some, but only some, of his laws? That is what is meant by saying that some of his penalties do not fit, and it is part of the essence of the Hammurabi mystery.

CHAPTER 11

THE HAMMURABI MYSTERY

THE HAMMURABI MYSTERY comes in two parts: the law of retaliation, and the problem of Hammurabi's position in Babylon with its consequences not only for Babylon but for the whole of the ancient Near East.

That Hammurabi may have based some of his laws on the principle of retaliation has been observed, but the time has now come to address the possibility in detail. The clue lies in seven laws which together make up the most ancient surviving statement of retaliation's nature and scope. The laws themselves have already been listed in Table 5 (b). Summaries of the individual laws are repeated below, but in a format designed to highlight the principles on which they are based and lead to a discussion of the possible background from which they might have arisen:

Table 7

SEVEN LAWS OF TALION IN HAMMURABI

(a) Laws of talion which punish only the guilty

196	Seignior destroys seignior's eye	destroy his eye
197	Seignior destroys seignor's bone	destroy his bone
200	Seignior destroy's seignior's tooth	destroy his tooth
229	Builder of house for seignior ... house collapses, kills owner	the builder to die

(b) Laws of talion which punish the innocent

116	Seignior caused death of distrained son of another seignior	seignior's son to die
210	Seignior struck pregnant woman who died; if she was daughter of a seignior	his daughter dies
230	Builder of house for seignior ... house collapses, kills owner's son	builder's son to die

---

Talion is shorthand for retaliation (Latin *lex talionis* = the law of retaliation). Talion is well known in history, and especially among peoples of the deserts whose life-style suits a justice that comes swiftly and cheap. Talion can be rough but in the desert it works.

What matters to nomadic peoples is that clan feuds should be smothered at birth. In *The Babylonian Laws*, G.R. Driver and John C. Miles describe feud and talion in these terms:[1]

> The family is the primitive unit ... If one member of the family injures another, the matter is settled by the head of the family ... The question is settled by family law and custom. If, however, one member of a family injures a member of another, as the family is a unit, a feud arises between the two families.

Driver and Miles add that these feuds are particularly damaging to small mobile groups since they deplete their complement of adult males and thus impair their chances of survival in a harsh environment, though adult males are not the only victims. Survival is threatened if feud (or vendetta) is continued over long periods of time and across vast distances. Feud is the background to talion. As Driver and Miles put it:[2]

> If a member of one family is killed by a member of another family, a member of the second family, though not necessarily the slayer, must be killed to avenge the spilling of the blood of the first family ...
>
> ... Here the germ of one of the principal limitations on the indiscriminate vengeance of the blood-feud appears, the principle of 'tit for tat' or talion. This principle is applied not only to slaying but to all corporal injuries, and the doctrine that the punishment must fit the crime begins its history.

The essence of feud is, basically, revenge. Striking back satisfies the injured and is supposed to put a stop to the conflict. Sometimes it does. When it punishes the guilty it can succeed, but when it punishes the innocent it can create a fresh grievance, so that revenge and grievance stimulate each other reciprocally into a cycle of killing which neither can bring to an end. One of the purposes of a public justice is to prevent feud. Talion was one method of trying to do that.

Whether the doctrine that the punishment must fit the crime begins with talion is a difficult question since that doctrine permeates the pre-Hammurabi Mesopotamian law collections whose relatively few surviving laws do not contain talion as such. That suggests that the source of the relationship between feud and talion is likely to be found outside the immediate area of the Mesopotamian cities. It also suggests that trying to make the punishment fit the crime may reflect a more basic sense of justice within which talion is one, but not the only, element.

If justice is represented as a social balance, a legal system can be seen as the machinery by which the balance is to be restored when it has been upset. At this point we turn to Anna Partington, philologist, specialist in ancient near-eastern languages and their modern relatives, and writer from whom I have been privileged to receive penetrating comment on many aspects of our common interests. Mrs Partington has gently suggested that the nature of justice in ancient Mesopotamia might be illuminated by tracing, at least in outline, the structure and meaning of the Sumerian word *nigsisa*. Mrs Partington writes:[3]

> The word *nigsisa* contains three elements analysis of which gives a little insight into the Sumerian notion of justice: *nig* is a nominal element indicating a noun; *si* describes fingers of the hand and also 'fingers' of antlers and horns, and of the crescent moon; *sa* describes equality and can be represented by the same ideogram as *di/din* which covers the sense of judge or judgement (cf Hebrew: Beth Din, the high court). So *nigsisa* is literally 'equal fingers' or, in contemporary English, 'even-handed' – the notion of equality, fairness or justice.
>
> Another approach is from the Latin *ius* or *jus* (Juris) meaning right, law or justice, and its derivative juror – the one who takes an oath. The parent of *ius* is the Greek *ison* or more especially *ise* which describes, among other things, punishment deemed equal to the offence.
>
> The Edict of Ammisaduqa, for instance, as a collection of laws is described in Akkadian as *misharum* (a variant of *isharu*), or in Sumerian as *nigsisa*.
>
> So there is a chain of related words meaning justice, including: *sisa* (Sumerian) = *isharu* (Akkadian) = *iasar* (Hebrew) = *sawiya* (Arabic) = *ison* (Greek) = *ius* (Latin) = *ju*stice (English)
>
> Bearing in mind that order or balance is an important notion in Sumerian culture, it is tempting to define all early Tigris-Euphrates river plain judicial activity in terms of maintenance and restoration of order or balance. Such an interpretation reduces or removes the distinction between impartial assessment and restitution, for the assessment is then the judgement about whether order or balance has been disturbed and restitution is the means of restoring the situation as it was before the disturbance.

The concept of balance may well have been the root of both restitution and talion; and that hypothesis is strengthened by Anna Partington's observation that the operation of systems of justice in Mesopotamia can be explained in terms of attempts to restore a balance that has been upset. Her selection of words for justice in many languages incidentally tells us not only how a common concept of justice may have existed across great distances despite language barriers, but also how far flung was the influence of the Sumerian and Akkadian languages from the ancient Near East to modern Europe.

Balance could be restored by action in either of two directions which were, predictably, incompatible with each other: under one the guilty party paid and the injured party received compensation identical or equivalent to the damage suffered, the principle of restitution; under the other the guilty party was made to suffer damage identical or equivalent to the damage he had caused, the principle of retaliation or talion. In both cases the social balance can be said to have been restored provided that the penalty did not exceed the original damage. Over-compensation or punitive damages might have achieved other ends, for instance separately penalising a defiance of the law; but that would have left the scales tilted, and conflict might not have ended. Hammurabi's laws of talion contain no punitive damages, though three of his other laws do (laws 8, 12 and 124).

The first principle, restitution, compensates the injured and is the basis of modern civil law; but courts of law are needed to operate it and they demand an environment of stability such as is found in a fixed settlement or a city. The second principle, talion, makes the guilty party suffer damage equal to the damage he caused, and it appeals to an altogether different instinct. It is known as 'getting even'; it is what many people really mean when they 'demand justice' and what moralists mean when they talk of 'revenge'. But under talion, justice is swift; it needs no apparatus beyond a decisive common sense and it involves the injured party in the penalty; it is accessible on the march or in the tent, and speaks of the nomad and the desert.

Talion first appears in writing in the laws of Hammurabi where, as Table 5 illustrates, it does not fit into the background of the other laws that Hammurabi collected. In a modified form it found its way into the Bible where it did not fit either, but it acquired there a divine authority that made it last. The nature of talion was summarised in the telling but literal phrase 'an eye for an eye and a tooth for a tooth'. Today, talion raises hackles; but the central doctrine of restoring a social balance, of which talion is only one expression, is symbolised in modern sculpture by an evenly balanced pair of scales.

Precise restitution and talion work in different ways. Restitution asks first 'who did it?' so that the guilty can be identified and the innocent go free. It then asks 'what damage was done?' and tries to restore the balance by calculating a figure and making the guilty pay.

Talion also asks 'who did it?' and uses the answer to identify the guilty; but the identity of the guilty is then seen not as the solution but as a description of the crime. Talion pauses there, saying nothing, while it asks the second question 'who suffered what damage?' Talion then uses the answer to that question to inflict as near as possible identical damage on the guilty. If the damage was loss of a seignior's eye then the guilty seignior lost his eye too and balance was restored, though at a lower level of minus two eyes; and in this case, as it happened, punishment fell only on the guilty. If the builder negligently killed the seignior's son, his own son must die and similarly the balance would be restored though at the level of minus two sons. In this case punishment, in the form of death, struck down the innocent son; and though it be argued that his loss was justified as a reciprocal and vicarious punishment for his guilty father, it was still the son who had to die, his innocence counting for nothing, while his guilty father lived on, punished only by his loss and his conscience.

So how did the ancient and so civilised world find itself embroiled in this kind of talion? We cannot be certain, but the answer may well lie in that other principle of the ancient world of which we have heard so much, the property principle. We have already observed that as far back as we can discern it wives were the property of their husband, children the property of their father (or parents), and slaves the property of their owner. If a wife or a child was injured or killed this was damage or destruction of their owner's property, and talion would in principle require that the guilty suffer an equal or equivalent damage to his property in return. That could mean killing the wife or child of the guilty who were themselves entirely innocent. In a combination of the principles of property and talion, logic was satisfied but innocence and humanity were destroyed.

But what of damage to a slave who was also the property of his owner? It is a curious but vital feature of Hammurabi's laws that talion applied, with one exception (law 229), as between persons of the seignior class or higher.

From the list of year names of the reign of King Hammurabi of Babylon:
Year 1 Hammurabi became king.
    2 He established justice in the country.
    3 He constructed a throne for the main dais of the god Nanna. . .
   21 The wall of the town Bazu was built.
   22 The statue of Hammurabi as king granting justice.

The list, containing 43 year names, was translated and annotated by A. Leo Oppenheim. The act of justice which identifies year 2 was probably the customary remission of debts on accession of a new king of which the 'Edict of Ammisaduqa', about a hundred and fifty years later, is a surviving example (see page 34). For year 3, Nanna was the city god of Ur, but he also had a temple in Babylon. Year 22 describes what was probably the stele, now in the Louvre, containing the laws of Hammurabi. If Hammurabi became king in 1792BC, the stele containing his laws will probably have been erected in 1770BC.

The device of year names identified years when there was no generally recognised event in the past from which they could be counted.

In Hammurabi, apart from the one case which might have marked a deliberate extension of talion, talion is never applied to a commoner or a slave.

Though the principles of restitution and talion are equally means of restoring a social balance, they are the thinking of incompatible worlds. It was part of Hammurabi's greatness that he succeeded in bringing the incompatible principles together into a single and acceptable set of laws and thus helped to reconcile the conflicting worlds they represented, at least in Babylon and the other cities governed by his laws.

The four laws in Table 7(a), 196, 197, 200 and 229 express the more acceptable face of talion: they happen not to punish the innocent; they state the amount of the penalty to be imposed as identical to the damage caused and thus exclude punitive damages; they restore the social balance and conflict can cease. That was the point. But although the injured party has the satisfaction of 'getting even', he receives no restitution and is left with his injury and the permanent disadvantage of its effects. The lack of any attempt to make up for the injury caused suggests that these laws may have originated in circumstances where restitution was usually impracticable; for instance, among nomadic peoples of the deserts.

The three laws in Table 7(b), laws 116, 210 and 230, are the *reductio ad absurdum* of the law of talion. Talion is understandable so long as it secures a balance by inflicting indentical damage on the seignior who caused it; but when it is a seignior's relative who is killed rather than the seignior himself, identical damage in return is impossible without killing the innocent. And then it ceases to be a principle for restoring the social balance, because the killing of an innocent is the killing of one not hitherto involved; and that extends the killing into a new cycle of the blood feud. That is the kind of contradiction produced when logic runs riot beyond the control of sense, a tendency of every legal system on record starting with the most ancient of all.

In Hammurabi's laws, talion is only applied in serious cases: three of maiming and four of death. As Hammurabi would hardly have included in his laws measures which were not intended to be used, we have to believe that there were cases where innocent people were actually put to death.

The characteristics of restitution and talion as they appear from the laws of Hammurabi can now be summarised:

Talion and restitution are different applications of the principle of restoring a balance, but they are incompatible with each other. However, they have in common that:

(i) Both prescribe a fixed penalty and exclude punitive damages, and
(ii) Both aim to stop conflict from degenerating into feud.

Talion applies only in the most serious cases and in Hammurabi its characteristics are:

(iii) Talion inflicts identical damage in return;

(iv) It applies only between seigniors, with one exception (law 230, including law 229) which may represent a deliberate extension of the principle;

(v) It punishes the guilty where both the injured and the guilty are independent members of the seignior class or above (with one exception);

(vi) But where the victim is a dependent relative of a seignior, talion requires that a similar relative of the guilty must die, and in that case the penalty falls on the innocent.

The main characteristics of restitution are:

(vii) Restitution punishes only the guilty;

(viii) It must not exceed the amount of the damage caused.

The extension of talion to the negligent builder in law 230/229 raises two questions: how far does the principle of talion pervade not only other laws in Hammurabi, but law in general? and why did Hammurabi extend talion to one builder not of the seignior class?

The answer to the first question depends on whether it is approached from principle or from its effects. Talion can be seen as one principle of law abstracted from its context, and applied regardless of its result in terms of humanity and balance; or it can be seen as a technique useful in specific circumstances, modern as well as ancient, but inappropriate elsewhere. A death penalty for causing death can be understood as a penalty necessary for the control of a particularly dangerous and abhorrent crime, or it can be seen as an expression of talion, a penalty chosen because it happens to be identical to the damage caused and an appropriate punishment for that reason. There is no absolute criterion for deciding the answer to a philosophical question but the favoured principle, whichever it may be, can certainly be presented as continuing to pervade legal systems in the modern world. A more relevant discussion will later consider, briefly, the place of revenge in the concept of justice.

And now for that builder. We have listed law 229 separately from law 230, although they are linked in the original, because there is doubt whether law 229 was really talion or a simple case of the death penalty in which the talion aspect was coincidental. What Hammurabi actually says is:

229. If a builder constructed a house for a seignior, but did not make his work strong, with the result that the house which he built collapsed and so has caused the death of the owner of the house, that builder shall be put to death.

230. If it has caused the death of a son of the owner of the house, they
      shall put the son of that builder to death.

These laws are clearly two parts of what in effect is a single law, and as 230
is talion without any doubt, law 229 could be classed as talion by associa-
tion; while if the death penalty is held in principle to derive from talion,
then 229 will be talion by that derivation. The probability that Hammurabi's
law 229 is talion seems rather more likely than otherwise, though that
does not mean that all death penalties must be so classified.

Law 229/230 is the only one (or two) of Hammurabi's laws of talion
which apply against a person not of the seignior class. This extension of talion to a builder suggests the existence a problem of city life so menacing as
to require something drastic to control it; and the application of talion in
this one case to a member of a social class not otherwise affected by it must
surely have been approved if not suggested by Hammurabi personally.
Furthermore, this law might indicate a more general decision that cases
which threaten life, or might provoke an old-fashioned blood feud, or
threaten the established hierarchy and civil order, require measures of the
severest cruelty even though the culprit may not be a seignior. Hammurabi's
laws of mutilation should probably be seen in this light.

Hammurabi's laws of talion are all concerned with balance, so the
penalty in each case equals but cannot exceed the damage caused. Punitive
damages have no place in talion, but they do appear in three of Hammurabi's
other laws:

8.   A seignior stole property from temple or state ... he makes thirty-
     fold restitution; if from a private citizen, tenfold.
12. (whose complex background includes laws 9, 10 and 11) If the seller
     of property stolen from a seignior has died, and the purchaser of
     that property has become liable for it, he may take from the estate
     of the seller fivefold the claim for that case.
124. A seignior who gave property to another seignior for safekeeping
     and later denied it shall pay double whatever he denied.

Punitive damages do not occur in any of the surviving laws earlier than
Hammurabi, so it is possible that the principle of punitive damages may
have been introduced by Hammurabi. If so, these laws imposing punitive
damages must rank within the generally greater severity of penalties introduced by Hammurabi; but they are not talion, and they are not feud.

Hammurabi's laws of talion are unlikely to have derived from the earlier
laws of Sumer and Akkad because the surviving laws from Sumer and Akkad
have no talion as such, and any implied basis in talion is arguable. Similarly,
punishment by mutilation occurs only in Hammurabi and not in the earlier
surviving laws, and although it is possible that earlier laws of mutilation

may have existed but not survived, the milder tone of the earlier laws which have survived makes it appear more likely that mutilation may not in fact have been among their punishments. Nor do Hammurabi's talion and mutilations fit with the moderate tone of the majority of his own laws which did derive from the earlier tradition.

Talion strikes a chord in the modern western mind because it appears in the Bible, identified by the phrase 'an eye for an eye and a tooth for a tooth'; but that verbal echo of Hammurabi's laws does not mean that the biblical laws of talion came directly from Hammurabi.

The function of talion as a means of limiting feud is expressed in the often repeated interpretation of the biblical phrase 'an eye for an eye' to imply 'and no more than an eye for an eye'. That is true but it understates the moderation of the Bible. It is now clear that the most cruel half of the law of talion, the half which punished the innocent, is omitted from the Bible altogether. Let us look at what the Bible actually says about talion.

The law of talion is set out in the Bible in two places, and in the setting of two different laws; but its substance is the same in each and so is the mystery that surrounds it. A legal authority and expert in the world's ancient laws A.S. Diamond in his *Primitive Law Past and Present* has this to say about talion in the Bible:[4]

> But the vogue of the talionic idea is short-lived: it was in practice unknown in the later Jewish law, and there was much debate as to the meaning of the rule and as to whether it had ever been literally applied.

And later:[5]

> The rule of the talion is an interpolation and addition wherever it occurs in the Pentateuch.

As talion continues to appear in the Pentateuch it is worth looking at what is actually said. One statement of the law of talion is in Exodus, Chapter 21, in the context of causing a girl to miscarry:

> 22. If men strive, and hurt a woman with child, so that her fruit depart from her, and yet no mischief follow: he shall be surely punished, according as the woman's husband will lay upon him; and he shall pay as the judges determine.
> 23. And if any mischief follow, then shalt thou give life for life,
> 24. Eye for eye, tooth for tooth, hand for hand, foot for foot,
> 25. Burning for burning, wound for wound, stripe for stripe.

This statement is in two parts. Verse 22 details the offence and says that if no mischief follows, the penalty shall fall on the guilty, (... he shall be surely punished ...), which excludes the possibility of punishing the innocent. If 'no mischief follows', the penalty is not talion but 'according as the husband will lay upon him'. The husband may ask for corporal punishment but 'as the judges determine' makes it clear that it is the judges who will decide. So, if a girl miscarries as a result of a brawl, Exodus: 21: 22 says that the penalty will be decided by the judges in the light of representations from the girl's husband, and it will fall only on the guilty. That is not talion.

If mischief does follow, the penalty in verses 23–5 is undoubtedly talion, and its precise nature depends, as a result, upon the nature of the mischief caused to the girl: a life for a life in verse 23 if the girl dies, but in verses 24 and 25 an eye for eye and so on through a catalogue of possible mischiefs and the penalties corresponding to them; while the 'he' in verse 22 continues to imply that the penalty will not fall on any but the guilty.

The difficulty is that the catalogue of mischiefs, and therefore of matching punishments, eye, tooth, hand, foot, burning, wound or stripe, while possible, seem a shade exaggerated in the context of a brawl in which a girl miscarried by accident. They can be argued of course, but an air of rhetoric continues to hang around them. They sound much more like a general statement of the principle of talion; and the mystery is why, if so, they should appear as appendages to a single incident rather than in the prominence of an independent declaration in their own setting.

The second statement of talion is in Deuteronomy, Chapter 19, verses 16 to 21, in the context of false witness:

16. If a false witness rise up against any man to testify against him that which is wrong;
17. Then both the men, between whom the controversy is, shall stand before the Lord, before the priests and the judges, which shall be in those days;
18. And the judges shall make diligent inquisition: and, behold, if the witness be a false witness, and hath testified falsely against his brother;
19. Then shall ye do unto him, as he had thought to have done unto his brother: so shalt thou put the evil away from among you.
20. And those which remain shall hear, and fear, and shall henceforth commit no more any such evil among you.
21. And thine eye shall not pity; but life shall go for life, eye for eye, tooth for tooth, hand for hand, foot for foot.

Verses 16, 17 and 18 detail the circumstances of the false witness, and verse 19 gives the penalty which is imposed only on the guilty (Then shalt thou do unto him ...). The penalty is talion. Verse 20 then makes plain the deterrent aspect of this case, and with that the incident would appear to be closed.

But it is not closed, because verse 21 follows as part of this statement but with a recitation of the full principle of talion which hardly relates to the preceding law. So Deuteronomy contains the same element of mystery as Exodus. In each, a particular law is laid down with a penalty tailored to the circumstances described, in both it is talion, followed by a full statement of the principle of talion whose terms are not related to the laws to which they are attached but whose status and setting are those of an appendage. In other words, precisely what A.S. Diamond said.

Hammurabi's laws of talion are of two kinds: those which punish only the guilty, and those which are applied to third persons and punish the innocent. Two things are now clear: that the most cruel half of the laws of talion, which would punish the innocent, occur in the laws of Hammurabi but do not occur in the Bible; and that A.S.Diamond is right that the presence of talion in the Pentateuch is as an appendage.

So now, there are two questions: how did the most cruel half of the laws of talion come to be omitted from the Bible? How seriously were the laws of talion which were included in the Bible meant to be applied in practice?

The image of the city states of the ancient near east can sometimes be distorted by the pattern of archaeological excavation which used to present them as separated, even isolated, islands of culture in an ocean of

THE REMAINS OF URUK, the home of Gilgamesh and the largest city of the third millennium BC. The city itself dates from the fourth millennium.

barbarism. What is now emerging is the very different image of a whole region peppered with cities, towns and villages whose population both urban and rural, with the exception of nomads, enjoyed what was in effect a highly complex common culture. The surviving laws, including the later Assyrian and Hittite laws, are similar enough in their general character to suggest that a common legal climate obtained throughout the whole region and may well have pervaded neighbouring regions as well; and that all must live within them who wished to have normal relations with their neighbours. Of course there were local differences especially in regard to severity; but those differences were not so great as to suggest a different kind of legal regime. A.S. Diamond describes it:[6]

> The Hebrew Code, though brief, is little less advanced than that of Hammurabi, and is perhaps nearer in its degree of development to the Laws of Eshnunna (of a millennium earlier), than to any other of the codes to which reference has been made. Yet it is true to say that all these codes give evidence of belonging to one great field of culture, for there are resemblances between them in language and content.

The common legal climate was not a copy of the laws of Hammurabi, but there is no doubt that Hammurabi's written laws had a powerful influence over its later development and character. The Hebrew (or Jewish) people shared many of their secular laws of daily living with their regional neighbours, as will soon be shown; but the most cruel half of talion, punishing the innocent, may well have fallen into disuse before they wrote their laws down; or they may have obtained talion from the same kind of desert source as did Hammurabi, and have rejected punishment of the innocent outright by their own decision.

The treatment of a wounded slave in example number 6 in the comparison (below) of Hebrew daily laws with the laws of Hammurabi shows that Hebrew law was capable of departing from the regional norm; and that part of the principle of talion that punishes the innocent may have been treated in the same way.

The half of talion that was included in the Bible does raise the question how seriously was it meant. The possibility that it might have been meant seriously cannot be dismissed out of hand. Its setting suggests a general statement that the principle of precise restitution shall be taken as the foundation of justice and be used widely when making actual judgements. In the ancient world, penalties were often administered by the injured parties even where a court had decided the question of guilt; but frequently there was no court, and guilt was judged and the penalty administered by those involved and their immediate elders. So a guide to what constituted acceptable justice, supported by examples, was far more use than any general and abstract law based on imagined circumstances. In an age when enforcement was difficult, acceptance of the law was vital, and an 'an eye for an eye and a tooth for a tooth' was a memorable guide to the administration of a justice that all could understand, accept and fear.

THE SECULAR AND DAILY LAWS IN THE BIBLE

There remain the secular, daily laws in the Bible, other than talion, which can hardly be passed over in total silence. These can often be seen to be similar to surviving laws of the region, a similarity that is not disturbed by the presence of relatively minor variations. Regional laws can broadly be identified for our limited purpose as those which appear both in the laws of Hammurabi and in the Bible, two written sources separated in both time and place. To list all the biblical laws which correspond, or seem to correspond, with the earlier laws of Hammurabi would use more space than is needed to make the point; so six rough correspondences covering a range of secular problems of daily life will suffice to illustrate concordance as well as the occasional difference:

1. Rape of a betrothed virgin

Hammurabi 130: If a seignior bound the betrothed wife of another seignior, who had had no intercourse with a male and was still living in her father's house, and he has lain in her bosom and they have caught him, that seignior shall be put to death, while that woman shall go free.

Deuteronomy 22: 25 But if a man find a betrothed damsel in the field, and the man force her, and lie with her: then the man only that lay with her shall die:

2. Honest weights

Hammurabi 94: If a merchant lent grain or money at interest and when he lent it at interest he paid out the money by the small weight and the grain by the small measure, but when he got it back he got the money by the large weight and the grain by the large measure, that merchant shall forfeit whatever he lent.

Deuteronomy 25: 13. Thou shalt not have in thy bag divers weights, a great and a small.

14. Thou shalt not have in thine house divers measures, a great and a small.

15. But thou shalt have a perfect and just weight, a perfect and just measure shalt thou have: that thy days may be lengthened in the land which the Lord thy God giveth thee.

3. Grazing a neighbour's field

Hammurabi 57: If a shepherd has not come to an agreement with the owner of a field to pasture sheep on the grass, but has pastured sheep on the field without the consent of the owner of the field, when the owner of the field harvests his field, the shepherd who pastured his sheep on the field without the consent of the owner of the field shall give in addition twenty kur of grain per eighteen iku to the owner of the field.

Exodus 22: 5. If a man shall cause a field or vineyard to be eaten, and shall put in his beast, and shall feed in another man's field: of the best of his own field, and of the best of his own vineyard, shall he make restitution.

4. Shepherd loses a beast

Hammurabi 266: If a visitation of God has occurred in a sheepfold or a lion has made a kill, the shepherd shall prove himself innocent in the presence of God, but the owner of the sheepfold shall receive from him the animal stricken in the fold.

Exodus 22: 10. If a man deliver unto his neighbour an ass, or an ox, or a sheep, or any beast, to keep; and it die, or be hurt, or driven away, no man seeing it:

11. Then shall an oath of the Lord be between them both, that he hath not put his hand unto his neighbour's goods; and the owner of it shall accept thereof, and he shall not make it good.

13. If it be torn in pieces, then let him bring it for witness, and he shall not make good that which was torn.

5. Striking a parent

Hammurabi 195: If a son struck his father, they shall cut off his hand.

Exodus 21: 15. And he that smiteth his father, or his mother, shall be surely put to death.

6. Wounding a slave

Hammurabi 199: If he (a seignior, law 196) has destroyed the eye of a seignior's slave or broken the bone of a seignior's slave, he shall pay one-half his value.

Exodus 21: 26. And if a man smite the eye of his servant, or the eye of his maid, that it perish; he shall let him go free for his eye's sake.

27. And if he smite out his manservant's tooth; or his maidservant's tooth; he shall let him go free for his tooth's sake.

There is no suggestion that the biblical daily laws are identical with the laws of Hammurabi or any set of the earlier laws of Mesopotamia, but the scale of coincidence between the Bible and Hammurabi suggests that in the rules of daily living there was a common legal tradition throughout the whole region which those who lived there generally, though not invariably, accepted.

Four of our chosen examples show acceptance of a common tradition while two suggest departures from it: In example 1, rape of a betrothed virgin, the Bible and Hammurabi are identical; in example 2, honest weights, the only difference is that Hammurabi imposes a fine where the Bible uses exhortation. In example 3, grazing a neighbour's field, and in example 4,. shepherd loses a beast, they are again identical.

In example 5, striking a parent, the offences are identical but Hammurabi removes a hand while the Bible puts to death; that suggests that both considered the offence to pose a serious threat to society. In 6. for blinding a slave or breaking one of his bones Hammurabi imposes a fine of half the slave's value while the Bible sets the slave free as an act of recompense; so in their treatment of this offence the contrast between Hammurabi and the Bible could hardly be greater. It is probable that this law reflects the Jewish memory of their own slavery in Egypt, and the spirit of humanity which that experience released.

We have said nothing about religious law in the Bible because that is outside our field, but just one thought about the form of religious laws may perhaps be permitted. The Bible's secular laws including talion generally take the form of a statement of particular circumstances followed by a penalty; they do not start from a general principle detached from circumstances or adopt an authoritative moral tone. One set of laws, by contrast, does just that. The ten commandments are the first known universal, moral injunctions, and their form reflects that they are intended to apply irrespective of circumstance. This unique statement of universal moral law

---

Sargon, the mighty king, king of Agade am I!
My mother was a changeling, my father I knew not . . .
. . . She set me in a basket of rushes, with bitumen she sealed
    my lid.
She cast me into the river which rose not over me.
The river bore me up and carried me to Akki, the drawer of
    water.
Akki, the drawer of water, lifted me out as he dipped his ewer.
Akki, the drawer of water, took me as his son and reared
    me . . .

From the 'Legend of Sargon' written in seventh-century BC Assyria, translated by E. A. Speiser. Sargon the Great was born around 2300BC, was king of Akkad (Agade) and founder of the Akkadian dynasty. This legend, which was reproduced in the seventh century, must have been written originally much earlier.

was to have a profound influence on future religious, philosophical and political thinking. The ten commandments are an historic departure from earlier tradition, and for that reason they stand above and outside all other biblical laws under discussion.

Biblical law is, for us, something of a diversion; but mention talion and the Bible springs to mind with its thunderous image of 'an eye for an eye' which cannot be ignored; and that in turn makes a glance at other biblical laws unavoidable. But the Hammurabi mystery now beckons.

HAMMURABI'S DILEMMA

Feud is not the only source of cruelty in the laws of Hammurabi's Babylon; but it does seem to lie at the root of talion a principle which, if carried to its logical extreme, can be met only with repugnance. But 'a life for a life' was not the same as a death penalty. In all the surviving collections of laws up to and including Hammurabi there are twenty-eight laws imposing the death penalty where no death at all had occurred and which cannot therefore be revenge by talion, compared with only seven in which someone had been killed and which probably were talion (Table 3). According to a count of the surviving laws, talion appears as a minority principle.

The apparent absence of talion from the surviving laws of Sumer and Akkad, and the seeming lack of any mention of either talion or feud in the literature, must mean that either the prehistoric legal systems had been so successful that feud had died out, or that the Sumerians and Akkadians had never been given to feud at all and therefore required no laws to prevent it or, possibly, that records of feud in fields other than those covered by the surviving laws have simply not survived.

'Yes, Atu? No, Please do . . . you have been silent a long time . . .'
'. . . *You have been talking much . . . and I think it is now time to put a few things right . . . some of what you say is true, but some is not . . . yes, feud had not been a problem in my world of Sumer for a very long time, but we knew it existed among those who had no cities. Feud belonged to the people of the desert, the Martu we called them and to you they are still Amorites. But Hammurabi's written laws of talion do not preserve the whole story. Within their families and clans the desert people did not punish the innocent, not just because each life was necessary to survival but because the clan remained together on the march and had time to reach the truth. Between different families or clans travelling for thousands of miles in different directions contact was intermittent, so if justice was to be done between them it must be done on the spot. Without permanent centres complex legal systems could not arise. Feud and retaliation kept the peace most of the time, and though a feud might continue to exist it subsided when the clans moved on . . .*

... That was all right for the desert people, but not for us in our vast settled cities. We had to and did establish structured legal systems with courts and judges that everybody knew, and we wrote our ordinary laws and kept records of our decisions. Most of us had never met feud in our lives ... or even heard tell of it among our own people ... but we knew what Hammurabi meant and what he had to contend with ... It was our cities that extinguished feud long before coherent records existed, and you must remember that our cities were immemorially ancient even to us.

... But the desert world was not all bad ... The principles of equal compensation and a balance of justice which are expressed in talion were the basis of our law and have never been abandoned, and you have yourself remarked that they are today at the root of much of your modern law as well. Guilt or innocence may be known and they usually are, but proving them is another matter; that takes time, and it can be impossible. Your city justice, and our's too, must have proof if the law is to be accepted; so, in what we both know as the civilised world, justice for much of the time does not get done because the only process that leads to it cannot get started. Yet, in cities, the legal process with all its gaps and faults is preferable to feud so we, like you, generally accepted the limitations of a careful justice which you rightly call the rule of law. But in the desert a careful justice would have meant no justice at all. Looking back, and looking round, we all need to adjust our minds to the fact that there is more than one kind of rule of law. When clans pause in the same oasis and tempers flare or knives flash, justice must be swift or there will be war; and war is even more terrible than a rough revenge which, defined and restricted, is still a rule of law ...

... You condemn our principle of retaliation ... yes, in your heart you do ... and I have to say as gently as I can in one of your own phrases: please, 'get real'... In the deserts which surrounded our city world, from which many of our people had come, justice could never be abstract: of course right and wrong mattered within the clan, but let others be involved and the clan closed mouths as well as ranks and the wall of silence was impenetrable. No outsider could prove that the man who did it was guilty, and no insider would dare tell. So feud and its endless killing loomed. But there was another way: if proof was impossible, why waste time chasing it? The individual might be out of reach but none could deny which clan it was: so we left the culprit to those who knew him, measured the loss and struck back at the clan who would not tell. That way the balance was restored, a balance of loss leading to a balance of fear, but also a balance of satisfaction and a justice all could understand ... To punish only the guilty is a high principle which requires a legal process to ensure that, paradoxically, for much of the time the guilty are not punished but allowed to go free; and in our world that would have meant that the conflict and the killing would go on. Talion

measures the damage and lets the injured get even; it restores the balance by striking back, and ends the conflict on the spot ... so who are you and I to say that the price was never worth it ... ? That, at least, was the argument ... '

'I suppose that still is the argument, Atu; but it is the vein of cruelty that runs through talion both in your world and, still, in parts of ours, that is one of the reasons why we reject it with a special repugnance. Yes, we have plenty of cruelty, and even in your laws, cruelty was not confined to talion; indeed, it might not even have formed part of talion originally. But it is not only cruelty that makes us reject talion, at least in what we call the western world; it was the principle of revenge. To us, Atu, revenge could never be part of an acceptable justice.'

'... Nor to us either, my friend ... Do not forget that talion was not really part of our world at all; it arrived late and came from the Martu ... But we knew its setting , and anyway it was imposed on us and we could not resist it ... But tell me ... do you not think there is an element of revenge in the very concept of justice? It is all very well to dismiss revenge as a base motive without going into what it is that is base ... but ... if you think about it, isn't it unlimited revenge that is dangerous and therefore evil while precise revenge sufficient to restore a balance is surely acceptable and, yes, necessary? ... You have to ask why we would restore the balance at all instead of just accepting that the old balance has now vanished and a new balance has been established? ... But to accept that would be to recognise violence and superior strength as a rule of law which is just what your world as well as ours escaped from ... Of course the wish to retore a situation that has been upset is part of the revenge motive ...'

'You may be right, Atu, that the impulse to repair an injury is essentially the same as the impulse to strike back by injuring the person who has injured you; but if the impulses are the same, there is still this difference between them in practice: that a payment equal to the damage suffered restores the situation and is acceptable justice, while the infliction of identical damage in return restores nothing and the satisfaction it gives exists only in the mind. We see the first as ethical and the second as unethical. The second might, of course, have emerged out of the first, though I think it more likely that they reflect different conditions of life rather than psychology.'

'... In our deserts ... my friend ... abstract principle was a luxury our nomads could discuss but seldom afford: they had to do what worked. But you have rightly pin-pointed the contradiction that arises if logic is followed too literally and too far. The nomads were not stupid; of course they too recognised the contradiction: when talion meant killing the innocent, it did not end the conflict but started a new cycle ... It was years before anyone got to grips with that, but they did in the end as your Bible makes plain ...'

160

With Hammurabi and his city laws, we are in two worlds. There is still no direct mention of feud, but some of his laws, including talion, suggest that feud must lie behind them. The date of Hammurabi's code is a matter of some doubt, but a rough and rounded estimate suggests about two hundred years between the laws of Eshnunna and those of Hammurabi. During that period important changes had taken place. Hammurabi's laws, unlike the earlier laws, are based on class distinction; some of his laws inflict outrageous physical mutilation as well as mere beatings, often in cases where there has been no personal injury and predominantly upon the seignior class; and they include the whole range of talion, even punishing the innocent, and with one possible exception they apply talion to the seignior class only. These elements of cruelty occur in Hammurabi especially in crimes which threaten the order of society or the security of the city; but in other fields, he broadly repeats the traditional and moderate laws of the region and administers them with a rational humanity that is studied and deliberate.

It is as if there were either two incompatible Hammurabi's, or a king under conflicting and irreconcilable pressures. We can almost feel the tensions within an ancient and kindly world that is being forced reluctantly to recognise that in great cities change is an irresistible natural growth which comes with two faces, and cruelty is one of them ...

HAMMURABI'S SOLUTION

Joan Oates, writing of the laws of Hammurabi, says:[7]

> A striking change from the Sumerian law is the appearance of lex talionis, 'an eye for an eye, and a tooth for a tooth', almost certainly a reflection of Amorite custom.

The Encyclopaedia Britannica:[8]

> The Code of Hammurabi differs in many respects from the Code of Lipit-Ishtar ... Its most striking feature lies in the extraordinary severity of its penalties and in the principle of the lex talionis ... It is often said, and perhaps rightly so, that this severity, which so contrasts with Sumerian judicial tradition, can be traced back to the Amorite influence.

H.W.F. Saggs in *The Babylonians* says that the harshness of some of Hammurabi's penalties was a reaction to the massive influx of Amorites during the early years of the second millennium BC, since they would expect to have their disputes settled in accordance with laws reflecting their own traditions; and a similar kind of conflict might arise between litigants from different cities within Babylonia: so Hammurabi's laws reflect the king's decision in cases where legal traditions conflicted. That confirms that the Amorite presence, and tradition, was the reason for Hammurabi's

new and harsh penalties, but there is more to be said about the nature of
Amorite tradition, about the contrast between Hammurabi's new brutal
laws and the benign laws which are the majority of his code and, for its
period, about the astonishing feat of balance that Hammurabi's law code
acheived and perpetuated.

Around 2000BC the city of Ur was destroyed by attacks from three directions: the Elamites invaded from the east and actually destroyed Ur; the
Gutians invaded from the mountains to the north-east, and the Martu or
Amorites invaded from the western deserts. The Martu were no strangers
in Sumer and Akkad having infiltrated the city civilisation for centuries,
where their unesettled presence was felt as a threat. After the collapse of
Sumer and Akkad which they had helped to bring about, the Martu settled
at last in the fertile lands and their leaders began their ascent from tribal
sheiks to regional kings. About two hundred years after the destruction of
Ur the Amorites, as we now know them, appear in two centres: as kings of
the city of Asshur from which Assyria derives its name; and as kings of
Babylon. The Babylonian king list records that the sixth king of Babylon
was called Hammurabi[9], while the list of the names of his regnal years[10]
gives a reign of 43 years. His dates in terms of the modern era are not universally agreed, but they are often taken to be 1792–1750.[11]

There are two basic assumptions: that the aristocracy of Hammurabi's
Babylon was drawn mainly from the more recently arrived Amorite settlers
and their descendants, of whom Hammurabi was one; and that the aristocracy retained features of the culture of their desert ancestors which clashed
with the ancient Sumero–Akkadian city culture of the Babylon born popu-
lace. That an Amorite monarchy may have given power and position to
their kin is an assumption, but a similar situation has been revealed in the
manner in which the Akkadian dynasty of king Sargon, some five hundred
years earlier, imposed their supremacy over the conquered Sumerians. The
land ownership aspect of that earlier process has been traced in detail by
Benjamin R. Foster in *Administration and Use of Institutional Land in
Sargonic Sumer* and the process as a whole is summarised in the final two
sentences of the book:[12]

> Royal lands and royal officials are found in Sumer, attesting to the aggres-
> sive expansion of the Sargonic royal household at the expense of local
> institutions. In the omnipresence and importance of the royal establish-
> ment and its dependents, one sees the economic foundation of this early
> empire.

The supposition that a similar process may have followed the Amorite
occupation of Babylon does at least have a precedent.

A question about feud is a good starting point: why are Hammurabi's laws so often characteristic of feud if they governed a society in which feud did not exist? The *Encyclopaedia Britannica* contrasts Hammurabi with the Sumerian Lipit-Ishtar and thus implies that the contrast introduced by Hammurabi is between his laws and a pre-existing common Sumerian–Akkadian tradition.

The surviving laws of different cities do not always match each other, but comparisons are occasionally possible. For instance, Hammurabi used mutilation as well as talion: the city of Eshnunna in equivalent circumstances used neither. Hammurabi's laws were based on class distinction: the laws of Eshnunna and the earlier laws were not. Hammurabi had seven laws of talion as set out in Table 7 above, and they are repeated here for convenience:

(a) Laws which punish the innocent

116	Seignior caused death of distrained son of another seignior	seignior's son to die
210	Seignior struck pregnant woman who died; if she was daughter of a seignior	his daughter dies
230	Builder at fault, house collapses, kills owner's son	builder's son to die

(b) Laws which punish only the guilty

196	Seignior destroys seignior's eye	destroy his eye
197	Seignior destroys seignor's bone	destroy his bone
200	Seignior destroy's seignior's tooth	destroy his tooth
229	Builder at fault, house collapses, kills owner	the builder to die

Five of these laws (116, 196, 197, 200, 229) deal with situations virtually identical to equivalent pre-Hammurabi laws, yet their penalties are very different:

Hammurabi's law 116 equates with Eshnunna's law 24: for causing the death of a wrongly distrained wife or child ... Hammurabi kills the son of the culprit where Eshnunna's penalty is death for the culprit himself.

Hammurabi's laws of personal injury, 196 an eye for an eye, 197 a bone for a bone and 200 a tooth for a tooth equate in principle with personal injury in Ur-Nammu laws 15 to 19 which deal with foot, unspecified limb, nose and tooth; and they also equate in principle with Eshnunna's laws 42 to 48 dealing with eye, tooth, ear, finger, hand, foot, undecipherable limb, and hitting; plus the final law 48 which decrees that cases involving 2/3 mina to 1 mina must come to court and that capital cases must go to the king.

Hammurabi's law 229 equates approximately but not precisely with

Eshnunna's law 58: if the owner of a building ignores an official warning, his house collapses and kills a free man... it is a capital offence, the penalty will fall on the culprit but the case must be referred to the king to decide the penalty himself; whereas Hammurabi kills the builder if the house owner was the person killed by the collapse of the wall but says nothing about what happens of the wall kills an unspecified free man.

The two of Hammurabi's laws of talion not matched by earlier laws are his law 210, the seignior who killed a pregnant daughter of a seignior for which the seignior's daughter must die, and his law 230, the builder whose house collapsed and killed its owner's son for which the son of the builder had to die.

Of the five of Hammurabi's laws whose penalties are talion one, law 229 equates only approximately with an earlier law, Eshnunna law 58. That leaves four of Hammurabi's laws of talion that do equate with earlier laws but whose penalties are very different. The penalties prescribed by both Ur-Nammu and Eshnunna, except for Eshnunna law 48, are all fines, financial penalties which do not inflict like damage, which fall on the culprit and have nothing of talion about them except that they may ultimately derive from a common first principle of balance. Hammurabi's penalties are certainly talion because they assess the damage caused and inflict equal damage in return ... an eye for an eye. So these penalties of talion are new to the surviving laws of the region.

If this is combined with the fact that Hammurabi's penalties of mutilation do not occur in the earlier surviving laws at all, it becomes possible, indeed necessary, to ask why Hammurabi should unpredictably add to what appears from the surviving laws to have been the legal tradition of Sumer and Akkad by inserting into his new collection of laws for Babylon penalties that arrive as new principles of talion and mutilation. Furthermore, both talion and mutilation are incompatible with the moderate, studied sense of justice which Hammurabi himself displays elsewhere in his laws. That is what we mean by two Hammurabi's.

The fact that Hammurabi was not an Akkadian, who were the principal pre-Hammurabi population of the city of Babylon, but an Amorite, a relative newcomer, is an important distinction. Both the Amorites and the Akkadians came originally from the deserts to the west of Sumer, but the Akkadians had been in Akkad for nearly as long as the Sumerians had been in Sumer and they shared the Sumerian city culture which by this time they had made their own; while the Amorites, or Martu as they were called by the Sumerians, were the desert dwelling ancestors of the modern Beduin. Their languages were related, but cultually they were at this time very different. This may be illustrated by two references from a poem, *The Curse of Agade*, written in Sumerian probably around 2000BC which gives a description of Agade the capital city of Akkad in the reign of Naram Sin (*c.*2250BC):[13]

> In those days the dwelling of Agade were filled with gold,
> Its bright-shining houses were filled with silver,
> Into its granaries were brought copper, lead and slabs of lapis-lazuli,
> Its silos bulged at the sides,
> Its old women were endowed with counsel,
> Its young men were endowed with 'strength of weapons',
> Its little children were endowed with joyous hearts ...
>
> ... Inside, the city was full of tigi music,
> Outside it was full of reed-pipe and zamzam music ...
>
> (The Curse of Agade, trans. S.N. Kramer)

Later in the same poem there is this:

> The Sumerians eagerly sailed their goods-laden boats to it [Agade],
> The Martu, the people of the lord that knows not grain,
> Brought her perfect oxen, perfect sheep ...

The Martu from the western desert did not cultivate (how could they?) but they brought perfect cattle and sheep for sale in the markets of Agade. They had long been infiltrating and settling in Sumer, indeed S.N. Kramer suggests that King Eannatum of the Sumerian city of Lagash may have been a Martu since he is said to have also been named Lumma, a Martu tribal name.[14] The Martu nomad presence had always been resented and feared, and shortly before 2000BC they joined the attack on Sumer which destroyed Ur. The Martu then settled freely in Sumer and Akkad ...

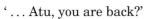

'... Atu, you are back?'

'... *Indeed yes ... you have nearly got it ... the Martu ...that was the problem facing Hammurabi. You will recall that when the Akkadians first conquered Sumer they made Akkadian the official language of the region and installed Akkadians in senior positions;* similarly, *after the fall of Ur, though the Martu, or the Amorites as you now call them, adopted the Akkadian language they installed fellow Amorites in leading positions of power. So Hammurabi found himself faced by two conflicting cultures: the ancient city culture of Sumer and Akkad and the desert nomad culture of a newly dominant class of Amorites, of whom he was one. And the clash was not just of two cultures, but of two irreconcilable sets of legal principles each with its established laws, the one written and the other oral. You have wondered why Hammurabi so badly needed to consolidate the laws of Sumer and Akkad, and what can have caused him suddenly to introduce laws involving mutilation and the punishment of the innocent.*

These harsher laws just do not fit and that, you are right, is the Hammurabi mystery...

... Well ... the answer lies in the dominance of the Martu, relatively newly arrived and now the Amorite aristocracy. Hammurabi seldom mentions this aristocracy, but you have noticed that he does so in law 207 '... and if it was a member of the aristocracy ...' The upper classes in Hammurabi's Babylon were substantially Amorite and, because of that, laws they would recognise and respect were necessary, laws with a familiar harshness and severe enough to enforce a recogniseable justice and prevent any return to feud. But the kind of law which would keep the aristocracy in their place would drive the ordinary civilised Babylonian to arms; so there had to be two laws, one for the Amorites and one for the rest, but they must be combined into a single document if they were to command obedience from both. With one exception, Hammurabi's laws of talion applied only to the Seignior class and above and not to other free men. The distinction between classes of free men, which Hammurabi so emphasised compared with earlier codes, may not have been perverse but have reflected a new ethnic as well as cultural reality on the ground. Laws applying to the seignior class may have covered most of the administrative and managerial levels of society. The earlier codes had only to deal with two ethnic communities, the Sumerian and the Akkadian, who shared a common culture and were rapidly coalescing. Hammurabi had that plus a third ethic component, the Amorite leadership, whose culture came not from centuries of civilised living and a legal system based on restitution but from the desert and its harsh laws of talion and mutilation...

... So Hammurabi's achievement is even more astonishing than you had thought. Not only did he impose a code of law which would bind equally on all sections of his kingdom, but he incorporated into the traditional laws of his dynasty's new home just those facets of his own stricter culture which might preserve the hierarchy of a city society and the Amorite dominance within it, and provide a set of laws which in a single document would make the desert blood feud impossible and which all could accept. The desert inheritance was not confined to laws dealing directly with feud but applied to sensitive areas in which weakness might endanger the whole. The most obvious extension is the builder whose wall collapsed and killed the owner's son, a situation which hardly existed in a desert society but which in a city could easily cause those still living in a desert culture to explode into feud. By extending the laws of feud from seigniors to the builder and thus condemning to death the builder's son who was in fact innocent, Hammurabi contained a crisis which otherwise might have spread ... he really had very little choice ...'

Atu has vanished again.

166

In personal injury, the laws of feud and the penalty of mutilation are joined; but the penalty of mutilation extends not only beyond personal injury but beyond the seignior class to other free men and to slaves. Hammurabi has fifteen laws which impose mutilations and these include the son, now one-handed, who struck his father, the seignior who could not prove his allegation against a nun and lost half his hair, the adopted son of a chamberlain who sought his natural parents and as a result has only one eye, as well as the one-handed physician whose operation had caused a seignior's death. It is hard not to see in this, Hammurabi's desert inheritance and the delicate situation of the Amorite aristocracy of Babylon.

If Hammurabi's purpose was not just to consolidate the existing laws of Sumer and Akkad but to bind the new Amorite aristocracy into his legal system by constricting feud; and if he then took the penalty of mutilation from desert law to reinforce key areas of city society, he was attempting something more far-reaching than he is usually given credit for.

With the presence of laws clearly from the desert thus accounted for, Hammurabi's decision to assemble and publish a fresh list of laws can be seen in a new light: a necessary collation of the traditional laws of Sumer and Akkad after two centuries of turmoil following the destruction of Ur about 2000BC, now to be supplemented by the insertion of laws from the desert needed to bind his Amorite aristocracy and their traditional desert culture into the city society and culture of Sumer and Akkad. Hammurabi's task and his achievement increase in stature the more closely they are studied.

'Atu, again . . . ?'

'*. . . Please . . . yes . . . I perceive that mutilation fascinates your world, and you still see Hammurabi in terms of penalties which were part of his policy rather than his nature; and you therefore underestimate the humanitarian debt you owe him. That no longer matters. What does matter is that your virtuous rejection of cruelty under the law may have led you towards an excess of disorder . . . Perhaps Hammurabi understood something that your world finds it difficult to face: that as society is human, there will always be cruelty somewhere; and if there is not a measure of cruelty under the law, there will be terrible and endless cruelty in the streets . . .*'

CHAPTER 12

LAW IN THE ANCIENT WORLD

OME PEOPLE SAY that the most ancient laws, up to and including those of Hammurabi, indeed all laws until early Greece, are not really laws at all but mere guides to the judges who were not bound by them. And those who say that are right: that is, they are right so long as they see the ancient world only through modern eyes and restrict their definition of law to the form given to it in the modern world. Some say the early laws were primitive, as A.S. Diamond did in his definitive book *Primitive Law, Past and Present*.[1] He related the development of legal systems to the level of economic development in the jurisdictions they served, and this enabled him to consider Hammurabi as the culmination of the stage of primitive law '... we have chosen to mark the closing stage of primitive law with the Code of Hammurabi[2]....' The development of law in the Code of Hammurabi by roughly 1750BC is compared approximately with that in Athens over one thousand years later: 'In Athens, Draco's legislation of 620BC or thereabouts seems to have represented the close of our primitive period[3]...'; while in his article 'An Eye for an Eye' in *Iraq*[4] he compared the laws of Hammurabi with those of England in the Middle Ages: 'The L.E. (Laws of Eshnunna), and the laws of Ur-Nammu, as far as they go represent the legal situation in England in AD1150. The C.H. (Code of Hammurabi) represents England in 1250.' So the word 'primitive' as used by A.S. Diamond describes a stage of development regardless of whether it is ancient, recent or current.

The development of legal systems tends to be presented as though they had grown from simple rules suitable for the governance of simple societies to the more complex rules needed for the governance of advanced societies. This unconsciously assumes that legal development started from the simple and advanced towards the complex. But that might not have been the case. Ancient legal systems whose written remains show that they recorded only outlines and left substance to the discretion of the judges, nonetheless gave legal form to ethical principle; and when the unwritten was added to the written the sum of law may not have been simple at all. Modern legal systems which write everything down (or try to) and leave as little as they can to the judges are more predictable than the ancient laws and much more voluminous, but they may not be more complex. The modern habit of dismissing ancient legal systems, or the legal systems of modern tribal societies for that matter, as mere custom means that they are not considered to be legal systems at all and should not therefore be discussed in that context. But legal systems cannot be categorised merely as simple or complex, because these are procedural terms and meaningless as descriptions of content. What matters is the kind of justice they aimed at and their efficiency in producing it. The humane quality of individual justice produced by the pre-Hammurabi laws, including those which Hammurabi incorprated in his 'code', may in many ways be preferable to the mass justice considered necessary by the modern world. Nostalgia for the small community may see Hammurabi as the point at which massive city populations revealed the inadequacy of legal systems based on the individual, the point after which the flat-iron of written law directed collectively towards the whole population began slowly to replace the discretion of the judges and the traditional flexibility of natural justice.

The situation in Mesopotamia was summarised by Roux:[5]

Indeed, the Mesopotamians were never ruled by any other system than a 'common law', handed down from reign to reign and occasionally modified to fit the social and economic conditions prevalent at a given period.

Jean Bottero[6] is among those who take issue with the word 'code' in relation to these early laws, on grounds that reflect the definitions in use within some modern legal systems:

The law code of a land is first of all a complete collection of the laws and prescriptions that govern that land.

Clearly, Hammurabi and the earlier collections are not 'codes' within this definition; but Bottero detects the presence of a body of unwritten law:[7]

Unwritten does not mean non-existent or unknown, but potential: because it was constantly presented to the people in the form of positive or prohibitive customs, transmitted together with education, or even in the form of traditional solutions to particular problems.

And he concludes:[8]

The 'Code' of Hammurabi is essentially a self-glorification of the king. But at the same time it is a political charter that synthesizes an entire detailed and organised vision of the 'right' exercise of justice. And it is, in that way, a real treatise on jurisprudence.

The situation is, perhaps, best summarised in five individual sentences extracted from a passage by Driver and Miles.[9]

... First, the laws were not enforced by the Babylonian courts as if the collection was a statute of the realm; they were rather something like

English case-law, which lays down a rule or norm of which the principle is to be followed and regard is to be had to the spirit and not to the letter of the text.

... Grammatical and logical rules must, of course, be observed in order to discover the meaning intended by the lawgiver, but certainly nothing like the English verbal interpretation of Statute Law was practised by the Babylonian judges.

... As, too, the laws are not exhaustive in the manner of a European code of laws, so they are not imperative.

... the laws, because they are ancient, are not necessarily primitive.

... The law, however, gave them the type of justice that they demanded, and there is no record of a case in which a man was deprived of justice by a technicality or by an error made by him in procedure.

Let us look once again at what Hammurabi wrote in the epilogue to his laws:[10]

Let any oppressed man who has a cause
come into the presence of the statue of me, the king of justice,
and then read carefully my inscribed stela,
and give heed to my precious words,
and may my stela make the case clear to him;
may he understand his cause;
may he set his mind at ease!

This appears to offer the citizen of Babylon a legal coverage and a level of certainty in the interpretation of the law that would be the envy of modern legal systems, but it shows the direction in which Hammurabi's mind was tending: towards increasing standardisation and a more predictable legal process. It also raises the question of the status given to the law under the Hammurabi regime. Jean Bottero[11] has something to say about this from a very modern point of view:

... the word, 'law', does not exist in their language. And laws are not found in their writings, because we have to admit that their so-called 'codes' are not that, and that they record in fact not laws but decisions of justice ...

... Let us not lose sight of the 'Code' itself. If it collects in fact *verdicts of justice*, it establishes by that very fact the existence of a system of justice.

The legal structure conveyed by Hammurabi through his laws acknowledges that the powers of political and ethical decision rest with the sovereign, that what constitutes justice is defined in outline by specific examples of how laws should be applied in practice, and that the implementation of justice in the individual case is left to the discretion of the judges subject, of course, to any subsequent appeal to the king. So the definition of justice is reserved to the ancient equivalent of the legisature but the judges are free to use their discretion in the individual case. This distribution of powers is broadly what obtains in the western world today, but the political and social conflict inherent in that distribution did not surface in the most ancient laws and has never, in fact, been resolved. We will ourselves soon have to confront it. It may turn out, for instance, that the advisory character of law in ancient times could have been a source of strength rather than a weakness.

By defining Hammurabi's laws as a treatise in jurisprudence Jean Bottero may have pointed towards one aspect of his legal regime that could

That the day be overturned, that 'law and order' cease to exist —
The storm is all devouring like the Flood —
That the me of Sumer be overturned,
That a favourable reign be withheld. . .

. . .That the me of Sumer cease to exist, that its rules of
    conduct be changed,
That the me of kingship and reign or Ur be overwhelmed. . .

. . .The me of heaven, the rules that govern people — may An
    change them there.

These words from the 'Lamentation over the Destruction of Sumer and Ur' summarise the decision of the gods to destroy the whole life of Sumer and take kingship away from the city of Ur (which happened a few years before 2000BC). The *me*'s were over one hundred principles on which human life on earth was held to depend. They were not gods and were not worshipped, but they were sacred. They included godship, royal insignia, shepherdship, truth, falsehood, descent into and ascent out of the nether world, sexual intercourse, prostitution, probably law, art, several musical instruments, lamentation, rejoicing of the heart, wisdom, several crafts, attention, peace, weariness...

Here the suggestion seems to be that the *me*'s were the foundation of law and order and their destruction would break down the cohesion of Sumerian society. The bare list of names of *me*'s does not describe how they may have been understood. One possible application in the field of laws provokes thought. Individual judges enjoyed wide discretion, but that does not seem to have resulted in judgements based on conflicting principles. An understanding and acceptance of the meaning of the *me*'s might go some way to explaining judicial compliance over many centuries with a common social ethos.

still be of practical relevance. We have already observed (Chapter 2) that one purpose of law in the ancient world was the preservation of the traditional order of society. We can now see something of how that was done. The principle of individual justice restricted the judge to a consideration of individual circumstance in relation to the law as known to the court, while the absence of any reference to a rule of precedent seems to underline the probability that policy lay firmly outside the judicial purview and within the sole province of the sovereign.

Undoubtedly, an idea of uniformity of principle underlay the very existence of the ancient oral law long before writing appeared. And undoubtedly a notion of precedent underlay the decision to write laws and publish them, after writing had developed sufficiently for the purpose. But that measure of practical precedent is a far cry from the formal legislative power of precedent that has been acquired by senior courts in the modern world. Precedent comes with at least two faces: an acceptable face of uniformity of treatment where circumstances are the same, which leaves the judge free to decide whether they are the same or not and, therefore, keeps his discretion intact. The unacceptable face is the one by which precedent has become the legal instrument of a doctrine of equality so that identical treatment is imposed by force on cases in which some of the circumstances are the same but others are not.

Behind the unacceptable face of precedent lies a peculiarly modern distortion: that what happens to other people can be unjust to me. A discussion of what is involved in the modern process of which precedent is a part must await our arrival (in the next chapter) at modern times. But a hard look at the meaning of equality and at what we really mean by justice is going to be necessary.

Meanwhile, a brief word about legal systems and social change in the ancient world, on this occasion as they appear to us. The social problem that faced Hammurabi in Babylon has been addressed, and a possible explanation of the process that led to it has been put forward. What has not been addressed is Hammurabi's use of written law to underpin a social policy which involved change. Hammurabi's laws in their social aspect might be classified as the beginning of the modern world rather than as

SUMERIAN PROVERB

The fox has a stick with him: 'Whom shall I hit?'

He carried a legal document with him: 'What can I challenge?'

A proverb from the period c.2000–c.1600BC. (Edmund I. Gordon, *Sumerian Proverbs: Glimpses of Everyday Life in Ancient Mesopotamia.*

the culmination of the ancient world; or, perhaps cynically, they may be seen as marking the point after which written law as a conscious organ of policy gradually came to replace impartial justice; and they may even demonstrate that once a legal system is used as an instrument of policy, however benign, individual justice will, eventually, vanish.

To preserve the existing order of society is one thing; to change it is something different. Hammurabi's introduction, in some circumstances only, of the principles of talion and punishment by studied cruelty was probably designed, at least in part, to preserve the supremacy of his own Amorite aristocracy and to ensure that they continued to behave in a manner which would not undermine their (or his) authority. The price which Hammurabi had to pay for doing this, and which he did pay without hesitation, was what we would describe as the sacrifice of a measure of equality, which was of course no sacrifice for Hammurabi for whom equality was a desirable but secondary advantage. The precise measure of equality that Hammurabi sacrificed was equality of treatment. He preserved equality before the law so far as procedure and the determination of guilt were concerned. The fact that the inequalities of treatment which Hammurabi introduced were in the form of harsher treatment for the privileged and the powerful may well help to explain why, despite his cruelties, his laws gained and kept their reputation for a sense of justice.

The modern world recognises the advisory character of ancient laws, but sometimes uses it to deny them the status of 'law' altogether. By this means the modern world avoids having to discuss those principles behind ancient legal regimes that differ from our own. That could be a kind of defensive wisdom. An advisory jurisprudence that leaves the judges free is unacceptable to modern collectivist philosophy, but that does not mean that the ancient flexibility was never justice, or has nothing to offer the modern world. The conflict of principles that forces modern legal systems into periodical injustice is not necessarily preferable to the ancient process in all circumstances, especially when an educated public are increasingly blaming their lawyers for faults forced on the system by the societies they serve. In any discussion of that predicament all previous experience has its relevance. Modern disillusionment is real and potentially dangerous, but the fault lies not with lawyers but with the public; and the time has come when someone, however ill-equipped, must at least try to say what it is that has gone wrong and how it has happened.

Ancient legal systems confronted by social and economic change could still serve for thousands of years, but eventually some of the means they used to discover the truth and some of their traditional penalties became problems. The horror of their cruelties dominates the modern image of the ancient world and prevents rational assessment of their principles and ideals. In fact, the prescribed cruelties of the ancient world were as nothing compared with the calculated and wholesale cruelties of our own. Legalised cruelty is not a field in which modern progress can reasonably be measured.

The term 'the rule of law' means only that conflicts must be settled by a public rather than a private process; it says nothing about the character and little about the status of laws under particular legal regimes. The advisory character of ancient laws ensured discretion for their judges and flexibility for their systems. Lack of flexibility may well explain the modern impression that justice has not just died but been killed. The discretion of the judge was first threatened by the rise of cities with their huge populations and new circumstances; these produced new laws that were not generally known and so could not be remembered or taught, and their legal regimes tended to look defensively more towards civil order than individual circumstance. But the judge's discretion was killed in modern times by popular movements fired with two principles, both modern and each incompatible with the other: the freedom of the individual, and the doctrine of equality. Neither of these appears in the surviving pre-Hammurabi laws or in the laws of Hammurabi, except by inference and negatively as dangers to be avoided. But they are two of the bedrock principles of the modern concept of justice.

CHAPTER 13

ANCIENT LAWS AND MODERN PROBLEMS: THREE PROBLEM PRINCIPLES

ANSWERS TO QUESTIONS of principle are unlikely to be found in a relatively superficial discussion. But it may be helpful to see if the ancient world, that achieved stability over periods of time vastly longer than we can even imagine, may be able to throw a glimmer of light on conflicts for which we shed blood but which they survived apparently in peace.

Discussion of ancient laws too often reflects the opinions of modern lawyers looking backwards, who criticise ancient legal systems according to modern criteria which do not fit either the form of those systems or the needs of the societies that used them. If ancient laws are simply dismissed as not being laws at all, discussion of modern legal problems is deprived of an important historical dimension. Driver and Miles are an exception to this criticism, and Bottero comes close to joining them with his 'treatise on jurisprudence'; and there is at least one even more recent source that hits the nail squarely on the head. Lord Ackner, a former Lord Justice of Appeal, in a letter to *The Times* of 20 May 1996 reminds Government that a White Paper issued in 1990 entitled *Crime, Justice and Protecting the Public* had stated:

> It is not the Government's intention that Parliament should bind the courts with strict legislative guidelines ... The courts will properly continue to have the wide discretion they need if they are to deal justly with the great variety of crimes which come before them.

Lord Ackner forebore to remind Government that their proposed policy for the criminal law was a return to the pre-Hammurabi legal regime of the third millennium BC. Even, as we saw in Chapter 1, right back to the old stone age which nurtured the most stable if not the most comfortable culture in human history. Lord Ackner's letter also lends weight to the contention that a study of ancient law may reveal not just coincidences between ancient and modern legal problems but patterns of fundamental principle that the modern world has abandoned and now misses. A brief search for the principles behind the laws we have reviewed may, therefore, be productive; though to confront some of the ancient principles, and the status of the individual is one, will require a measure of detachment.

Three fundamental concepts demand special attention immediately: the concept of the individual, the rule of law, and the principle of equality. A number of other important principles, including the composition of justice, will be considered in the next chapter.

THE INDIVIDUAL AS AN INCONVENIENCE

Even when the problems our ancestors faced were similar to those we face today, their circumstances and the means available for dealing with them were very different; so we must be careful about interpreting the ancient world in the light of modern practice. And we must be equally careful about the reverse: judging the modern world by reference to ancient practice. But comparison is permitted, and there need be no dismay if it exposes contrasting principles that provoke thought.

In the ancient world crisis was never far away so public safety had to take priority over the individual rather more often than it does today. Public safety was held to depend upon all those institutions through which social order was enforced: the family, the occupational and class hierarchy, the temple, the palace, the bureaucracy. Individual freedom fosters personal and public growth so long as society is stable enough to survive the shocks that freedom administers; but if society is fragile, unlimited freedom can destroy the social structure together with the lives of those within it. For this reason, the person visualised in the ancient laws and in the societies they reflected was very different from the individual he was later to become. Survival of the city was the governing principle. Supremacy of the individual and unfettered personal freedom were unknown; and if they had been known they would have been dismissed not just as socially dangerous but as irrational and unnatural. Freedom of the individual does not appear in the surviving tablets ... and yet, there is a seeming paradox: the ancient world which did not recognise the individual as an independent entity in any modern sense has left us laws based largely on the concept of individual justice. By contrast, the modern world in which individual freedom is held to be axiomatic and sacrosanct has evolved legal systems in which justice is another name for equality, a principle by which the individual and his circumstances can be suppressed.

In evolutionary terms the family or clan, which were essential for physical survival, may have been the primary unit by which early man identified himself; and it is still the family, the firm and the club that we principally identify with and by which we are identified. Man's image of himself as an independent individual came late, and then only in part; but it still came well before human society was ready for it. So the birth of the individual was indicated by a marked increase in the severity of the laws. In the oldest societies only very little coercion must have been needed and this is reflected in the surprising mildness of their penalties.

The last five thousand years have seen the emergence of the concept of the individual as an independent entity, but also dramatic increases in the variety and power of groups. Four thousand years ago prologues and epilogues to the earliest sets of laws tell us that conflict between the power of the group and the rights of the individual already underlay the search for justice. So, what we often consider to be a modern conflict must already have existed in prehistory: '... the man of one shekel was not delivered up to the man of one mina ...' writes Ur-Nammu in his prologue to the earliest laws to survive. Ur-Nammu recognised that wealth was power, but insisted that the principle behind his laws should be protection for the individual and for the weak. He could hardly have avoided also recognising that the power which wealth made possible consisted of the ability to command the services of others, in other words leadership of a group. In the four millennia since Ur-Nammu conflict between the group and the individual has continued, with the balance shifting as the one is temporarily promoted to compensate for perceived excesses in the power of the other.

As the individual cannot be dealt with in the mass it is the needs of representative groups that carry weight today. The doctrine of the supremacy of the individual has led to a weakening of the individual and an increasing dominance by groups, because representation promotes the power of the group and subordinates the individual and his particular circumstances to a common policy. The political and social machinery of the modern world differs from that of the ancient world; but the realities behind the machinery are sometimes curiously similar. The seeds of many a modern dilemma can be seen germinating in the ancient world, and the problem of individual freedom is one of them. That is another reason why ancient solutions may well contain a germ of contemporary relevance after all.

In the ancient world, including that of Hammurabi (in spite of his epilogue, see Chapter 10), the citizen in search of certainty must consult his conscience and the traditional oral law rather than a document. The published laws indicated an idea, but they did not offer certainty; and the judge retained his discretion over the individual case. In our world, the citizen discovers from statute and precedent what the law has hitherto been held to mean and, if the facts fall within the written law, he knows what the judge must do. In our eyes, the principal function of the courts is to interpret and apply the written law, and the courts' discretion is restricted to what the written law omits, or specifically allows. Though recognisable justice is often the outcome it is not necessarily the intention: a predetermined political philosophy may decide the nature of legislation while the machinery of the law is artificially restricted to its enforcement.

The ancient codes were addressed to the individual and led from the particular to the general: 'If a man ... ' they begin, and choose a case whose facts illustrate a principle. Modern law does the reverse: the principle is defined in advance, and as many applications of it as can be foreseen are described so that the individual may have the certainty he craves. In the ancient world the deciding factor was individual justice, with the written law as guide to what justice ought to mean in representative circumstances. In the modern world the deciding factors are the written law, the political or social principles it is intended to promote and what its wording has hitherto been interpreted to mean, leaving little room for the individual or for the justice of particular circumstances. The individual is sacred in modern political theology, but an impossible inconvenience in court.

Modern scholarship often presents ancient law as uncertain and arbitrary. The ancient judges would accept the charge of uncertainty, replying that certainty is just what the lawbreaker needs. The importance of being able to rely on what the wording of a law must be held to mean excludes any consideration of right and wrong in the particular case, and thus takes ethics out of the legal process. The consequent transfer of the ethical dimension from the court to the legislature ensures a measure of uniformity and makes life easy for the judge, but it is food and drink to the criminal. By contrast, a background of ethical principle that leaves room for the court to use its discretion will make the legal process unpredictable and equality of treatment impossible, but it focuses judgement on the individual and his case and prevents the edifice of justice from being destroyed by a quibble. The law which is supposed to protect the innocent and the weak can be annihilated not so much by a public parliament or by supposedly wicked and devious lawyers, but by the sincere and conscientious working of the modern legal system. Impartial justice within a regime determined by the legislature is the public aim of the legal process but the frustration of justice is too often the result.

While the ancient world would accept, even welcome, the charge of uncertainty they would deny that they were arbitrary, unless judging each case separately on its merits is to be so described. But at once there is an ambiguity: the word 'arbitrary' can mean either that a particular judicial process is merely accidental and random, or that it may be logical and orderly but that its outcome cannot be predicted in advance. Of course, judging each case on its merits is not a random process, but it is so described by many modern lawyers because it means that individuals would be treated differently instead of equally, and that the result would be uncertain instead of predictable. In an article in *The Times* of 23 May 1996, Lord Chief Justice Taylor wrote: 'Certainty in sentencing can be achieved only by sacrificing justice'.[1]

Everyone has a right to know where they stand under the law, says the politician. But the ancient world did not agree, if that meant that the evil-minded must be provided in advance with a map of ways round the intention of the law. Here also, embedded in the debate about the individual and his freedom, is the doctrine of equality, the third of our three basic principles. It raises its controversial head and threatens a devastating possibility: in modern philosophy, equality and individual justice are so closely associated with each other that they are often held to be obverse and reverse of the same coin; whereas a moment's thought suggests that they may be not only different coins but incompatible with each other.

Ancient societies were smaller than ours. Small size undoubtedly made it easier to find acceptable procedures, because individuals were known and their circumstances could be allowed to matter. Thus our ancestors could accommodate many of their problems without actually solving them. For instance they did not have our range of punishments: people could be held pending trial, but imprisonment was not available as a punishment because the administration needed to operate it punitively was not there. Corporal punishment and mutilation seem to have been rare in earlier times, and even in Hammurabi the number of crimes for which they were the prescribed punishment may overstate the frequency with which they were actually used. Small size where people were known may well have fostered a climate of accommodation, whereas large size, anonymity and minutely defined issues of principle may produce mass reactions that are less tractable.

It was accepted as a fact of life that the individual owed an over-riding duty to his clan and his city; they were his relatives and his life-support. It was the ancient cities that created civilisation, though the forced labour by which they did so was an odd preparation for the liberties to which they were later to give birth. In the modern world when the physical, as opposed to the financial, demands of the state began to bear less heavily on the individual, the cry of freedom began to be heard. But that cry was deceptive: the vast populations and the services that had been created for them which made freedom possible, ensured that instead of strengthening the individual, freedom ended by weakening him.

The individual's ancient duty to the state or society has been so diminished that it is often denied entirely. On occasion the doctrine of freedom for the individual conscience is held to justify not only exemption from public service, but violent opposition and active betrayal; and the possibility of betrayal has been defended as a necessary safeguard against bureaucratic abuse. The ancient world could not have coped with the consequences of individual conscience and personal freedom on this scale, so the ancient and the modern situations differ. Our solutions and the social turmoil they foster would not have been practicable in the ancient world any more than the ancient solutions with their social rigidity would be acceptable in ours, so it would be wrong to think in absolute terms. And there is a necessary aside: if small size was a factor in the stability of the ancient world and large size is a factor in the instability of the modern world, the policy of continuing to construct ever more gigantic institutions needs to be challenged more and more loudly.

The question whether the individual or society should have priority under the law has been debated probably since mankind acquired speech. It has not been solved. If society is placed first the individual is considered only in so far as he is useful: that society is efficient, and personal growth is encouraged because it contributes to the prosperity of the whole; but there is little personal freedom. So a disciplined society arises in which lack of freedom is the price paid for prosperity, security and, within limits, personal growth. The adjective that best describes such a society is 'totalitarian'. On the other hand if the individual is placed first, cohesion is lost and society is permanently in danger of collapse. That is known as 'anarchy'.

The freedom and personal growth of the individual have always had to be weighed against the security necessary for his survival. It may be that the way in which most of the modern world defines the individual and his place in the scheme of things could profit from a cold gaze at the way our ancestors defined him (and her); and the modern world might also profit from a glance at the obligations which ordinary people acknowledged and undertook in the age when the modern world was being founded.

Today the individual is widely held to be the purpose for which society exists. That makes him a nuisance to those with visionary or collective ambitions; but it also means that his demands for self-destructive liberties may, in his own interests, need to be trimmed.

In much of the modern world, the pendulum has swung so far towards the individual that prosperity seems threatened and anarchy looms. Of course prosperity will survive and anarchy will not prevail; but the problem of the individual cannot be avoided for ever, and his place in society will one day have to be redefined. Indeed, the continuous advance both of scientific knowledge and of the techniques of management may dictate a reassessment of the status of the individual at fairly frequent intervals.

There is a considerable gap between the expensive near anarchy in which privileged societies at present choose to live and the 'totalitarianism' that characterised the ancient world, which some modern states have recently experienced and all rightly fear. The condition of near anarchy, which is fashionably described as 'market forces', has proved invaluable as an instrument for taking impossible decisions. Nevertheless, between anarchy and totalitarianism there is room for a shift of balance away from the headlong pursuit of personal self-interest and towards the individual identifying himself as an essential, integral component of society as a whole. That does not necessarily mean narrowing the differences in financial and social rewards available to success or failure, still less is it a comment on whether such narrowing may be desirable: but it is suggesting an adjustment of personal outlook irrespective of where an individual may stand on society's ladder. Even a cursory glance at our ancestral world of four or five thousand years ago suggests that a corrective movement of our personal identity away from the private and towards the public would help to remedy the lack of public cohesion in today's societies, and that a more vivid awareness of the public interest would surely be aided by a wider acceptance of one uncomfortable fact: that whether the individual likes it or not he is organically locked into the society of the whole range his fellows by laws of nature whose immensely varied characteristics appear to include a sense of humour.

THE RULE OF LAW

It is clear that the ancient world knew the rule of law because laws existed and were published; and we know something of how they defined it, partly from the form of the surviving collections of laws and partly because not one of the many hundreds of court records that have survived refers to any specific written law. At the same time these records show that courts generally, though not always, reached decisions and imposed penalties that were consistent with the surviving written laws. Whether that reflects the authority of the written laws or the continued presence of an underlying oral tradition that acted directly both on the written laws and on the courts is uncertain; but whatever the origins of their legal tradition may have been, the collections of written laws that have survived carry some important messages: they tell us that law was guide and servant to the court, but not its master; that the rule of law was seen as obedience to a public legal process as opposed to private action and that the legal process judged individual circumstance in relation to principle rather than imposing on the individual case the meaning attached to a particular set of words.

From the earliest accounting records of the late fourth millennium BC to the beginning of the Christian era, a period of over three thousand years, the building blocks of future change were being evolved but the actual structures of daily life in city, town or country hardly altered at all.

That was an immense period of incubation which saw the birth of writing and, much later, the invention of the alphabet; the improvement of technology in bronze, then iron, the emergence of mathematics out of engineering; the birth of democracy as a constraint against tyranny. But it also saw the promotion of law from flexible guide to guardian deity of society. It

SUMERIAN PROVERB
An unfavourable legal verdict is acceptable, but a curse is not acceptable.

A proverb from the period *c*.2000–*c*.1600BC. (Edmund I. Gordon, *Sumerian Proverbs: Glimpses of Everyday Life in Ancient Mesopotamia*)

was a period in which the search of wealth and peace took the form of conquests and empires while the real threat to the fabric of daily life was already stirring in the associations and minor power centres within the cities, but it would be another millennium and a half before that particular threat would burst out.

Throughout this whole period, society was hesitantly evolving in a way which would permit the individual to emerge as an independent entity. The old, strict patterns of family sustenance and support co-existed with the beginnings of mass production, and the latter gradually spread while the former reluctantly contracted. The tensions which forced efficient administration upon late fourth millennium BC Uruk went on to replace the medieval village by the manufacturing town as the social and economic centre. The stability of a community in which the individual was known could not compete in opportunity or adventure against personal mobility, which provided industry with its workforce and offered the twin advantages of wealth and anonymity. So a new economic and social climate allowed the free independent individual to emerge.

Freedom enlarged the horizons of life. The worlds of science and culture opened their doors, after some persuasion, to all who wished and had the ability to enter. A huge expansion of knowledge and technology resulted, but the legal framework continued to reflect the human relationships of an earlier age. So there were, and still are, two incompatible worlds governed by two interlocking but incompatible regimes of law. In the social world of daily living, of property, of free leisure, of family, of children, the ancient bases for human relationships are valid still and the basic age-old laws continue to rule. But let those people enter the world of work and power, and the individual and his personal responsibility is replaced by the employing institution or the representative group; and the institution and the group are treated by the laws as though they were persons when they are nothing of the kind. Relationships between individuals are small, personal, detailed and specific with all the ambiguities and accommodations which these imply. Relationships between institutions and groups are formal, economic, massive, logical, general, therefore defined, precise, inflexible, clear, and hard as ice. An orderly production process requires laws that reflect the needs of institutions and groups and it is the laws of that character whose principles increasingly apply to all. Wherever the law intrudes, the human relationship is steadily reduced to the mechanical so that a steel thread of logic is felt, and genuinely felt, as the preferred content of justice. Except that ordinary people are increasingly condemning their legal systems as inhuman and unjust, and rebelling against them; and they are condemning the judges for faults which originate in society as a whole and which the judges, at a loss, have no choice but to reflect.

The written words in which an ancient law happened to be framed were carefully, sometimes expertly, chosen but they were still essentially accidental, merely one of many possible ways in which the substance and intention of a law might have been expressed. It was the substance and intention of the law that mattered not its accidental wording. In the modern world the wording of a law is just as accidental as it was in the ancient world, but it is open to different interpretations in a way that the ancient law was not. The wording of a law has become identified with the law itself, and that has led, in many cases, to the law being interpreted by the judges to mean something that the legislators had not intended. The power by which modern judges make law by attaching their own meaning to its accidental wording is an interpretation of the rule of law that does not appear in the ancient tablets. The ancient rule of law left judges free to use their discretion within the principles which the carefully chosen written cases illustrated; so the individual case was what they judged and individual justice was what they tried to do.

One problem of principle with the rule of law is how to define the limit of dissent. In fragile societies very little dissent can be permitted, and fragile societies include those that are poor, stressed or threatened. Modern advanced societies when going to war contract the area of permitted dissent as one of their first acts; but in time of peace, dissent has become a constitutional posture whose limits are open and undefined. That does not mean that the boundary of the acceptable is never crossed. For instance, the terrorist bomb is real even though everyone, and especially the terrorist, knows that it is not acceptable: the terrorist is bombing public opinion in the hope that it will weaken and draw policy with it. Protesters can destroy military weapons of whose probable use they disapprove, and the court is powerless to intervene if the jury representing public opinion will not convict. The disruptive strike becomes legally acceptable provided certain procedures have been followed, but the disruption of essential services damages the public whose fury may turn against the groups sufficiently to support a new government that will strike back. In the ancient world, informed public opinion was present in court in the persons of part-time judges who had normal occupations; so that judges drew strength not only from the law but from the same public sources as those from which the law itself drew strength. The jury system brings public opinion into the courtroom, originally in the form of local people who knew the participants and probably most of the circumstances; and they were free to judge according to their sense in ways in which the judges no longer could. Today, local knowledge has been replaced by impartial outsiders using their sense, and occasionally their instinct. But in the modern world of an educated and informed public, the jury system brings to the court, in the shape of both

sweeper and captain of industry, a strong mix of social and political attitudes, so that in jury cases the power balance inside the court reflects, and
is meant to reflect, something of the range of social background in the real
world outside. At the point of decision, the pure logic law can, occasionally
and unpredictably, be diluted by a popular social attitude which rounds in
anger on the whole legal process and judges a single issue in isolation and
according to popular sentiment. The fact that, like any judge, the jury is
occasionally wrong does not annihilate its importance. But public opinion
is still felt by some lawyers as a problem in court, an intrusion into the
legal process, a sniff of the mob, a threat to the rule of law rather than
what the rule of law ought really to be about. How abstract and impartial
can justice be and still be justice? That, of course, is a political question;
but political attitude is not a new problem in the court of law and it does
not only affect the jury.

Active opposition is expected to cease, and indeed generally does cease,
at the point when a measure becomes law. After that, discontent and political action may continue but generally disruption does not. Sometimes the
possibility of dissent is prescribed by law: the modern citizen may often
legally refuse military service if he can show that war is against his conscience, though less often if he merely considers that his national state is
in the wrong. But conscience is never a ground for refusing to pay taxes,
even though the taxes concerned be used to finance a war from which the
citizen could claim, and may indeed have been granted, exemption on conscientious grounds.

During the nearly four thousand years since Hammurabi, a fresh source
of complexity has gradually been emerging with the growth of private corporate entities which are recognised by, but are not part of, the state.
Today the citizen can sometimes be excused from committing a crime if he
did so as agent of a corporation, when he would not be excused if he had
acted as a private citizen; in our world, corporate behaviour is not always
subject to the moral or legal constraints considered necessary for individuals. Our trade unions, our press, our business enterprises, our self-govern-
ing professions are corporate entities that are treated as individuals; as a
result, the individuals they employ become mere agents who are not
wholly responsible for what they do. Huge areas of our public and private
lives are affected by individuals whose personal conduct is absorbed into
that of the institution, and escapes the personal responsibility by which
alone it can be constrained. The rule of law binds equally on all individuals
but it does not bind equally as between individuals and groups.

In the modern world the rule of law on the one hand, and individual
freedom on the other, balance each other in practice most of the time. But
that balance is not easy to maintain. For instance, the modern citizen

may commit a crime if he uses force to stop a thief; the thief may then assume the role of innocent victim of assault, and the courts may convict and penalise the aggrieved citizen while letting the thief go free. Sometimes the injured citizen is even forced to apologise to the thief and pay him compensation for the humiliation he, a criminal, has suffered at the hands of an honest man. In the early years of the modern world, only those with clean hands could expect the full protection of the law, and judges used to say with public approval 'the dirty dog shall have no dinner here'. In those days the law breaker could enjoy some, but only some, of the law's protection. The rule of law, deified as a sovereign principle to whose interpretation only the judges as a trained and exclusive priesthood have access, has, like other exclusive cults, not always led to either truth or justice. The fault does not lie with the rule of law as a principle; nor does it lie with a particular legal procedure, for instance the adversarial procedure. The fault lies at the very core of our whole legal system, with the way in which the modern world defines the rule of law. By itself the rule of law says that conflict must be decided by a defined public process. It says that the private citizen must submit his own important conflicts to decision by the legal process within whose jurisdiction he lives. He must not take his own private action to settle a conflict outside of the legal process; but it does not say that only one kind of legal process can be accepted as embodying the rule of law. The particular interpretation that the modern world has given to the rule of law is related to the written nature of the law and is often self-defeating. Blind adherence to previous definition of particular forms of words makes it impossible for the judge to decide the individual case and forces the court into decisions whose effect in practice is to deny justice to the individual. This is not the fault of the judges; it is forced upon the judges by the expectations of society, and specifically by the expectation of equal treatment to which we shall shortly be turning. But it does mean that the written law so binds the judges that justice cannot breathe, and wronged individuals find, to their dismay, that their only hope of practical redress lies in their taking the law into their own hands. It is one of the miracles of the modern world that wronged individuals denied access to justice will still abide by the rule of law, and prefer the public interest and the orderly society to direct personal action – and long may that be so.

In principle as well as in practice the emergence of the individual as the fulcrum of society altered the balance of justice. In the most ancient world, the property principle safeguarded lives at the expense of personal freedom. In return for safety and an ordered life, the individual sacrificed the possibility of action which might lead to his independence. The web of reciprocal and enforced obligations permitted individual development, but inhibited the growth of subsidiary power centres such as corporations and unions in which demands for change tend to germinate.

The free individual is, in principle, the crowning achievement of five thousand years of city-based civilization and he is the entity whose activities threaten the continuance of the human species, if not of the planet. The threat does not come from the concept of the individual as such; but a glance at the ancient world where modern problems originated can tell us that today's problem is one of principles that contradict each other: the interests of society, that is the survival of mankind, and the freedom of the individual can become incompatible. They are not, of course, incompatible for most of the time or in most circumstances; both are precious, and neither must be destroyed: but they are not infinitely compatible with each other. The concept of the free individual does not need to be challenged, but the sacred and absolute status which the modern world has given to freedom in all circumstances, allowing it to be carried to the last extremity, and adopting the principle of unfettered freedom as the one and only moral basis for an acceptable state, does need to be challenged. It needs to be challenged because it is an inflexible element in a changing world within which human society is constantly required to adapt or die. It needs to be challenged as a principle which, if taken to its logical extremity, becomes self-contradictory and threatens the continued existence of humanity; it needs to be challenged as a principle which no state does or ever could apply as it stands.

The free individual demands adaptability from others but resists it for himself. The status of the free individual does need to be reviewed from time to time in relation to changes in the patterns of consumption and their impact on the various capacities of the planet. One starting point for any review might be to look closely at what are frequently claimed as human rights to see how many of these individually desirable principles become, if universally applied without any constraint, in practice incompatible with each other. Freedom and the rule of law are two principles that if carried to extremes are incompatible with each other. That does not mean that either must be denied the status of a principle; but it does mean that no principle can be taken as absolute in all circumstances.

THE PROBLEM OF EQUALITY

The emergence of the individual as the fundamental social and political concept has produced, in the democratic election, a reservoir of support for political leadership and an alternative to civil war as a means of changing it; and the referendum has become an occasional escape route for governments with a problem. The transfer of decision making from leadership to citizen has led to massive manipulation of public opinion, but that is accepted as preferable to ignoring it; at least it permits government by a measure of consent and ensures civil peace for most of the time. But the birth of the individual has raised a fundamental issue of justice which is so sensitive that most people refuse even to discuss it; and it is a problem which is still unresolved: that problem was, and is, equality.

Equality means equal status, which sounds simple enough; but it can also mean equal treatment, which is not simple at all. The ideal of equality, which popularly includes both status and treatment, has a long history. It lies behind the concept of balance apparent in the precise compensation of the earliest laws as well as in the 'eye for an eye' of the laws of Hammurabi and the Bible: it was the law of the cities as well as of the desert, and it was probably also the law of prehistory.

But in crowded city societies precise compensation was not always possible. There were two sources of difficulty. One lay in the dual nature of the term equality: all came equally before the law and in that sense were of equal status in the eyes of the law; but all people were not the same, so when equality of status was extended to include equality of treatment, an element of falsehood was introduced which led to injustice. A second source of difficulty was the inflexibility with which the principle of equal treatment had to be applied in those cases where people were not the same but were expected to be treated as though they were. At that point an element of envy crept into the doctrine of equal treatment. To the question 'can what happens to other people be unjust to me?' the answer became, and still is, 'yes'. So the unspoken bitterness of envy began to colour people's assessment of each other, not because of anything they had done but because of some involuntary circumstances of their lives. And so the acceptable sounding doctrine of equality became both pretext and slogan for tyranny.

In the world of the earliest surviving laws, women were treated differently from men, the child differently from the adult, the master (or mistress) differently from the slave; but the principle of equality before the law survived. It survived too, just, in the laws of Hammurabi even though the powerful and privileged were sometimes treated more harshly than the weak and the poor. All – including slaves – came equally before the court so far as guilt or innocence, or winning or losing their case, were concerned; but they were treated differently when it came to punishment or disposal of property. That the ancient world considered many kinds of discrimination to be justice which the modern world calls, or tries to call, injustice is half the story: the profounder half is whether judgement is based on truth or on falsehood, because when a judgement is based on truth justice is possible but when it is based on falsehood injustice is inevitable. That women should be treated as though they were in all respects the same as men is a policy based on falsehood. That women should have special privileges so that they can be equated with men in particular circumstances is often justice but it is not equality. The modern world is reluctantly being forced to recognise what the ancient world always knew, that equality and justice are not invariably compatible with each other; and that where they conflict a choice has to be made between them. So, in significant areas we treat women differently from men because truth and justice, but not equality, require it; and therein we discover an example of at least a limited return to ancient values by which truth, not equality, was recognised as being the one fundamental component of justice.

The ideal of equality has always roused public emotion whether in appeal (sincerely) to the unity and brotherhood of Man or (cynically) as a chance for the less able to be accepted at a higher level than their abilities would otherwise enable them to reach. The ideal of equality overlooks the fact that though it may be argued that men are born free (and argued it must be) they are manifestly not born with equal talent; so to achieve equality, the more able must be constrained. But the constraints that shackle the advancement of the more able do not equip the less able to achieve beyond what their abilities make possible; so society degenerates into tyranny on the one hand and incompetence on the other. Great empires have collapsed from this cause.

By contrast, the more restricted (and modern) ideal of equality of opportunity is widely welcomed because it does not involve artificial constraint or inappropriate advancement. But equality of opportunity does not lead to equality: on the contrary, it reinforces inequality by liberating talent, and by doing that it incidentally disarms the most able of its probable opponents. Thanks to what we see as the perversity of nature, the pursuit of equality is incompatible with personal freedom, and equality of opportunity is incompatible with equality of result. These incompatibilities did not trouble the ancient world because they did not see that people were in fact equal to each other in the first place, while their power structures – like their human power source – depended upon inequalities being accepted as part of the natural order. They had no basis on which to evolve an aspiration for equality, and they did not do so.

In the ancient world the individual was important as a member of a group, whether city, clan, family, social class, occupation, or nation. These groups were not mutually exclusive: the individual was required to defer to the interests of the particular group within whose context he was currently acting. That was the foundation for order within the city and the framework for public safety. Individual freedom operated within defined and accepted constraints which preserved for centuries, indeed for millennia, the institution of the city as the principal life-support and the centre for, in the modern sense, civilised living. The opportunity for individual prosperity and creativity within a safe society generated city loyalty, while fear of disorder and its inevitable consequences made a high level of constraint acceptable.

Constraints against freedom were always open to abuse of which slavery was one, and forced labour stopping short of slavery was another; but the principle that there must be some constraints on individual freedom was accepted as the preferable alternative to violence and civil war ...

'... You are in fine voice this evening, my friend ... '

'Atu! I thought you had deserted us ...'

'... I very nearly had ... but if you are going to talk about freedom, equality and the individual in my world it is only fair that you should get the facts right ... and that you have not so far done ... My friend, it is far more simple than you seem to have understood ... The reason why we placed the individual and his freedom low down in our priorities was not that we did not recognise the ideal but that we could not afford it. The history of our world has surely made clear how fragile our areas and periods of prosperity were, and how even a small disturbance could wreck a city. The fact that we would fight to the death against the slightest defiance of our order or our hierarchy, and against principles such as freedom or equality whose acceptance might lead to such defiance, is a measure of the wafer thin cushion of wealth upon which our cities rested. In your world that cushion is thick and can absorb the damage wrought by defiance, and even by rebellion and sabotage. You can afford to indulge, almost worship, the idea of the individual and pay for the consequences; but we could not. The difference between us lay not in our theoretical ideals but in our wealth. To create wealth we needed to control the people and direct their labour; but once the wealth has been created and the means to go on creating it have been established then you, who seldom acknowledge your good fortune in being our heirs, can indulge the individual with his freedom and his defiance and all his other luxuries as well. Indeed, you no longer even recognise them as luxuries ...

... Your concept of the individual has caused you to manufacture a whole new set of indirect controls operated from a distance which you call government by consent, or sometimes economic management, or social engineering ... you have many techniques and you have to thank us for some of them, and many names; but within the constraints of your unobtrusive procedures, your enormous numbers enable you to deal only with the mass and leave the individual free to go his own way, and free to go as far as his energy or his ability will carry him; you can afford tolerance and the pleasant life, and for that I do not criticise but envy you. Had we done that we would have starved. It is your wealth and the science that wealth has given you, public and private, that enables you to indulge each other and still prosper ...'

189

'Thank you, Atu. Perhaps we deserve that. Yes, there are many countries today less wealthy than you were, who we blame for not providing the same freedoms as we enjoy. We attribute their failure to adopt 'civilised principles' to lack of those personal and public qualities that are basic to civilisation, such as integrity, co-operation, public generosity, acceptance of the rule of law, qualities which they have in fact in abundance, but we do not recognise them because they use them differently from the way we do. We no longer know what the cost of freedom can be when the difference between a full stomach and starvation is as little as a day's rain. Nor do we always appreciate that the opportunity to get your foot on the ladder can come as a gift from your brothers and sisters, who may be less able than you are but they pay your fees; and that this gift which you receive when you are young and struggling involves duties when you are adult and employed. They are the duties created by scarcity, duties that are not understood in societies that have forgotten what scarcity is, societies that describe as corruption the repayment of obligations by those who will not (or are not allowed to) forget their debts. Among the more subtle differences between poor and rich societies, modern as well as ancient, is a difference in the kind of ethics they can afford. And this is the difference, Atu, which I fear that we do not allow for ... We are so used to thinking of ethics as absolute that we have forgotten that different levels of wealth need, perhaps not so much different kinds of ethics, as the universal principles of ethics applied in ways that are going to help rather than destroy them; we have to accept that, for instance, individual freedom can be a right in one setting but disaster in another.'

'... *A right in one setting but disaster in another ... my friend, you destroy the very nature of rights and principles ... but I suppose you might not be so very far wrong at that ... In my world individual freedom was never a right ... It is your world not ours that has made it so and that, really, is what has happened during the four thousand years that separate us ... Your great men and women have created such wealth, and such sustainable methods of making wealth, that you can afford to make freedom into a right and survive, and if there are times or places where that does not work, and a military setting is one of them ... you simply recognise them as either temporary or exceptional ... No, I am not criticising you ... your personal freedom is something my world, and particularly our young, would have envied ... for heavens' sake, do not give in to the temptation to destroy freedom merely because it sometimes threatens to destroy you ... But you must find some way of directing freedom away from destructive ends, and of enabling the young to use their natural energy, a wonderful but temporary gift for which, curiously, you seem to have no real use at all ... you must find some way of curbing freedom without destroying it ...*'

'Atu, this may be a good moment for us to go back to the rule of law because that too bears upon the status of the individual in different societies and ages. We have already observed that in your world law was guide rather than master of the court. Of course your laws had to be obeyed; that is not in question. But when our experts search your records for evidence of your laws in action, they find that in all the court cases that have come down to us there is not one that refers to any particular law that appears in a published 'code'. So what sort of laws were they if they were never even referred to in the courts? Clearly, they were very different from anything that we would recognise as law. We have provisionally thought that what mattered in your courts was the facts of the particular case, and your laws were there to guide the judges not to dictate to them. In your world, the laws that were written seem to have emerged from judgements in real cases and they could not have been known for certain in advance; but the fact that some judgements were recorded and then published in a code suggests an attempt to introduce what we know only too well as precedent; so the law codes look like an attempt to introduce a greater measure of certainty into the legal process, and perhaps also a measure of uniformity which is another way of saying the same thing. Your laws may have been written as a guide to the part-time judges about the sort of principles they were expected to apply, and as a guide to the people about the sorts of decision they might expect to receive in certain kinds of circumstance; but they suggest that no one expected the published laws to bind a court in advance of the facts.'

'... Yes, my friend, that is about right ... of course we could not foresee where writing laws might lead us, but in the cities the laws were multiplying and writing them became unavoidable ... but I think we would have wanted to write our laws in any case ... When thinking about the meaning of justice we generally felt the same as most of you about equality, that people should so far as possible be treated alike; not just come equally before the court but receive equal treatment when they got there, and that writing laws down was one step towards that; but we did not consider that equal treatment was always justice or press equality to the point where justice was annihilated. The difference between your world and ours over equality was large in the result but not so very great in its cause ... and it may be that our world could tolerate a measure of inconsistency which your world because of its enormous size has to reject ...'

'No sooner had you written your laws down, Atu, than, unknown to you, the process which we have identified as deification of the law began. Of course law had always been revered; it had to be or it would not have been law; but the written body of the laws was a physical reality which easily assumed the mystical presence and then the inflexible power of deity; and like deity the law came, over many years, to be served by its own exclusive priesthood. They alone could interpret the hidden meaning of the laws, not just because they had the power to enforce their interpretations, but because their exclusive community generated a special use of language whose interpretation became the expertise of a professionally qualified elite. What other meaning can we attach to the presence in your schools of tablets listing technical legal terms? Of course, this process was not confined to law; medicine, surveying, every one of your professions had its own language as part of its freemasonry as did, and do, our professions today. It is necessary to professional communication and there is nothing so very wrong about it. But it had its effect on the nature of justice.'

'... *Indeed* ...'

The hope that writing laws would produce uniformity and therefore certainty was to be disappointed. The uncertainties of judicial discretion were replaced by those of interpretation which a hierarchy of courts would eventually do something, but not enough, to stabilise.

The demand for equality came later, but when it did come it overrode the fragmented, individual justice of the ancient world. The simplistic wish for equality was a reaction against centuries of social abuse by powerful minorities, and it was adopted as it stood as the only acceptable principle for a moral society. The demand for equal treatment that was forced upon the courts stifled their discretion so that as equality prevailed individual justice died. A lingering regret for what was lost still surfaces from time to time as in this report in *The Times* of 8 June 1994, when the Justices Clerks' Society in a paper to the Law Commission, said:

> There is still room in our over-complex legal system for discretion, common sense and flexibility. These qualities are becoming increasingly difficult to exercise as laws become more prescriptive.

Laws were probably first written simply to let people know what they were. To provide the public with certainty and the law with uniformity were probably only secondary advantages. Individuals, indeed developing enterprises, needed to know in advance what they could do and what they must avoid so that they could plan and invest in safety; and they wanted to be reasonably sure that the same laws would govern them whichever city they were in. But the written word conveyed only an imprecise message; it lacked both intonation and those subsidiary explanations and repetitions which are characteristic of an oral tradition and form so large and vital a part of clarity. So long as the law could be transmitted by word of mouth it was relatively simple and everyone knew what it was; as soon as it was written it became ambiguous and no one could be sure. Writing originally increased the number of laws recorded and fixed their form, and by doing so seemed to offer a new opportunity for certainty; and the scribes predictably responded by writing laws that tried to cover all eventualities. The result was not more certainty but less, and individual justice was the casualty. The age-old discretion of the judge was destroyed at last by the written word.

The intention was not unreasonable. In crowded cities, written laws were inevitable and they had to be given an accepted meaning; and that could only emerge gradually from successive judgements in particular cases. The law as defined in one set of circumstances must be binding in all cases where key circumstances were similar. Thus precedent was born. Soon, the court would no longer be guided by natural justice and the facts of the case, because more powerful entities would be breathing down its neck in the shape of the written word, precedent and official policy. And before those powers, the court itself would be forced to bend.

But at the period of the early laws the court had not bent yet. It was still free to reach its own conclusions and, if necessary, to make its own enquiries. The court's duty was still to seek the truth and do justice: social policy was not yet in sight. The written laws were a public guide, but no court was yet shackled by someone else's interpretation of a word. So when the modern world looks back at its roots, as in this case by chance it can, it may observe the death process of individual justice, and begin to understand that the cause of that death lay not in any particular legal process or its practitioners but in the extension of a few individually admirable principles of society to a logical extreme where they began to contradict each other.

In a way, the originating fault was a misunderstanding of the nature of logic. Logic is not actually found in nature. It is a human intellectual arte-fact, a construction of the enquiring mind in search of a principle that might make sense of the way in which an apparently rational but impene-trable universe is organised. As an intellectual tool, logic has unveiled sci-ence and made technology possible. But science and technology have not explained the universe: they tell us something about 'how' but nothing about 'why'. The logic on which science and technology are founded is prob-ably the best indication we have of one aspect of a universal law, but logic is not a sufficient explanation of the universe partly, but only partly, because it cannot explain itself. So, in dealing with many practical prob-lems of which justice is one, logical reasoning can be carried too far.

Of the three basic principles under discussion, which boil down to indi-vidual freedom, the rule of law and equality, it is now clear that no one of them, if carried to its logical extreme, is compatible with the other two. In other words, none of these can be adopted as a principle in any absolute sense. And yet, there are contexts in which each is furiously defended as a principle absolute and beyond challenge.

The fact that people are born with different talents dictates that freedom and equality contradict each other at a fairly early stage, so that almost any individual freedom will make equality impossible; similarly, equality can be secured only by force varying between the tolerably subtle and outright tyranny. The rule of law is a phrase that describes the extent to which a society will accept constraint upon the exercise of individual freedom and is prepared, in the general interest, to forego some of the privileges of inequality. But freedom, equality and the rule of law continue to be proclaimed as the ideals of civilised society. The three principles are not wrong in themselves: what is both wrong and dangerous is the illusion that all three can be pursued to infinity separately and simultaneously.

The ancient laws did not proclaim abstract principles but they did deal in balance. They thus suggest to us that our ancestors well knew that the secret of a stable society was to be found not in the practice of noble ideals but in maintaining a balance between individual ideals that are less than perfect and contradict each other. No one ideal, however noble, can be followed in isolation, but each must be tempered to allow for the operation of others. In the modern world, the ideal of equality is often held to override the claims of individual freedom, and tyranny and war are the result. At other times freedom, of the individual or the group, is held supreme so that bankruptcy and anarchy threaten. At all times, the incompatible claims of freedom and equality combine to threaten the operation of the rule of law so that, desperate for an acceptable balance, the judges follow after public opinion, but at such a distance that the interpretation of the law lurches between one precipice and the other, leaving the public dizzy.

The modern world demands answers; but what it should not look for is perfectly consistent answers, because the pursuit of consistency is part of the problem. Nor should it expect anything resembling real solutions which can be described in general terms and applied in the particular case. No world known to mankind has ever been like that. But like our guesses about laws in the stone age (Chapter 1), there are a few things that suggest themselves. One is that the intractable problems within a legal system are unlikely to be merely legal problems, but the fruit of the society within which that legal system has evolved. The characteristic which principally distinguishes ancient from modern societies is size. In the ancient world, cities were big and crowded compared with the towns out of which they had grown, even though in modern terms they were small; while outside the cities populations were scattered and the expectations of those who lived in the country were almost as rural as they had been in the stone age. The beginnings of modern legal problems can be seen emerging from the still rural legal systems of the ancient cities. Modern populations are enormous and rural life has vanished; even in the country the character of life, the buildings, the goods traded, the services expected, the machinery employed, the personal mobility are urban in character. 'The global village' is an affectionate diminutive for the global city which the developed world lives in, and whose legal systems which are made for the mass trample, as a result, on the individual.

Chris Stringer and Robin McKie in their book *African Exodus* make a fascinating comment about the efficient size for an operational group, which the research they quote suggests is about 150 persons:

> In short, the number (150 persons) looks like the fundamental unit of human social cohesiveness. Above this level, peer pressure can no longer control individuals and the group breaks apart. By using language to create this largest of all primate or hominid assemblies, *Homo Sapiens* was able to generate a healthier, more effective culture.[2]

In the village of the ancient world, justice could be individual because people and circumstances were known and differences in treatment were not only accepted but required. In modern cities, law has to be administered impersonally because numbers are large. In the small towns and early cities of the ancient world, problems generated by increasing numbers were already beginning to appear, and the search for solutions can be detected in their surviving laws. The story of the evolution of writing tells of the struggle for control over the city economy; the surviving laws tell of similar problems with city society.

'Small is beautiful' may be a cliché, but if individuals seek justice from the state, small is essential or justice is not the result. On the one hand, we are offered large size with its equality, uniformity and considerable certainty; on the other, we find the small unit, the local knowledge, the individual justice, but accompanied by loss of equality, lack of uniformity, and uncertainty. Those who wish to preserve the free individual and the principle of equality shout their wares but seldom explain how the conflict between the two is to be resolved.

The global city has given birth to global crime, and the criminal is no longer necessarily an individual but can be an institution or even a state. So today we look for, and indeed find, a hierarchy of national courts leading up to international courts which are just beginning to obtain powers appropriate to the level of the crimes they are required to judge. But the administration needed by international courts includes obedience to a framework of international laws, investigative facilities and punitive powers. In the name of equality, these threaten the sovereignty, even the existence, of nation states. So legal processes are being sucked upwards and outwards while law and its priesthoods become ever more mighty. Meanwhile, individual justice like some golden age retires into legend and even myth.

CHAPTER 14

ANCIENT LAWS AND MODERN PROBLEMS:
JUSTICE AND OTHER HAZARDS

I F INDIVIDUAL FREEDOM, the rule of law, and equality are so incompatible with each other that none can be called a principle, what becomes of mankind's search for a concept of justice and a legal system that all can accept?

The search for a common basis for a legal system is not simple, but it is certainly not pointless. A brief look, however superficial, at the nature of justice is not a bad starting point.

JUSTICE

Law and justice are not the same: both are abstract, but law is precise and as real as a number whereas justice is an aspiration and impossible to define. Except that martyrs have usually fought on behalf of justice and against law.

Justice is a compound concept whose elements can vary both in their identity and their proportions. Absolute justice has never existed in the real world, and what is accepted as justice has varied with time, place and circumstance. The unstable balance of conflicting and partial principles which make up the concept of justice and form the basis of any actual legal system requires that both justice and legal system be kept under permanent review; and the impermanence which that implies is entirely compatible both with continuity and with authority.

A glance at the most ancient laws suggests that some of the principles which are fundamental to justice could be listed, though not all will be immediately acceptable to all modern opinion. First, the most general of our three problem principles, the rule of law. The rule of law declares that some constraints on individual freedom are necessary, while it gives law the authority without which it could not operate; but it says nothing about the character of any particular legal system. That opens up the possibility that if the character of a legal system becomes incompatible with the other components of justice, there may be occasion for defying the principle of the rule of law by which the offensive legal system is being sustained. So the rule of law is another double-edged principle: if carried to an extreme it can become incompatible with other principles of justice and end by contradicting itself.

The point at which rebellion can become moral or even legal has been debated incessantly but never defined, except that a missionary idealism which rebels against other people's ills can create more problems than it solves. Here, only the converse need be noted: that so long as the definition of justice and the principles and operation of the legal system derived from that definition are sufficiently acceptable to the public they serve, a rule of law will be the result.

The free individual and regard for equality can be listed without hesitation as ingredients of justice, so long as justice is defined as a combination in which no one principle can be considered absolute. These, together with the rule of law, can then become three of our main ingredients of justice. But there are two other main ingredients of which one comes as near as may be to supremacy, while the other would be rejected as totally immoral if its presence could only be denied in fact.

The fourth of our ingredients of justice, an ingredient which comes near to supremacy is, of course, truth. The ancient laws are full of the search for truth, while later laws emphasise how indispensable truth is by permitting torture as a means of obtaining it and death as the penalty for withholding it. In the ancient world the water ordeal could be described as torture too, but its motive was not to extract truth by fear of agony but to appeal to the gods for a decision when certainty was unobtainable. If truth can be obtained, justice is relatively easy: the problem has always been how to do justice, and avoid doing injustice, when the truth is not available.

The adversarial system of justice evolved precisely because truth could not usually be obtained directly. That system hopes that truth may be detected if both parties to a conflict are free to make the best case they can and to fight each other – usually with a jury as referee – on the basis of evidence available to both sides and to the public. But there is a dilemma: on the one hand, a process aimed at winning an argument may not always be compatible with discovery of the truth, so the adversarial system contains at least a possible conflict of internal principle. On the other hand, the realities of concealment ensure that to make truth the supreme ingredient of justice would destroy the adversarial system without improving the investigative element in the legal process. All known systems are imperfect, but the adversarial system succeeds for most of the time and especially in the lower courts. It fails spectacularly, and predictably, when the techniques of conducting an argument are stretched to include various methods of suppressing or distorting evidence. The adversarial system is probably the most effective safeguard in history against the arbitrary abuse of power, but its essential nature as a tool for eliciting truth must be preserved, notwithstanding the occasional cause for a raised eyebrow, until a superior system has been found and proven. But obstacles to the discovery of the truth were being erected long before the adversarial or any other modern system could be blamed for them. The search for truth was inadvertently hampered at least three thousand seven hundred years ago when Hammurabi promulgated his law 3 in Babylon, and that is unlikely to have been the first time when it was hinted that the discovery of truth might be obstructed by subtlety:

> If a seignior came forward with false testimony in a case, and has not proved the word which he spoke, if that case was a case involving life, that seignior shall be put to death. (Hammurabi, law 3)

This law has two preconditions: if the seignior's evidence was false and if he could not prove it true, then the consequence followed: if the case involved life the seignior must suffer death. That may have been effective in the context of Hammurabi's Babylon, but even then, and certainly in a modern context, a more devious question must arise: what if the evidence was false and, within the procedures accepted by the court, it could be proved to be true? In that case, false evidence would be accepted by the court on procedural grounds, the seignior would walk free and injustice would both have been done and have been seen to have been done. The modern world is as familiar with that kind of tactic as it is with that kind of result.

The insistence on proof was and is a necessary safeguard against false accusation; but Hammurabi's law almost makes explicit the possibility of suppressing evidence as a means of manipulating justice. Nowadays it is not only an accused who may wish to suppress evidence: the suppression of evidence is almost a legal speciality whose beneficiaries include commercial or research institutions and even governments with a secret. And what must be hidden is by no means typically the guilty secret, but truths whose revelation would imperil public safety, or new discoveries on whose exclusive exploitation scientific or commercial prosperity depends and whose premature disclosure in court would not only deprive their owners of a just reward but damage the lives and prospects of thousands. But procedures intricately designed to allow cases to continue when relevant evidence is concealed from judge and court are based on two misconceptions: that justice can be separated from truth; and that relevant evidence is irrelevant. Occasionally the procedures work, but too often they end in scandal. As a result, the guilty may not be prosecuted when to do so might be embarrassing, which is not only an injustice in its own right but potentially at least surrender to a form of blackmail. There is nothing odd about these predicaments: they are part of the real world and every legal system has to adjust to them. Acknowledgement of their existence suggests sincerity rather than cynicism, but the problem is not necessarily unsolvable. In war, the public press is controlled by censorship operated with public consent, but censorship in time of peace is an invitation to its own abuse and is not usually the solution. The final problem is, of course, one of trust in circumstances where trust cannot always be justified.

There may be two criteria. That those who really take the decisions whether or not to prosecute, or whether or not to conduct a trial when evidence is being suppressed, must of course continue to act in secret, but it must be made publicly verifiable that they all had the full known facts before them when they did so. To deprive those taking this kind of decision of access to the truth can only be self-defeating, so some machinery must be created by which the public can be certain, not what the facts were, but that all facts were made known to, and none were hidden from, those who decided. The penalty for hiding the truth from those who take these decisions in secret must be severe and inevitable; and the fact that a wrongdoer has paid a penalty could be made public.

The other criterion must surely be that those who make these decisions should be at least potentially identifiable to the public. Permanent officers of state need confidentiality if their advice is to be honest and free from pressure; but when they occasionally assume a judicial role the cloak of secrecy can conceal public danger. If a tribunal of enquiry becomes necessary they must be available to stand or fall by what they have done. The prevailing ethos that the buck need never stop but can be kept in play for as long as need be, might be replaced by an alternative ethos that the public has a right to know that the wrongdoer has paid a penalty even if not the details of who and what.

The fifth of our main ingredients of justice, the one that really does raise hackles, is the principle of revenge. Revenge lay at the heart of talion which kept peace in the desert (more or less) for unrecorded millennia in prehistory; and talion survives in the modern world where its cruelties are condemned more loudly than its orderly results are praised. But where does acceptable punishment stop and revenge start? The answer can be found in the ancient concept of balance. Balance tells us how much must be paid in fine or punishment in order to return to the status quo. That amount of fine or punishment is not held to be revenge, but any excess or damages beyond that is revenge. The principle of balance says that no man should suffer loss as a result of the accidental negligence of another, but nor should he profit from it; and, conversely, it also says that each must have a care for his neighbour and pay back in value any loss which he has caused. So, in strict logic, a financial penalty equal to a proper restitution as agreed by a court is not revenge, but anything more than restitution, and that includes most punishment especially if it is not financial, is revenge.

But logic, balance and precise restitution are not a sufficient justice in the popular mind where the need for punishment as a mark of revenge has been embedded for so long that it has become part of human nature. If this is primitive it is still with us, for what else are penal damages but a legalised revenge, a non-violent striking back in retaliation for malice?

199

Nor is mankind the only animal that punishes the wrong doer. Punishment is revenge for most of the time; and the importance of punishment is reinforced by our daily experience of the consequences of trying to avoid having to inflict it. Once again we are confronted by a conflict between social philosophy and the facts of nature. There are two questions: first, whether to accept nature or to try to cope with the effects of defying it; then, if punishment or revenge have to be accepted, the second question is only what and how much. So long as human nature contains that kind of defiance which is part of initiative, or that streak of creativity whose other name is rebellion; so long as human beings are not born equal in status or talent; so long as damage is caused by malice as well as negligence ... for so long will a controlled and publicly approved measure of revenge be a necessary ingredient of an effective penal policy; and for so long will a sufficient revenge be present in fact among the main principles that make up an acceptable definition of justice.

Traditional legal opinion would have penal policy determined in principle by the legislature but applied in the individual case solely by the judiciary in public court. That raises the ancient question of a right of appeal to the sovereign. A right of appeal to the sovereign has always been part of the nature of kingship; it is not derived from any laws made under the king's authority nor from convention. It stands outside and above the generality of laws, and that is probably why appeal to the king does not appear in the surviving written laws of the ancient world, at least up to and including Hammurabi. A right of appeal to the sovereign also means that the judges' penal power has never been absolute. The sovereign's decision to delegate particular appeals to a minister he has appointed to act in his name is consistent with the nature of his office and of his own authority; but for appeals to be referred back to the judiciary as a matter of course for final solution would be for the sovereign to abandon his authority and deny his office. The question how appeal to the sovereign should be handled is not dependent on whether the sovereign is king, queen or president. They need to be dealt with by procedures outside the legal process since they are, in effect, appeals against the legal process, and the procedures must respect the nature of sovereignty from which they directly derive.

So far as justice is concerned, the time has come to record that if a single principle is sought then there is no such thing. The age-old search for a concept of justice has inevitably been fruitless because it was looking for what never was. Justice is neither a single concept nor an absolute; it is a compound of different and often contradictory elements whose claims have to be balanced against each other within the variable context of a real society and a popular culture. Popular feeling expressed in an orderly way can no longer be dismissed as mob rule, a cry that for too many centuries has provided cover for judges acting in the (perfectly sincere) belief that civil order depends not only on the power of the judiciary but on the prestige of the individual judge. Now that the leaders of the people are at least as educated as their judges, a new relationship based on realities can be encouraged between them.

The main principles competing against each other for supremacy within the definition of justice can be listed quite simply. They are: the freedom of the individual, the rule of law, the principle of equality, truth, and a sufficient revenge.

The rule of law, truth, and a sufficient revenge are principles that appear in full operation in the ancient laws. The freedom of the individual and the principle of equality do not appear as they stand in the ancient laws, but their negative influence as disruptive ideas to be avoided or suppressed at almost any cost can be inferred. The adoption of the principles of freedom and equality was in the end inevitable, and they have exhanced beyond recognition the quality of life in the modern world as compared with the ancient; they have brought science and technology to the service of daily life, supremely in the form of medicine and the control of pain; and they have expanded horizons so that ordinary people can live at a level and intensity that our ancestors could not dare to dream of. But the records of our ancient ancestors are not entirely devoid of a kind of canny wisdom, a suspicious foresight that the modern world might be incautious to ignore. For all the advantages they have brought, the freedom of the individual and the principle of equality are not panaceas to be applied indiscriminately and without restraint, but policies with limitations. Like nuclear energy, their extention to extremes threatens the destruction of the civilisation they serve.

Justice does not consist only of the five great principles which are its main components. There are innumerable ideals and considerations of lesser status also competing for a share of influence. These include an ethical dimension, the desirability of certainty which is a product of equality, uniformity which is a product of certainty, mercy which is not the same as individual justice, and many others. Some are considered below, some are referred to in course of discussion; and their number is equal to the number of separate elements which make up the compound known as common sense.

No one person can balance the components of justice; no one profession can supervise the institution that does so. But there is a need for some point within our society where debate about fundamental social principle can be conducted and advice about a balance of principles can be evolved. That point should not be the property of one political or religious persuasion; and it must have no power, except the power to publish. Modern history almost cries out that those who wield power should be separated entirely from those who define it, though both will derive their wisdom from the common pool of knowledge and experience. If such an advisory body can be brought into existence, a starting point for its first debate might well be the question whether the doctrines of the freedom of the individual and of equality do not need peripheral trimming at least in some areas, even though they may well need more obvious encouragement in other areas. But that body must have regard to the expectations of society at large when deciding what advice to publish about the contemporary balance of at least the main components of justice.

THE ETHICAL DIMENSION

The question whether law should have an ethical dimension is controversial. Some say that ethics is the sole province of the legislature which can choose, if it wishes, to make ethical laws, but that the legal system should be confined to an executive role as the instrument of policy. That opinion maintains that the law must be comprehensive, uniform and certain, it must be applied to all equally, and the judge as a consequence must have as little discretion as possible. If there is an ethical failure, responsibility must lie with the legislature. It was not like that in the ancient world. Jean Bottero described the Code of Hammurabi as '... real treatise on jurisprudence';[1] and in that, Hammurabi did not differ from the earlier collections of laws whose format he followed. In the ancient world the discretion of the judge was the cornerstone of justice; and the cases chosen for inclusion in the written laws illustrated how ethical principles should be applied by the judges in representative circumstances. Responsibility for the ethics of the individual case rested squarely with the judge. This comes from the earliest surviving collection of laws of the late third millennium BC:

> If a man had leased an arable field to another man for cultivation, but he (the lessee) did not plow it, so that it turned into wasteland, he shall measure out (to the lessor) three kor of barley per iku of field.
>
> (Ur-Nammu, law 29)

Ur-Nammu illustrates how a legal judgement embodies an ethical precept. The arable land was leased out to be cultivated, so cultivation was a duty accepted by the lessee. When the lessee failed to perform his duty, he not only lost his own share of the produce but had to make good the lessor's loss of expectation as well; and to make the ruling generally applicable the court stated in cold figures the proportion in barley per square unit of field that any lessee in these circumstances must pay. The ethical duty of precise restitution did not have to be argued; it was already accepted by society at large, probably in the form of oral law, and incorporated into the individual written law. These laws left no room for legalistic argument about the meaning of terms; they were indeed jurisprudence in action.

Today the written law has subverted the traditional progress from ethical principle through law into judgement, by inserting into the law by means of precedent a new principle not found in the ancient world: that anything is lawful that is not specifically forbidden. This extension of the principle of personal freedom is based on two propositions: first, that the individual is fundamentally free and his freedom can only be restricted by an accepted process of law; second, that a citizen cannot be required to abide by an ethical principle unless the law specifically defines and imposes it. And behind these lurks a deeper proposition: that ethical principles are arbitrary and without force until they have been adopted by a parliament, after which they are still arbitrary but there is a duty to abide by them.

The surviving written laws of the ancient world suggest that it has never been possible to prosecute someone simply for doing wrong. But it was possible to prosecute for a specific deed considered wrong under the contemporary ethos, probably as expressed in a continuing oral law, when the accused if guilty would face the wrath of the judges. He might, of course, appeal to the king if he thought that such an appeal would be likely to arouse the king's sympathy; but he could not be sure of that result. In the modern world, it is the duty of the legislature to insert ethics into the written laws, and this is held to relieve the court of the necessity for making ethical judgements of its own. Thus the pursuit of individual freedom has weakened the very concept of right and wrong by excluding it from the daily working of the legal system.

In the ancient world, the written word was supposed to make the meaning of the law available to all; it did not do so. In the modern world, the written word has annihilated the ethical dimension and opened the way to evasion by sophistry. This is another example of pursuing one ideal, in this case the freedom of the individual, to its logical extreme without regard to the other components of justice: and it is the end product of having denied the judge any substantial measure of discretion. The freedom of the individual has not only excluded right and wrong from the legal process but has come near to destroying the ordinary distinction between right and wrong in principle.

The need for an ethical dimension is not, of course, a legal problem at all. We do our judges an injustice if we blame them for a defect forced on them by society. No one wishes to be caught preaching but there is a real need for an acceptable ethic in society at large. An acceptable ethic is not the property of any particular religious persuasion, though it has quite a lot to do with religion; nor is it the property of any one political party, though it has to do with politics; and it has a great deal to do with education in its widest sense. Be that as it may, until we have a generally acceptable ethic in society we will continue to look in vain for such an ethic in either the law or its practice.

THE DISCRETION OF THE JUDGE

The rule of law is unavoidably linked to the discretion of the judge: the wider that discretion, the less detailed the law itself becomes; and as the law becomes less detailed, it becomes less binding, less certain, and less uniform. The judge versus the law is a problem of balance that is seldom identified but needs to be addressed. The dilemma may be encapsulated in a reciprocal contradiction: individual justice if carried to its extreme will end up by destroying law; but deification of the law ends up by destroying individual justice.

A balance has to be struck; but before that can be done, the principles which need to be balanced against each other must be identified. Two such principles are, once again, the freedom of the individual and the principle of equality.

The judge's discretion safeguards the existence of the individual because it is the one procedure that enforces consideration of individual circumstance. The disadvantage is that judicial discretion is neither uniform nor predictable, and it is open to the charge of denying equality of treatment. Equality of treatment produces high levels of uniformity and certainty, but if extended to its extremity it destroys the individual. The balance between equality and the individual is, again, not a legal problem and any solution must start from the recognition of that fact. It is a social problem to be decided through the political process. So here is another candidate for consideration in that body which may be called into existence to highlight and advise on contradictions between principles within the definition of justice.

But there is one path that may make progress easier in balancing the conflict between judicial discretion and the individual on the one hand and equality and the uniformity of the law on the other. That path is the appeal process. Any judge may simply get it wrong; or he may mistake the public's legitimate expectation for the growl of the mob. All humanity is permitted a measure of error, and judicial error need no longer involve the personal prestige or the authority of the judge. An appeal process that looks only at procedure is cheap to operate, but it does not dig down into the substance of a case and so is not necessarily capable of dealing with the matters that are the real subject of appeal. An appeal that does dig down into substance could amount to a full re-trial, and in any case it would be expensive and time consuming. But it would not necessarily be more expensive or more time consuming than the massive miscarriages of justice which have been revealed on the small number of occasions when a conscientious appeal process has reluctantly been conceded in recent times.

THE PRESTIGE OF THE JUDGE

The authority of a legal system can no longer be described in terms of the personal authority of judges. In Hammurabi's day it was different. He expressed concern about the authority of the judge in admirably clear terms:

> If a judge gave a judgement, rendered a decision, deposited a sealed document, but later has altered his judgement, they shall prove that that judge altered the judgement which he gave and he shall pay twelvefold the claim which holds in that case; furthermore, they shall expel him in the assembly from his seat of judgement and he shall never again sit with the judges in a case. (Hammurabi, law 5)

We can imagine the effect such a law must have had on the judges to whom it was addressed, and there must still be Lord Chancellors (or their equivalent) who would read Hammurabi with a tinge of envy; but we must also ask why Hammurabi should have needed such a law. Clearly, some judges (perhaps only one) had been changing their mind and, as a result, reducing the legal process to chaos. The legal system in the ancient world depended very much on the authority of the judges, and they derived their authority in no small measure from universal acceptance that their judgements could be relied upon to be final. Of course there was an appeal to the king; but that was risky at the best of times, and it would become ridiculous if the judge might have changed his mind meanwhile. In the ancient world, judges could occasionally be overruled and keep their authority; but if they themselves denied their authority by changing their mind, the whole system would be threatened with collapse. Today, appeal processes are so well established that judges can be overruled and survive; indeed, the layman might be forgiven for suspecting, if not hoping, that very occasionally judges may possibly rely on being overruled so as to be free to use their judgement to make a point.

The more real and deep the appeal process the wider the discretion of the judge can be and the safer the remnant of individual justice becomes. An expensive appeal process could do much to relieve the dilemma of the judge versus the desirable certainty and uniformity of the law.

DRAFTING LAWS

It is clear that in the ancient world there were immense advantages in allowing judges a wide discretion within the general principles laid down by law. Framing laws in terms of general principle, without attempting to prescribe imagined detail, allowed the courts to deal in justice rather than pedantry. In the modern world, such freedom would immediately open the way for a judiciary to make law in competition with a legislature, and occasionally in defiance of it; and if that became possible there is no doubt that it would happen. But that is not necessarily an insuperable difficulty.

Judges occasionally do just that at present, on a limited and unpredictable scale, when they use their power to interpret the law in those cases where its wording happens to be ambiguous.

If laws were drafted more with the unpredictability of the real world in mind, and less in fear of lack of uniformity between courts; if judges had more room to use their discretion in the individual case; if the public could be acclimatised to a measure of uncertainty as the price of individual justice; if people could be educated out of the belief that what happens to another can be unjust to oneself, and out of the principle that anything is legal unless specifically forbidden by law; if a more ambitious appeal process could be envisaged; if access to the courts could be freed from fear that the financial cost, win or lose, could wreck a lifestyle; if saving public money could be denied precedence over the destructive consequences of justice denied ... if ... if ...

LAW AND THE PLANET

Another subject for inflamed debate might well be the population of the planet. To stabilise the population of the planet and see population as one component within the planet's natural character and capacities is an ideal much discussed, but it crashes headlong against the principle of the freedom of the individual. 'We have an absolute human right to bear children as and when we please ... ' some women say, and men agree. But the creation of human rights which are not found in nature is bound to end in conflict between idealism and the facts. Left to itself, nature controls population at the level it can support, and it does this through infant mortality, disease and shortage of food, all of which have been diminished and almost eliminated by science; as a result, human population has exploded while animal populations, vegetation and even climate are under threat. Perhaps belief in the power of Almighty Man to create a new universe is one feature of today's theology that needs to be questioned; and the various lists of today's ideals that have been deified as 'human rights' may be another. The very concept of human rights as something separate from the real world of nature, that can be created by mankind at will and operated indefinitely without contradiction or coercion, may be ripe for challenge. The act of questioning will, of course, be controversial: the contemplation of heresy always is. But it does not have to be destructive if it takes as its objective, as well as its method, an investigative rather than an accusatorial stance.

A justified fear of war and giant processes of production demand international co-operation whose machinery can override national governments; but in the process, that machinery converts persons into units. The modern world, or parts of it, is beginning once more to look at population size as the source of many problems, and as a result there is much dispute between freedom of the individual and the capacities of the planet. The problem which concerns the future of mankind has not, basically, altered over nearly five and a half thousand years, but this time our choices might have to be different.

THE CHALLENGE

The list of topics that can be discussed in relation to the ancient laws is so nearly endless that the range and quality of those laws never ceases to amaze. The third and early second millennia BC were no golden age, but that remote world continues to command respect because so many of the principles out of which the modern world is built, and so many of its problems, can be seen emerging in response to pressures being generated within the earliest cities. Many of the ancient solutions such as slavery, forced labour, the river test, mutilation, appal us; but the quality of intellect applied to problems which they had to confront with no previous knowledge or experience to call on, demonstrates that their best minds were forward looking and creative. Nissen and others[2] illustrate that somewhere among those ancient cities a succession of brilliant scribes met the challenge of feeding a mass population by inventing writing. The quality of intellect has not diminished in four thousand years, but many social and legal problems which they had solved in terms of their culture, we have not solved in terms of ours. We face a challenge of enormous numbers which they did not face; and we also face the principled criticism of a mass social conscience whose mere shadow terrified them into suppressing developments whose consequences they knew they could not afford. But within the limitations of their knowledge and their resources they had the courage to stand four square for social order and against anything which might threaten it such as individual freedom or a doctrine of equality; and it may have been only their suppression that prevented those contradictory principles from declaring their nature by clashing with each other. Theirs was the civilisation of the ant heap and the hive, intelligently directed, cleverly controlled, orderly, rich, creative and safe. We have released the genie but have not yet learnt to direct it. Perhaps what we most need from the ancient world is the clarity of vision we attribute to them and which they may indeed have possessed. We have found two golden principles which they did not find; but they recognised, what we have not recognised, that freedom and equality are not manna but come with dangers that can annihilate all their advantages and mankind along with them. The challenge is whether we can collectively persuade ourselves to acknowledge the facts of nature and, confronted with a choice between ambition and probable destruction, find the courage to choose that which offers a future for us all.

LIST OF REFERENCES

A GENERAL NOTE

The abbreviation ANET refers to J.B. Pritchard *Ancient Near Eastern Texts*, Princeton University Press, 1969. Translations of the laws of Hammurabi and earlier laws come from ANET. References to the Edict of Ammisaduqa, to the Hittite laws and to the Middle Assyrian Laws are also to ANET.

Biblical quotations are from the Authorised (King James) Version of the Bible of 1611.

CHAPTER 1: EMERGENCE FROM PREHISTORY

1. Gibbon, Edward, *The History of the Decline and Fall of the Roman Empire*, Bohn edition, London, 1854, vol. IV, 1788. Chapter XXXVIII, p.241: spelling as printed. In his autobiography 'an extract from Mr Gibbons Commonplace Book' says that vol. IV was begun on 1 March 1782 and completed in June 1784.
2. Nissen, ed. Curtis, 1993 p.60
3. Ibid, p.58
4. Ibid, p.56
5. Green, 1989 p.46ff
6. Bottero, 1995 p.80
7. Nissen et al, 1993 p.11
8. Schmandt-Besserat, ed. Senner, 1989 p.29
9. Ibid, p.34
10. Sjoberg, 1975 p.164
11. Schmandt-Besserat, 1989 p.32
12. Kramer, 1963 pp.187–8

CHAPTER 2: THE LAW CODES

1. Meek, ANET p.178
2. Diamond, 1971 pp. 9ff
3. The individual collections of laws come from ANET:

The Laws of Ur-Nammu (J.J. Finkelstein)	p.523ff
The Laws of Eshnunna (Albtrecht Goetze)	p.161ff
The Laws of Lipit-Ishtar (S.N. Kramer)	p.159ff
Sumerian Laws, to avoid possible confusion referred to here as 'A Law Fragment', (J.J. Finkelstein)	p.525ff
The Laws of Hammurabi (Theophile J. Meek)	p.163ff

4. Finkelstein, ANET p.526ff
5. Finkelstein, ANET p.526 Introductory Note
6. Goetze, ANET, The Hittite Laws, p.188ff
7. Meek, ANET, The Middle Assyrian Laws, p.180ff
8. Finkelstein, ANET, the laws of Ur-Nammu, p.523ff

CHAPTER 3: THE BURDEN OF PROOF

1. Sollberger, 1976 p.442
2. Ibid, p.447
3. Finkelstein, ANET, Additional Mesopotamian Legal Documents, p.545, (translated by V. Scheil)

CHAPTER 9: WOMEN ACCORDING TO THE LAWS

1. Kramer, 1963 p.329

CHAPTER 11: THE HAMMURABI MYSTERY

1. Driver and Miles, 1952, vol.1 p.501
2. Ibid, pp.501–2

3.   Unpublished personal correspondence with author
4.   Diamond, 1971, pp.150–1
5.   Ibid, p.153
6.   Ibid, p.19
7.   Oates, 1991 p.75
8.   *Encyclopaedia Britannica*, 15th Edition, 1995, vol.23, p.875
9.   ANET, The Babylonian King List B, p.269
10. ANET, Hammurabi's Regnal Years, pp.269–70
11. Oates, 1991, p.200
12. Foster, 1982, p.116
13. ANET, The Curse of Agade, translated by S.N. Kramer, pp.646–51
14. Kramer, 1963, p.55

CHAPTER 12: LAW IN THE ANCIENT WORLD
1.   Diamond, 1971 passim
2.   Ibid, p.20
3.   Ibid, pp.21–2
4.   Diamond, 1957, p.155
5.   Roux, 1985, p.190
6.   Bottero, 1995, p.161
7.   Ibid, p.181
8.   Ibid, p.183
9.   Driver and Miles, 1952 vol.1, pp.52–3
10. Meek, ANET, p.178
11. Bottero, 1992, p.179

CHAPTER 13: ANCIENT LAWS AND MODERN PROBLEMS: THREE PROBLEM PRINCIPLES
1.   Taylor, *The Times*, 23 May 1996, p.20
2.   Stringer and McKie, 1996, p.198

CHAPTER 14: ANCIENT LAWS AND MODERN PROBLEMS: JUSTICE AND OTHER HAZARDS
1.   Bottero, 1995 p.183
2.   Nissen, Damerow, Englund, 1993, passim

BIBLIOGRAPHY

The following have been of direct help in researching this book:

ABDULWALID, Ali Fadhil *Sumerian Letters: Two Collections from the Old Babylonian Schools*. University of Pennsylvania PhD 1964, University Microfilms, Ann Arbor, Michigan.

ADAMS, Robert McC. 'Ancient Mespotamian Settlement Patterns and the Problems or Urban Origins'. *Sumer* XXV, 1969.

BERMANT, Chain and WEITZMAN, Michael *Ebla*. Weidenfeld and Nicolson. London, 1979.

BOTTERO, Jean *Mesopotamia*, translated by Zainab Bahrani and Marc Van De Mieroop. University of Chicago Press, 1992.

BOYER, Carl B. *A History of Mathematics*. John Wiley and Sons Inc, USA, 1968.

CRAWFORD, Harriet *Sumer and the Sumerians*. Cambridge University Press, 1991.

DALLEY, Stephanie *Myths from Mesopotamia*. Oxford, University Press, 1989; World Classics paperback, 1991.

DIAMOND, A.S. *Primitive Law, Past and Present*. Methuen, 1971.
'An Eye for an Eye'. *Iraq* XIX, 1957.

DRAPKIN, Israel *Crime and Punishment in the Ancient World*. Lexington Books, 1989.

DRIVER, G.R. and MILES, John C. *The Babylonian Laws*. Clarendon, 1952.

FOSTER, Benjamin R. *Administration and Use of Institutional Land in Sargonic Sumer*. Akademisk Forlag, 1982.

FRIEDMAN, Lawrence M. *Law and Society*. Prentice-Hall, 1977.

GIBBON, Edward *The History of the Decline and Fall of the Roman Empire*. Bohn edition, London, 1854.

GOETZE, Albrecht 'Fifty Old Babylonian Letters from Harmal'. *Sumer*. Vol XIV, 1958.

GORDON, Edmund I *Sumerian Proverbs: Glimpses of Everyday Life in Ancient Mesopotamia*. The University Museum of Pennsylvania, Philadelphia, 1959.

GREEN, M.W. 'Early Cuneiform', in Wayne M. Senner (Ed) *The Origins of Writing*. University of Nebraska Press, 1989.

GURNEY, O.R. *The Hittites*. Penguin, 1975 edition.

KRAMER, S.N. 'The Ur-Nammu Law Code: Who was Its Author?", *Orientalia*, Vol. 52, Fasc. 4, 1983.
The Sumerians. The University of Chicago Press, 1963.

LEEMANS, W.F. *Legal and Administrative Documents of the Time of Hammurabi and Samsuiluna*. E.J. Brill, Leiden, 1960.

NISSEN, Hans J., DAMEROW, Peter and ENGLUND, Robert K. *Archaic Bookkeeping*. University of Chicago Press, 1993.

NISSEN, Hans J. 'The Context of the Emergence of Writing in Mesopotamia and Iran', in John Curtis (Ed) *Early Mesopotamia and Iran*. British Museum Press, 1993.

OATES, Joan *Babylon*. Thames and Hudson, 1991.

PINCHES, Theophilus G. 'Some Early Babylonian Contract Tablets or Legal Documents II', *Journal of the Royal Asiatic Society*, January 1899.

PRITCHARD, J.B. *Ancient Near Eastern Texts*. Princeton University Press, 1969.

ROUX, Georges *Ancient Iraq*. Pelican, 2nd edition 1980, reprinted 1985.

SAGGS, H.W.F. *The Babylonians*. The Folio Society, 1999.

SCHMANDT-BESSERAT, Denise 'Two Precursors of Writing: Plain and Complex Tokens' in Wayne M. Senner (Ed), *The Origins of Writing*. University of Nebraska Press, 1989.

SENNER, Wayne M. 'Theories and Myths on the Origins of Writing: a Historical Overview', in Wayne M. Senner (Ed), *The Origins of Writing*. University of Nebraska Press, 1989.

SJOBERG, A.W. 'The Old Babylonian Edubba, Sumerological Studies in Honor of Thorkild Jacobsen on his Seventieth Birthday, June 7th 1974'. *Assyriological Studies* No.20, University of Chicago Press, 1975.

SOLLBERGER, Edmond *Some Legal Documents of the Third Dynasty of Ur*. Kramer Anniversary Volume, Ed. Barry L. Eichler, Verlag Butzon and Becker Kenelaer, 1976.

STRINGER, Chris and MCKIE, Robin. *African Exodus*. Jonathan Cape, 1996.

WALKER, C.B.F. *Cuneiform*. British Museum Publications, 1987.

INDEX

DATES	SOCIAL DEVELOPMENT
Before c.7000BC	OLD STONE AGE Hunting and gathering; clans.
From c.7000BC	NEW STONE AGE (NEOLITHIC) Beginning of farming – both animals and crops. (Hunting and gathering slowly diminish.)
c.3500BC	Early cities in existence. Probably some ruling bureaucracies.
c.3200BC	Cities growing larger. Ruling bureaucracies expand.
c.2800BC	Developed city states. Centralised bureaucracies.
c.2600BC	
c.2300BC	Regional kingdom of Akkad Collapse of Akkad
c.2100BC	Sumer reaches its peak
c.2000BC	Destruction of Ur
c.1975BC	Sumerian civilisation continues, led by the cities of Isin and Larsa.
c.1930BC	
c.1800BC	
c.1792BC	Hammurabi becomes king of Babylon
c.1770BC	
c.1750BC	Death of King Hammurabi